P9-CKT-357

NOW
DON'T TRY
TO
REASON
WITH
ME

NOW DON'T TRY TO REASON WITH ME

Essays and Ironies for a Credulous Age

Wayne C. Booth

THE UNIVERSITY OF CHICAGO PRESS
Chicago and London

ISBN: 0–226–06579–0 (clothbound); 0–226–06580–4 (paperbound)
Library of Congress Catalog Card Number: 73–123359

THE UNIVERSITY OF CHICAGO PRESS, CHICAGO 60637
THE UNIVERSITY OF CHICAGO PRESS, LTD., LONDON

For Phyllis

CONTENTS

PREFACE

Everyone who collects his occasional pieces does so with some embarrassment, or ought to, regardless of how many of his devoted readers have wished they could get hold of this or that marvelous passage. The whole assemblage is so terribly scattered, so piecemeal, compared with the books one imagines oneself writing. What excuse could a man have—a retired dean and not even into his fifties!—for cobbling these things together rather than getting on with the business of writing a real book?

Mine is, I think, quite straightforward: having been a full-time, absurdly harassed administrator for five years, I am turning back now to "teaching and scholarship." I hope to produce something more systematic and—I suppose this is the word—professional than most of the pieces I have chosen to include. As I am freed of those daily pressures (or so I dream), I shall lose the excuse for being "unscholarly." I may very well become more cautious, and though I could wish that many of my colleagues would show a bit more caution, *my* dangers lie, I think, the other way. I do not intend to stop issuing jeremiads to a credulous age, but it is unlikely that I shall ever again be tempted into as many outbursts timed to specific occasions.

I confess that I think most of the pieces still, in 1970, very timely, though hardly fashionable in either content or style. I could never bring myself to publish them if I waited ten years; the prose here, though by now repeatedly revised, is scarcely deathless, and the thought often cries out for the fuller development that the forty-five minute lecture or the twenty minute sermon did not allow for. My excuse—except for the self-indulgence that accounts for part IV—is that the forces I attack in the academy and the nation may very well be winning; if I wait until every argument satisfies the scholar in me, the battle will have swept past me, or over me: we can never take for granted the continuing freedom to say what we believe.

Since most of these pieces would lose much of whatever value they have if torn from the occasions they tried to meet, I have not usually expunged signs of their time and place. Some readers may be put off by references to unknown students and colleagues, but to change all of these to anonymous or pseudonymous folk—"a student I know," "one of my colleagues"— would be to populate the book with those nonpersons invented by clever journalists: "Last week, in Denver, Colorado, an alert young professor of physics was heard barking into his dictation machine. . . ." Everybody here is real; the occasions have not been invented; the thought is almost always under the pressure of the impending moment when I must stand up and speak, pretending to a knowledge and confidence that I do not possess.

What tampering I have done with these moments, in preparing them for print, has been mainly to remove repetition and awkwardness. I have not tried to change the American of the speaker into the English of the scholar: the stuff was spoken, most of it, and it should be read as if spoken.

Part

THE NEW
CREDULITY
AND THE
NEW
RHETORIC

To go on preaching reason to an inherently unreasonable species is, as history shows, a fairly hopeless enterprise.
          —Arthur Koestler
... a beast that wants discourse of reason ...
          —Hamlet

THE NEW CREDULITY
AND THE
NEW RHETORIC

Every man trusts his own forms of credulity, and we all are angered by an opponent's unreasonableness, especially when he claims to be a defender of reason. "I'll not listen to reason," a character in *Cranford* says. "Reason always means what some one else has got to say." A student in our recent sit-in at the University of Chicago (1969) told me he was shocked to find that the faculty had succumbed to a "gut reaction" when they were attacked. "They weren't being reasonable and they didn't care about reason. I don't care what they said; they were just defending what they loved—like us!"

These essays in defense of a rational persuasion are not, I hope, either gutless or heartless. The reasonableness they defend is not "mere logic," as I try to explain in parts 2 and 3. Nor is there any rigorous system here that will prove, to those determined to doubt, that reason can or should be applied in human affairs, much less that I, in contrast to my opponents, am a man of reason. It is true that in almost every piece, I *set out* to prove, once and for all, that sweet reasonableness can and should prevail in the affairs of men. In those beginning moments, I always feel very noble and unassailable. But the occasion and my own limitations intervene, and I end up writing another academic sermon, exhorting or teasing my auditors in a fashion that in retrospect leaves the would-be philosopher in me dissatisfied and even humiliated.

A literary critic who believes in philosophy, a literary critic who believes in the pursuit of pure critical and philosophical knowledge for its own sake, I am almost invariably deflected into the everyday job of the rhetorician. The rhetorical stance can be defended in theory, and it can even be built into a philosophy, as Cicero and others have shown. But here it is defended by a man who in his heart of hearts would prefer to live in an age when a purer philosopher's stance could be maintained. The reasonableness of this rhetorician, in other words, is always slightly tainted by the inability of reason to defend itself except in the courts of philosophy. Part I, in short, needs part II; but when we get to part II, we find the inept gropings towards philosophy of a philosopher manqué who wishes that he and his fellows could have built a wiser age by making themselves wiser.

"NOW DON'T TRY
TO REASON WITH ME!"
RHETORIC TODAY,
LEFT, RIGHT, AND CENTER

I

When I began teaching English twenty years ago, I saw myself as taking up the weapons of reason against a world committed to emotionalism, illogical appeals, and rhetorical trickery—a world full of vicious advertisers and propagandists who were determined to corrupt the young minds I was determined to save. Now, as a professor of rhetoric and dean of a liberal arts college, I may seem still to present myself in the same melodramatic light: the valiant champion of rationality against the forces of darkness. But bravely as I may try to hold my pose, both the world and the reasonings of men look more complicated than they did twenty years ago. Even as I turn my weapons on the enemies of reason, you will catch me revealing that I am not quite sure who they are, or whether I am qualified to challenge them.

But let me at least begin boldly, with a defense of reason that implies more clarity than I feel about how men ought to proceed when they set out to change each other's minds. The

Revised from speech "commissioned" by the Student Government at the University of Chicago. Reprinted with permission from the *University of Chicago Magazine,* November–December 1967.

defense begins, quite properly, with the claim that we are in a time of intellectual crisis, a time when confidence in reason is so low that most men no longer try to provide good reasons for what they believe. Of course the very question of what constitutes a good reason is itself under debate, now as always—and I shall be returning to it later. But suppose we begin with the simple notion of proof—the presentation of evidence and arguments in a causal chain intended to pull the mind toward belief.

When we consider how much time teachers spend insisting that students exhibit genuine arguments in their papers, it is perhaps surprising to find the very notion that such forms of proof are desirable, or even obtainable, largely ignored in our public discourse. The simple painful task of putting ideas together logically, so that they track or follow each other, doesn't seem to appeal to many of us any more. I once heard Professor George Williamson of our English department explaining his standards for accepting articles for *Modern Philology.* "Considering the level of argument in the stuff that comes in, I can't really insist on anything that could be called a 'standard,' " he lamented. "I'm happy if I can find essays which show *some* kind of connection between the conclusions and the evidence offered."

You don't have to read much of what passes for literary criticism, or political argument, or social analysis, to conclude that the attention of most authors has not been primarily, or even secondarily, on constructing arguments that would stand up under close scrutiny. Leslie Fiedler spoke at Chicago a couple of years ago and said that the younger generation is really imitating Negro culture, and that the cultural warfare between what he calls palefaces and redskins accounts for our literature today. I protested to a student afterward that Fiedler had offered no evidence, no proof. "That doesn't matter," the student replied, "because it was so interesting."

But it is not simply that our practice is sloppy: open mistrust of rational argument is in the air. The first really modern form of this mistrust was Freud's claim that our conscious efforts at systematic thought are mere superstructures for the fundamental processes which are pre- or sub-logical. But Freud's own attack is, by recent standards, radically tainted with a faith in reason and logical argument. Norman O. Brown, one of the most widely quoted speculative anti-thinkers of the sixties, attacks psychoanalysis for relying on logical processes that alienate us from the realities of selfhood which, he says, are the only truths that we should care about. "The reality-principle," Brown says, "the light by which psychoanalysis has set its course, is a false boundary drawn between inside and outside, subject and object, real and imaginary, physical and mental. It gives us the divided world, the split or schizoid world." The psycho-analyst is, in Brown's view, simply using reason as a defense against the truths which can be found only by realizing the "surrealist" forces that lie too deep for reason.

Marshall McLuhan is an even better-known source of attacks on the intellect—or at least on that part of it that he calls "linear reasoning." Like Brown, McLuhan admits that most of our scientific, technological, and economic life depends on the linear thinking that was brought to its perfection with the invention of printing. But he says that the price we have paid for our "phonetic alphabet" is the diminished functioning of our senses of sound, touch, and taste. "Consciousness is not a verbal process," McLuhan says, with that blissful faith in half-truths which frequently illustrates his own theses. "Yet during all our centuries of phonetic literacy we have favored the chain of inference as the mark of logic and reason. In Western literate society it is still plausible and acceptable to say that something follows from something, as if there were some cause at work that makes such a sequence." McLuhan reminds us that Hume and Kant—or so he believes—both recognized that nothing ever *follows* as effect from something else as cause. Unfortunately, however, neither Hume nor Kant went far enough, McLuhan says, because they did not recognize that what had misled Western man into thinking that reasoning could be linear was the alphabet and printing!

The attack on "mere logic" in the name of intuitive truths that are deeper, more profound, and not amenable to logical testing is by no means a new thing in the world. Everyone who has ever really thought about it, from Plato to the present, has known that logic is by itself at best a weak though necessary tool—a tool that can be used by the devil as well as by angels. But if you read closely in McLuhan, Brown, and many others in recent years, you find that they are expressing a dissatisfaction with reason that goes far beyond a simple mistrust of logic or linear thinking. At its extreme it is a repudiation of anything that deserves the name "thought" at all, in favor of feeling or of the "wisdom of the body."

One of the most seductive expressions of this spirit is the development of what one might call the anti-essay. The word *essay* used to mean "an effort to try out," an attempt. One "essayed" to deal with a topic adequately. Today we have the anti-essay which is a non-attempt. Listen to how Susan Sontag introduces her famous non-essay into the regions of "camp":

> To snare a sensibility in words, especially one that is alive and powerful, one must be tentative and nimble. The form of jottings, rather than an essay (with its claim to a linear, consecutive argument), seemed more appropriate for getting down something of this particular fugitive sensibility. It's embarrassing to be solemn and treatise-like about Camp. One runs the risk of having, oneself, produced a very inferior piece of Camp.

We have grown used to such demurrers and to the kind of disjointed and self-contradictory "notes" she then offers: these are the marks, we tell ourselves, of a "nimble" mind. Surely it is not fair to ask whether the effort to grapple with the notion of Camp is really more difficult than the efforts of Plato and Hume and Kant to "snare" matters like justice and human understanding and the aesthetic order. But fair or not, the suspicion will not down: Miss Sontag simply has not done as much for us as she could have done by repudiating the fashion for non-attempts and pushing herself to some old-fashioned linear thought about how her genuinely clever "notes" relate to each other. She is capable of such thought; I have seen her do it. Why, then, should she deprive us of it?

But the truth is that Miss Sontag is coherence itself by comparison with some of her elders. If you want an interesting exercise in futility, just try sometime to construct an outline of one of McLuhan's chapters. As Edgar Friedenberg says of both Brown and McLuhan, their style "honestly derives from and expresses" their point of view.

I must confess that when I read what passes for argument in these attacks on traditional modes of arguing, I experience a succession of body blows that I'm sure would please these folks immensely. They would argue that my being offended by incoherence results from my bad upbringing: I am a product of an education oriented to print, to the visual, to the organized, the sequential, the analytical, the linear. They may be right. Some of us professors would no doubt be less ashamed if caught beating our wives than if caught in a logical fallacy. McLuhan would tell us all to stop worrying and relax: the time of linear thought, the time when "rational" meant "uniform and continuous and sequential," is over. We have entered a time of "creative configuration and structure," whatever that is, a time of the "inclusive form of the icon," a time when "the medium is the message," a time when what we say no longer matters but only how we say it.

Now I know that I'm being slightly unfair to McLuhan (though I think only slightly). On his descriptive side, as he points to what is happening to our minds under the non-verbal onslaught of the mass media, he is doing part of what must be done. The trouble—aside from his seeming pleasure in his *own* incoherence—is that in most of his recent utterances he seems to have stopped worrying about the loss of our traditional powers of reason. He says, in fact, that the new media, as "extensions of man," are capable of revealing synthetic, simultaneous truths perhaps more important than the old analytical hogwash. What I would want to insist on is that, even though the older forms of rationality are obviously limited, our need for them is as great as ever. To gloss over our need for defenses against irrationality with such phrases as "the medium is the message" is to sell out a major part of our humanity—even if the claim to bring to light neglected abilities proves justified.

II

Suppose we look at a bit of irrational message-mongering, done by one of the "new media," to see if we can be satisfied with saying that the content no longer matters. Everyone knows that journalism has been transformed in recent years, especially in the news magazines, from reportage into new forms of para-logical rhetoric: political argument disguised as dramatic reporting. It would be fun to spend the rest of my hour simply describing the new rhetorical devices, and the new twists on old devices, that *Time* magazine, only the most successful of many, exhibits from week to week, all in the name of news. Mr. Ralph Ingersoll, former publisher of the magazine, has described the key to the magazine's success as the discovery of how to turn news into fiction, giving each story its own literary form, with a beginning, a middle, and an end, regardless of whether the story thus invented matches the original event. Everyone I know who has ever been treated by *Time*—whether favorably or un-favorably—has been shocked by the distortions of fact for effect, and the more they know about a subject the more they are shocked. A doctor friend at the University says one cannot trust the medical reporting. Eric Bentley, the drama critic, says they cannot be trusted about drama. Igor Stravinsky says, "Every music column I have read in *Time* has been distorted and inaccurate."[1]

More important to us than all of this testimony is the *way* the distortions operate. Though much of the distortion is simply for the sake of being interesting, much of it is done to put across political and social viewpoints. I open an issue of *Time* at random to an attack on *Ramparts* magazine. It is of course not called an attack. It is made to look like a regular news account, objective, olympian. But it is a highly loaded attack, neverthe-less. What troubles *Time* about *Ramparts,* amusingly enough, is that "*Ramparts* is slick enough to lure the unwary and be-dazzled reader into accepting flimflam as fact"—a description which I would take as fitting *Time* exactly. "No other left-wing publication in the United States," *Time* says, "pursues shock

1. As I read proof in May, 1970, I have an impression that *Time* has been somewhat improved lately. Am I simply reacting to the attacks on the "media" by Vice President Agnew? And to the fact that lately *Time*'s sur-reptitious editorializing is often employed against presidential policies and methods that I, too, deplore?

more relentlessly or plays around more with fact." Now you may think, for a moment, that *Time* added that adjective "left-wing" in order to add one more charge to six other charges of leftism skilfully planted (to use a favorite *Time* word) in the account. But I prefer to think that *Time* is being unusually honest: by confining the competition for fact-distortion to left-wing magazines, *Time* has considerately ruled itself out of the running.

It is always instructive to follow *Time's* shenanigans closely. Ask yourself, for example, how you would headline the following quotation, if you worked for *Time:* " 'Quite frankly,' says Hinckle, the publisher of *Ramparts,* 'there weren't enough Catholic laymen [we soon discovered] to write for and to buy the magazine. Besides, we got bored with just the church.' " Now think of a headline. Isn't it obvious? Your headline for this section will be "Bored With The Church." And that, of course, is the headline used, with an important shift in meaning.

Let's go on with the game. How would you describe where *Ramparts* is published? Where else but in "one of those topless streets in San Francisco's New Left Bohemia." What kind of humor does *Ramparts* publish? "Clever if sophomoric humor" —clever, or there would be no threat, sophomoric, or it might really be funny. How would you describe an article in *Ramparts* purporting to show that one million children have been killed or wounded in the Vietnam war? Could you do better than this: *Ramparts* "produced a mere juggling of highly dubious statistics." How would you describe the pictures of dead or wounded children? Why naturally as "a collection of very touching pictures, some of which could have been taken in any distressed country."

Time is, of course, only one example of a kind of nonrational persuasion that is practiced on us all the time, and *Ramparts* is also guilty of the disguised and dishonest rhetoric I am describing. Another good instance of this same kind of transformation of journalism into degraded rhetoric is *Fact,* the magazine from which I collected, perhaps somewhat naively, some of the testimony I earlier used against *Time.* I originally subscribed to *Fact* on the basis of a one-paragraph ad in the *New York Times;* it claimed that with so much editorializing in all other journals (that word "all" should have alerted me, perhaps) America needs a magazine devoted to objective reporting of the truth. I should have predicted what would come: a collection of shrill exposés, most of them with a touch of scandal and few of them providing enough solid evidence or argument to allow a reader to know whether there was anything to them or not. "A Psychoanalytical Study of Baseball," "A Study of Wife-Swapping in California," an argument that Dag Hammarskjold was a psychotic who committed suicide (*could* be, one says, but not on the basis of *this* evidence), another argument that Goldwater has been declared insane by thousands of psychiatrists (yet if you look closely at the evidence here it turns out to mean, at most, far less than the headlines claim) [2] —why, it's as hard to read *Fact* as it is to read *Time!*

The important point is that McLuhan's current cheerful response to such corruptions of the media is not enough. (He used to be much less complacent; now he says that TV advertising is the greatest art of our time. Even allowing for self-protective ambiguity, *what happened?*) To say that the medium is the message is entirely inadequate when a definite message has been sneakingly and very powerfully conveyed by the medium. The content of *Time,* and of *Ramparts,* and of *Fact* is very important indeed, once we have dug it out of the seemingly neutral prose. The medium is *not* the message nor is it that exciting new kind of "iconic presentation" that enables us "to live mythically and integrally." Rather, it is that very old-fashioned kind of manipulation of rhetorical distortions, skillfully placed in non-McLuhanesque sequences designed to take us in. And if we are not to be taken in, we must learn now as in the past to think *through* the medium *to* the message, to think critically about that message, to ask what reasons if any have been given to support it. In short, we must do exactly what McLuhan

2. It was recently announced that Goldwater has won his libel suit against *Fact.* But of course in the four years since I wrote my preliminary verdict, the editor has gone on feeding his gulls—many of whom no doubt think of themselves as wise birds indeed.

deplores: continue to *think* in what he calls the old, fragmented space and time patterns of the pre-electric age.

What I have been trying to suggest, with these examples, is that we live in a world in which men show little esteem for logic, little respect for facts, no faith in anyone's ability to use thought or discourse to arrive at improved judgments, commitments, and first principles. The consequences that one would expect in such a world, when honesty of observation, care with logic, and subtlety with dialectic have declined, can of course be seen wherever men try to change each other's minds. What is left to rhetoric when solid substantive argument is denied to it? Obviously only emotional appeal and appeal to the superior moral integrity and wisdom or cleverness of the rhetorician— what was formerly called "ethical appeal" (whether the appeal was moral or immoral). Emotional appeal and ethical appeal can never be expelled from the house of rhetoric; all the great rhetoricians are passionate in their rationalism. But when men are reduced to using these properly subordinate appeals as if they were the sole means of persuasion, they produce the kind of rhetoric that we now find flowing at us, left, right, and center.

I have time only for two examples. They both will seem extreme and therefore unrepresentative to some of you, but the test is that they have apparently been effective on large numbers of Americans. Can you recognize who is speaking in the first quotation?

I can see a day when all the Americas, North and South, will be linked in a mighty system, a system in which the errors and misunderstandings of the past will be submerged, one by one, in a rising tide of prosperity and interdependence. We know that the misunderstandings of centuries are not to be wiped away in a day or an hour. But we pledge that human sympathy—what our neighbors to the south call an attitude that is "simpatico"—no less than enlightened self-interest will be our guide. I can see this Atlantic civilization galvanizing and guiding emergent nations everywhere. Now I know that freedom is not the fruit of every soil. I know that our own freedom was achieved through centuries by the unremitting efforts of brave and wise men. And I know that the road to freedom is a long and challenging road. And I know also that some men may walk away from it, that some men resist challenge . . .

No doubt you have placed the speaker by now in a general way. His is a political rhetoric appropriate to the campaign trail, and his platitudes are mostly the platitudes of the conservative center: the combination of human sympathy and self-interest building an Atlantic civilization (God knows how!) and the appeals to freedom might be offered by any Democrat or Republican of slightly jingoist cast. Only with the move toward the vaguely ominous charge that some men *resist challenge* do we suspect that this may be a different kind of conservative; we are thus not really surprised at the concluding phrase:

. . . accepting the false security of governmental paternalism.

The vapidities of a Goldwater, representing a nation that does not ask that its political candidates give reasons, are now clear! (I am not saying that only Goldwater could have written the passage, just that it is typical.)

Where on the left was I to find an equally revealing piece of bombast. It ought to be one that would make a few of my listeners mad—and a few more think. Obviously something by a student; obviously something from the new student left. Listen closely now to excerpts from a long "Letter to Undergraduates," by Bradford Cleaveland, former graduate student of the department of political science at Berkeley; it was written during the troubles of '64–'65.

Dear Undergraduates, . . . On the one hand there [is] substantial agreement that the University stamps out consciousness like a super-Madison Avenue machine; on the other, people [are] saying, "So what?" or "Bring me a detailed and exhaustive plan." *But there is no plan for kicking twenty thousand people IN THEIR ASSES!* No plan will stop excessive greed, timidity, and selling out. At best the university is a pathway to the club of 'tough-minded-liberal-realists' in America, who sit in comfortable armchairs talking radical while clutching hysterically at respectability in a world explosive with revolution. At worst the university destroys your desire to see reality and to suffer reality with optimism, at the time when you most need to learn that painful art. . . .

. . . The first set of facts [is that in your undergraduate program] you are puppets. You perform. But when do you think? Dutifully and obediently you follow, as a herd of grade-worshiping sheep. If you are strong at all, you do this with some sense of shame, or if you are weak, you do it with a studied cynicism . . . as jaded youth with parched imaginations that go no further than oak-paneled rooms at the end of the line . . . BUT WHETHER YOU ARE STRONG OR WEAK YOU PERFORM LIKE TRAINED SEALS, AND LIKE SHEEP YOU FOLLOW . . . WITH THE THOROUGHBRED PHI BETA KAPPA SHEEP LEADING YOU! ! ! up the golden stairway to the omnipotent A, to the Happy consciousness, to success and a very parochial mind.

[The second set of facts is that the Charter Day is an unmerciful sham; an example of unparalleled demagoguery.]

Having elaborated these two sets of facts, which were of course not facts at all but deeply personal judgments, Mr. Cleaveland then moved to his clincher:

Dear Undergraduates!! I am no longer interested in cajoling you, arguing with you, or describing to you something you already know. I . . . entreat you to furiously throw your comforting feelings to duty and responsibility for this institution to the winds and act on your situation. . . . There is only one proper response to Berkeley from undergraduates: that you *organize and split this campus wide open!* From this point on, do not misunderstand me, my intention is to convince you that you do nothing less than begin an open, fierce, and thoroughgoing rebellion on this campus.

My point here is not to argue that Mr. Cleaveland was right or wrong in urging revolution. What interests me is the kind of reasons he felt were adequate to persuade undergraduates to strike against the university. The notion that thousands of highly selected American undergraduates should find this sort of thing appealing ought to frighten us all. Indeed, there is a kind of contempt for the intellect and its efforts running throughout the literature of the Berkeley revolt—and through other literature of the new left—which seems to me far more threatening to the future of the American left itself than has been generally recognized. When the left stops thinking, we should all know by now, it becomes as destructive of human values as the unthinking right—and I must say that there is a tone in much of this literature which suggests that thinking is itself a suspect activity. Cleaveland is fond of using the word "scholars" in quotation marks: he talks of "scholars" and "so-called liberals" who adopt "the hideous posture of studying" or analyzing the "problem."

Now I cannot really prove that these two rather special examples are in any way representative of right and left, or that their similar tendency to shout and chant rather than reason is representative of American rhetoric today. But I suspect that you have found, in your daily reading, enough that is like these two to bear out my hunch that there really is a predominance of irrational persuasion at work here. You may, in fact, have concluded—subjected to so much slick advertising and political propaganda as you are—that this is all there is to rhetoric, that in fact men cannot persuade each other rationally in such matters since, in matters of judgment and action, all choices are equally irrational.

And of course this is precisely why everyone in any academic community should be deeply disturbed whenever the Goldwaters and the Cleavelands begin to attract large numbers of listeners. We claim to be committed to free and honest and relentless inquiry. This almost everyone takes for granted; only a few on the extreme right and the extreme left have questioned this basic commitment of colleges and universities. What is not so frequently recognized is that the very notion of free inquiry depends on the possibility of valid, genuinely justified persuasion—that is, of a rhetoric not like Goldwater's and Cleaveland's but rather a rhetoric built on the use of reason to persuade men to believe one proposition—a true proposition—rather than another, a false or less adequate proposition.

III

My point is not, as I'm sure you realize by now, to indict either the left or the right, but to plead for what I take to be the very fragile twin values of honest inquiry and honest rhetoric. I have said so far that these values are under steady attack, both in theory and in practice, by men of both left and right—some of them presumably sincere, some of them no doubt knaves. Wherever men find themselves too impatient to think together about their problems, wherever immediate action based on "unity" becomes more important than men's determination to achieve genuine unity by discovering the truth together, my twin values disappear—often never to reappear in a particular society. They *always* risk annihilation in a major war, and it is not surprising that the Vietnam war, which seems to most of us self-evidently a horrible national disaster and which to many Americans seems self-evidently a righteous crusade, should have led us to shout rather than reason. My twin values disappear in any society whenever enough men decide that victory is worth whatever it costs. They disappear whenever men decide, as Bradford Cleaveland decided in California, that there is "only one proper response" to a political situation—the effort to destroy the opponent through force or political pressure. (I would not want to suggest that these twin values are the only values for mankind, or that I would never be willing to risk them for other values. Though it is fairly easy to show historically that most revolutionary efforts work more harm than good, I can think of situations when I would be forced to stop thinking and talking and start overthrowing: Nazi Germany, say, or *perhaps* Boston in 1775—but note how many of our revolutionaries managed to go on thinking as well as fighting. It is clear that the force of my plea for more reason and less shouting depends in part on my conviction that we are not yet in such an extreme situation. If you really believe that the only action possible in America is to choose one of two sides and then use violence to win, we may as well close the College and load our weapons.)

It is important to recognize that none of the attacks on reason —either theoretical or in the form of shapeless writing or biased reporting or open invitation to riot—none has pretended that reason is ineffective in dealing with practical, prudential affairs. Everyone admits that reason has produced fantastic results in science and technology. The protests seem, often enough, to be against the very success of rational calculation in the hands of statisticians, logicians, computer analysts, or army officers, when applied to human affairs without starting from humane premises. Atomic bombs and doomsday machines and calculations of overkill all seem to show what happens when reason is left to its own devices without the control of—of what?

Traditionally the answer might have been "the control of reason itself." Reason did not, in earlier centuries, mean simply logical calculation but rather the whole process of discovering sound first principles and *then* reasoning from them to sound conclusions. What seems distinctive in our time is the widespread conviction that our choice of first principles is itself irrational or capricious. Most teachers and students I talk with seem to have concluded that the choice of one's starting point is always an arbitrary act of faith, and that to debate about such choices is a mark of immaturity. After all, we have been shown in so many different ways that even in the physical sciences hypotheses are discovered intuitively; that the first principles are not subject to proof; that even the most seemingly objective knowledge is, as Michael Polanyi says, *"personal* knowledge"—infused with personal meanings and values and thus not really what we ordinarily mean by objective at all. Though most professional philosophers now as in all times are not relativists, the predominant lay philosophy is, I would say, a kind of relativism. Men make their own values; values change from society to society, and even from group to group within a society—"How can one reason about such things?" we seem to say to each other. It is not hard, in fact, to see why McLuhan and Brown and others feel that they must speak, even if in a distorted form, for truths that lie beyond reason.

The first part of my title comes from a *New Yorker* cartoon which showed a woman, quarreling with her husband, saying: "Now don't try to *reason* with me." The cartoon reflects, it seems to me, one of our attitudes toward reason. It is of course a male cartoon, and it betrays first of all the American male's traditional contempt for the female's unreasonableness. To be reasonable has in our folklore been the male's prerogative, one sign of his superiority. In this view, reason is of course a good thing to have; to be irrational, "like a woman," is somehow funny. But it is not hard to develop a different view of the cartoon; to think oneself into "the woman's point of view" and imagine how a brutal and irrelevant logical argument can cover up or violate fundamental needs or feelings while seeming to have all of the right on its side.

Man was traditionally known as the rational animal; in that view reason was of man's very essence. But it takes no great learning to remind us that much that we think of as distinctively human—love, poetry, martyrdom—can present itself in forms that seem to violate reason—or perhaps to transcend it. We can all quote Pascal, who said that the heart can be turned on by reasons that reason cannot dig—or words to that effect. Tertullian is supposed to have said that he embraced his religious belief just *because* it was absurd. In the last several centuries, many have seen man's peculiar humanity not in his rationality, not in the common grounds of truth and right action that reason leads to, but rather in his capacity for individual freedom, whether rational or mad. For them, the act of freely choosing an error or falsehood confers greater human dignity than the act of passively accepting that which reason seems to require and which many men consequently believe. Stephen Dedalus, in Joyce's *Portrait of the Artist as a Young Man,* is by no means the only literary portrait of a soul electing what he believes may be eternal damnation for the sake of doing things his own way, according to his own feelings. The romantic soul has for at least two centuries been shouting defiance at traditional reasonings, though one should hasten to add that the relation between reason and romanticism is laden with the same ambiguities as are our attitudes toward the coldly rational male and the weakly intuitive female: if the romantic hero can be portrayed as a representative of individualism gone mad, seeking what in modern jargon we might call a personalized truth which to everyone else will be damnable falsehood, he can also be portrayed in Faustian terms, as the man who is willing to violate intuition, love, and the value of religious faith and salvation all for the sake of knowledge—that is, for what reason reveals.

In either view, somehow, the Garden of Eden is threatened by man's quest for knowledge—not just knowledge of good and evil, but the whole search for intellectual mastery. A life led according to what the mind can test and prove seems somehow to threaten much that all of us hold dear. The young student who is impatient with the cautious weighings and probings and refusals of commitment that go on within every university is plainly in one great tradition of a mistrust of reason that all of us must feel at one time or another. Men are starving throughout the world; men's souls are being destroyed in Harlem and Mississippi; children are being bombed in Vietnam—and here you sit, training your intellects to savor the pleasures of art and literature and elegant argument!

IV

So you see, we can make the emphasis fall either way: attacks on reason are vicious because reason, properly defined, is our most precious gift; or attacks on reason are needed, because no matter how you define a "reasonable life" much of what is most valued by men is left out. As a university professor I am committed to the supreme professional standard of rationality: insofar as I am an honest professor, worthy of my own respect, I am sworn to change my mind if and when someone shows me that there are *good reasons* to change my mind. But both as a man who loves art and literature that I cannot fully explain, and as a human being who holds to many values the correctness of which I cannot easily prove with unanswerable rational arguments, I know how much of my life is not readily explicable at the court of what is usually called reason.

The question is whether reasonable debate is in *any* degree possible about such basic commitments, political and moral and personal. What we call rhetoric is usually used only when scientific proof is not available—about such matters as whether to oppose or support the Vietnam policy, or whether to join a church or commit suicide, or whether to vote for Goldwater or join a strike against the University of California. Can such questions be debated rationally, or do we have available only those forms of persuasion used by Goldwater and Cleaveland—emotional appeals and appeals to the character of the speaker or references to the enemy's viciousness?

Though I have no time to undertake the difficult argument such a question demands, I should like to suggest that in losing our confidence in the possibility of finding genuinely good reasons for important human actions, in losing our belief in a reasonable rhetoric, we have laid ourselves open to the kinds of perverted rhetoric I have described. My main point is to argue that we must preserve and extend our capacity for a rational persuasion about the most important questions. If we don't, liberal education in any meaningful sense will die, leaving us at the mercy of propagandists and protected only by the superficial slogans of the propaganda analysts.

What has happened, I am convinced, is that we have fallen victims to an all-or-nothing kind of argument that we should be ashamed of. Of course we cannot find, in social and political and ethical questions, the degrees of certainty in proof that scientists—at least some of them—boast of. But does this mean that we are reduced to emotional appeal, shouting, lying, trickery, and ultimately, warfare? That it does not is in itself a conclusion to be proved with the kind of proof that is in question—and the intellectual problems are not simple. For now, perhaps you will be willing simply to record one man's strong conviction that a reasonable persuasion is not only possible but indispensable if we are to live well together.

Whatever such a rhetoric might be, it will not be a dry, unemotional kind of argument for the middle of the road. To believe in reason doesn't mean that one believes only in reason —one might recognize the truths of the heart without having to launch an attack on the head. The trouble with our present situation is that the defenders of logicality or rationality seem too often to be men who want to reason only about the means to unquestioned ends—they would "rationalize" society, make us efficient, lead us to social usefulness, rather than try to humanize us. This leaves the defenders of the heart to operate in a whirlwind of emotions, convinced that to be reasonable is somehow to be cold and calculating. Well, there *are* some causes worth dying for, and there are many causes not worth a hoot. I will not die for a cause unless I feel deeply about it. Imagine Churchill using only a chain of syllogisms trying to persuade the British to fight. But on the other hand I cannot distinguish the good causes from the circus acts unless I have learned to think about them, and the good rhetorician will, like Churchill during the war, show me by his arguments as well as by his character that he is on the right side.

V

We should be quite clear about what all this means to us. If we cannot find a defense of reason that makes of it something more than a useful weapon in the arsenal of each warring faction, if there is not some sense in which men can reason together about even their most precious commitment, if basic faiths and loves and first principles are entirely arbitrary and hence beyond discussion, then we may as well succumb to the McLuhanesque glow, or to the polymorphous perverse pleasures offered by Brown, or to the revolutionary inanities of Cleaveland. And, incidentally, we English teachers are on very shaky ground when we scribble in the margin "logic bad here" or "not clear how these propositions relate." We are on shaky ground in teaching *composition* at all. Who cares, after all, whether the logic is bad or good unless the conclusions that good writing might persuade to are in some sense superior to the conclusions produced by bad writing? But this can be true only if some first principles are themselves superior to others, only if they are in some sense *demonstrably* superior.

Plato said that the worst fate that can befall a man is to become a misologist, a hater of reason; for him it was clear that since man is essentially reasonable, when he ceases to reason he ceases to be a man. I happen to believe this unfashionable doctrine—assuming the broad definition of reason that I have been implying here. I also believe that when any society loses its capacity to debate its ends and means rationally, it ceases to be a society of men at all and becomes instead a mob, or pack, or a herd of creatures rather less noble than most animals. In America in recent years we have seen far too many such herds—self-righteous fanatics who know without listening that the speaker is wrong. There are many of our universities, so-called, where Karl Marx, say, or Miss Aptheker would be booed from the platform, even if the administration were to allow them to speak. And on the other hand there have been some disturbing instances lately of left-wing students in first-class universities coercing a speaker into silence. Whatever defenses may be offered for such rhetoric—the rhetoric of shouting a man down

—it is not the rhetoric of a student, and those shouting mobs are not students, no matter what else they may be. It is one mark of an honest man, as it should be the mark of an educated man, that he tries not to use a double standard in judging his friends and his enemies. Self-righteous bullying fanatics are self-righteous bullying fanatics regardless of the cause they support, and they are as much a threat to the central values we defend when they bully on our side as when they bully on our enemy's. Men—at least some men—aspire to a life of sweet reasonableness, but all men seem engaged in a verbal warfare that leaves them perpetually teetering on the brink of actual warfare, local, national, and international. Our hold on reason is precarious; our institutions for giving it a chance are highly fragile. The very tradition out of which I speak of a rational rhetoric is itself fragile. It would not really be surprising if fifty years from now no one in America would even know what I'm talking about tonight—such a transformation would not be greater than many that history has known. Men in that time would know something that most of you do *not* know—what it *feels* like not to be *allowed* to follow a thought wherever it might lead, openly, publicly. Whether we move toward that genuine garrison state, that really total institutionalization of the mind, will depend in part, in very small but very real part, on how many of us here can manage—not in sermons like this, which are easy superficial substitutes for the day-by-day thinking that counts, but in our life as teachers and students—to reason together about what we care for most.

THE RHETORICAL STANCE

Last fall I had an advanced graduate student, bright, energetic, well-informed, whose papers were almost unreadable. He managed to be pretentious, dull, and disorganized in his paper on *Emma,* and pretentious, dull, and disorganized on *Madame Bovary.* On *The Golden Bowl* he was all these and obscure as well. Then one day, toward the end of the term, he cornered me after class and said, "You know, I think you were all wrong about Robbe-Grillet's *Jealousy* today." We didn't have time to discuss his objections, so I suggested that he write me a note about them. Five hours later I found in my faculty box a four-page polemic, unpretentious, stimulating, organized, convincing. Here was a man who had himself taught freshman composition for several years and who was incapable of committing any of the more obvious errors that we think of as characteristic of bad writing. Yet he could not write a decent sentence, paragraph, or paper until his rhetorical problem was solved—

Revised from an address delivered to the annual meeting of the College Conference on Composition and Communication in 1963. First printed in *College Composition and Communication,* October 1963. Reprinted by permission of the National Council of Teachers of English.

until, that is, he had found a definition of his audience, his argument, and his own proper tone of voice.

When I think back over the experiences which have had any effect on my own writing, I find the great good fortune of a splendid freshman course, taught by a man who believed in what he was doing, but I also find a collection of other experiences quite unconnected with a specific writing course. I remember the professor of psychology who pencilled one word after a peculiarly vacuous paper of mine: *Bull.* I remember the day when P. A. Christensen talked with me about my Chaucer paper and made me understand that my failure to use effective transitions was not simply a technical fault but a fundamental block between him and my meaning. His off-the-cuff pronouncement that I should *never* let myself write a sentence that was not in some way *explicitly* attached to preceding and following sentences meant far more to me at that moment, when I had something I wanted to say, than it could have meant as part of a pattern of such rules offered in a writing course. Similarly, I can remember the devastating lessons about my bad writing that Ronald Crane could teach with a simple question mark on a graduate seminar paper, or a pencilled "Evidence for this?" or "Why this section here?" or "Everybody says so. Is it true?"

Such experiences are not, I like to think, simply the result of my being a late bloomer. At least I find my colleagues saying such things as "I didn't learn to write until I became a newspaper reporter" or "The most important training in writing I had was doing a dissertation under old Blank." Sometimes they go on to say that the freshman course was useless; sometimes they say that it was an indispensable preparation for the later experience. The diversity of such replies is so great as to suggest that before we try to reorganize the freshman course, with or without explicit confrontations with rhetorical categories, we ought to look for whatever there is in common among our experiences, both of good writing and of good writing instruction. Whatever we discover in such an enterprise ought to be useful to us at any level of our teaching. It will not, presumably, decide once and for all what should be the content of the freshman course, if there should be such a course. But it might serve as a guideline for the development of widely different programs suited to the widely differing institutions in which we work.

The common ingredient that I find in all of the writing I admire—excluding for now novels, plays, and poems—is something that I shall reluctantly call the rhetorical stance, a stance which depends on discovering and maintaining a proper balance among three elements: the available arguments about the subject itself; the interests and peculiarities of the audience; and the voice, the implied character, of the speaker. I should like to suggest that it is this balance, this rhetorical stance, difficult as it is to describe, that is our main goal as teachers of rhetoric. Our ideal graduate will strike this balance automatically in any writing that he considers finished. Though he may never come to the point of finding the balance easily, he will know that it is what makes the difference between effective communication and mere wasted effort.

What I mean by the true rhetorician's stance can perhaps best be seen by contrasting it with three corruptions, unbalanced stances often assumed by people who think they are practicing the arts of persuasion.

The first I'll call the pedant's stance: it consists of ignoring or underplaying the personal relationship of speaker and audience and depending entirely on statements about a subject—leaving out, that is, the notion of a job to be done for a particular audience. It is a virtue, of course, to respect the bare truth of one's subject, and there may even be some subjects which in their very nature define an audience and a rhetorical purpose so that adequacy to the subject can be the whole art of presentation. For example, an article on "The Relation of the Ontological and Teleological Proofs," in a recent *Journal of Religion*, requires a minimum of adaptation of argument to audience. But most subjects do not in themselves imply in any necessary way a purpose and an audience and hence a speaker's tone. The writer who assumes that it is enough merely to write an exposition of what he happens to know on the subject will produce the kind of essay that soils our scholarly journals, written not for readers but for bibliographies.

In my first year of teaching I taught a whole unit on "exposition" without ever suggesting, so far as I can remember, that the students ask themselves what their expositions were *for*. So they wrote expositions like this one—I've saved it, to teach me toleration of my colleagues: the title is "Family relations in More's *Utopia*." "In this theme I would like to discuss some of the relationships with the family which Thomas More elaborates and sets forth in his book, *Utopia*. The first thing that I would like to discuss about family relations is that overpopulation, according to More, is a just cause of war." And so on. Can you hear that student sneering at me, in this opening? What he is saying is something like "you ask for a meaningless paper, I give you a meaningless paper." He knows that he has no audience except me. He knows that I don't want to read his summary of family relations in *Utopia,* and he knows that I know that he therefore has no rhetorical purpose. Because he has not been led to see a question which he considers worth answering, or an audience that could possibly care one way or the other, the paper is worse than no paper at all, even though it has no grammatical or spelling errors and is organized right down the line, one, two, three.

An extreme case, you may say. Most of us would never allow ourselves that kind of empty fencing. Perhaps. But if some carefree foundation is willing to finance a statistical study, I'm willing to wager a month's salary that we'd find at least half of the suggested topics in our freshman texts as pointless as mine was. And we'd find a good deal more than half of the discussions of grammar, punctuation, spelling, and style totally divorced from any notion that rhetorical purpose to some degree controls all such matters. We can offer objective descriptions of levels of usage from now until graduation, but unless the student discovers a desire to say something to somebody and learns to control his diction for a purpose, we've gained very little. I once gave an assignment asking students to describe the same classroom in three different statements, one for each level of usage. They were obedient, but the only ones who got anything from the assignment were those who intuitively imported the rhetorical instructions I had overlooked—such purposes as "Make fun of your scholarly surroundings by describing this classroom in extremely elevated style" or "Imagine a kid from the slums accidentally trapped in these surroundings and forced to write a description of this room." A little thought might have shown me how to give the whole assignment some human point, and therefore some educative value.

A complete and pedantic divorce of writing from human purposes is revealed in a recent publication of the Educational Testing Service, called "Factors in Judgments of Writing Ability." In order to isolate those factors which affect differences in grading standards, ETS set six groups of readers—business men, writers and editors, lawyers, and teachers of English, social science, and natural science—to reading the same batch of papers. Then ETS did a hundred-page "factor analysis" of the amount of agreement and disagreement, and of the elements which different kinds of graders emphasized. The authors of the report express a certain amount of shock at the discovery that the median correlation was only .31 and that 94% of the papers received either 7, 8, or 9 of the 9 possible grades.

But what *could* they have expected? In the first place, the students were given no purpose and no audience when the topics were assigned. And then all these editors and business men and academics were asked to judge the papers in a complete vacuum, using only whatever intuitive standards they cared to use. I'm surprised that there was any correlation at all. Lacking instructions, some of the students undoubtedly wrote polemical essays, suitable for the popular press; others no doubt imagined an audience, say, of *Reader's Digest* readers; and others wrote with the English teachers as implied audience. An occasional student with real philosophical bent would no doubt do a careful analysis of the pros and cons of the topic assigned. This would be graded low, of course, by the magazine editors, even though they would have graded it high if asked to judge it as a speculative contribution to the analysis of the problem. Similarly, a creative student who has been getting A's for his personal essays would write an amusing, colorful piece, graded "F" by all the social scientists present, though they would have graded it high if asked to judge it for what it was.

One might as well assemble a group of citizens to judge

students' capacity to throw balls, say, without telling the students or the graders whether altitude, speed, accuracy, or form was to be judged. The judges would be drawn from football coaches, jai alai experts, lawyers, and English teachers, and asked to apply whatever standards they intuitively apply to ball throwing. Then we could express astonishment that the judgments did not correlate very well, and we could do a factor analysis to discover, lo and behold, that some graders concentrated on altitude, some on speed, some on accuracy, some on form—and the English teachers were simply confused.

One effective way to combat the pedantic stance is to arrange for weekly confrontations of groups of students over their own papers. We have done far too little experimenting with arrangements for providing a genuine audience in this way. Short of such developments, it remains true that a good teacher can convince his students that he is a true audience, if his comments on the papers show that some sort of dialogue is taking place. As Jacques Barzun says in *Teacher in America,* students should be made to feel that unless they have said something to someone, they have failed; to bore the teacher is a worse form of failure than to anger him. From this point of view we can see that the charts of grading symbols that mar even the best freshman texts are not the innocent time savers that we pretend. Plausible as it may seem to arrange for more corrections with less time, they inevitably reduce the student's sense of purpose in writing. When he sees innumerable W13s and P19s in the margin, he cannot possibly feel that the art of persuasion is as important to his instructor as when he reads personal comments, however few.

This first perversion, then, springs from ignoring the audience or over-reliance on the "pure" subject, whatever that could be. The second, which might be called the advertiser's stance, comes from *under*valuing the subject and overvaluing pure effect: how to win friends and influence people.

Some of our best freshman texts—Sheridan Baker's *The Practical Stylist,* for example—allow themselves on occasion to suggest that to be controversial or argumentative, to stir up an audience, is an end in itself. Sharpen the controversial edge, one of them says, and the clear implication is that one should do so even if the truth of the subject is honed off in the process. This perversion is probably in the long run a more serious threat in our society than the danger of ignoring the audience. In the time of audience-reaction meters and pre-tested plays and novels, it is not easy to convince students of the old Platonic truth that good persuasion is honest persuasion, or even of the old Aristotelian truth that the good rhetorician must be master of his subject, no matter how dishonest he may decide ultimately to be. Having told them that good writers always to some degree accommodate their arguments to the audience, it is hard to explain the difference between justified accommodation—say changing *point one* to the final position—and the kind of accommodation that fills our popular magazines, in which the very substance of what is said is accommodated to some preconception of what will sell.

At a dinner about a month ago I sat between the wife of a famous civil rights lawyer and an advertising consultant. "I saw the article on your book yesterday in the Daily News," she said to me, "but I didn't even finish it. The title of your book scared me off. Why did you ever choose such a terrible title? Nobody would buy a book with a title like that." The man on my right, whom I'll call Mr. Kinches, overhearing my feeble reply, plunged into a conversation with her, over my torn and bleeding body. "Now with my *last* book," he said, "I listed 20 possible titles and then tested them out on 400 business men. The one I chose was voted for by 90 percent of the businessmen." "That's what I was just saying to Mr. Booth," she said. "A book title ought to grab you, and *rhetoric* is not going to grab anybody." "Right," he said. "My *last* book sold 50,000 copies already; I don't know how this one will do, but I polled 200 businessmen on the table of contents, and . . ."

At one point I did manage to ask him whether the title he chose really fit the book. "Not quite as well as one or two of the others," he admitted, "but that doesn't matter, you know. If the book is designed right, so that the first chapter pulls them in, and you *keep* 'em in, who's going to gripe about a little inaccuracy in the title?"

Well, rhetoric is the art of persuading, not the art of seeming to persuade by giving everything away at the start. It presupposes that one has a purpose concerning a subject which itself cannot be fundamentally modified by the desire to persuade. If Edmund Burke had decided that he could win more votes in Parliament by choosing the other side—as he most certainly could have done—we would hardly hail this party-switch as a master stroke of rhetoric. If Churchill had offered the British "peace in our time," with some laughs thrown in, because opinion polls had shown that more Britishers were "grabbed" by these than by blood, sweat, and tears, we could hardly call his decision a sign of rhetorical skill.

One could easily discover other perversions of the rhetorician's balance—most obviously what might be called the entertainer's stance—the willingness to sacrifice substance to personality and charm. I admire Walker Gibson's efforts to startle us out of dry pedantry, but I know from experience that his exhortations to find and develop the speaker's voice can lead to empty colorfulness. A student once said to me, complaining about a high school teacher, "I soon learned that all I had to do to get an A was imitate Thurber."

But perhaps this is more than enough about the perversions. Balance itself is always harder to describe than the clumsy poses that result when it is destroyed. But we all experience the balance whenever we find an author who succeeds in changing our minds. He can do so only if he knows more about the subject than we do, and if he then engages us in the process of thinking—and feeling—it through. What makes the rhetoric of Milton and Burke and Churchill great is that each presents us with the spectacle of a man passionately involved in thinking an important question through, in the company of an audience. Though each of them did everything in his power to make his point persuasive, including a pervasive use of the emotional appeals that have been falsely scorned by many a freshman composition text, none would have allowed himself the advertiser's stance; none would have polled the audience in advance to discover which position would get the votes. Nor is the highly individual personality that springs out at us from their speeches and essays present for the sake of selling itself. The rhetorical balance among speaker, audience, and argument is with all three men habitual, as we see if we look at their nonpolitical writings. Burke's work on the Sublime and Beautiful is a relatively unimpassioned philosophical treatise, but one finds there again a delicate balance: though the implied author of this work is a far different person, far less obtrusive, far more objective, than the man who later cried *sursum corda* to the British Parliament, he permeates with his philosophical personality his philosophical work. And though the signs of his awareness of his audience are far more subdued, they are still here: every effort is made to involve the *proper* audience, the audience of philosophical minds, in a fundamentally interesting inquiry, and to lead them through to the end. In short, because he was a man engaged with men in the effort to solve a human problem, one could never call what he wrote dull, however difficult or abstruse.

Now obviously the habit of seeking this balance is not the only thing we have to teach under the heading of rhetoric. But I think that everything worth teaching under that heading finds its justification finally in that balance. Much of what is now considered irrelevant or dull can, in fact, be brought to life when teachers and students know what they are seeking. Churchill reports that the most valuable training he ever received in rhetoric was in the diagramming of sentences. Think of it! Yet the diagramming of a sentence, regardless of the grammatical system, can be a live subject as soon as one asks not simply "How is this sentence put together" but rather "Why is it put together in this way?" or "Could the rhetorical balance and hence the desired persuasion be better achieved by writing it differently?"

As a nation we are reputed to write very badly. As a nation, I would say, we are more inclined to the perversions of rhetoric than to the rhetorical balance. Regardless of what we do about this or that course in the curriculum, our mandate would seem to be, then, to lead more of our students than we now do to care about and practice the true arts of persuasion.

THE REVIVAL OF RHETORIC

As teachers of language and literature, you have all noticed that my title is even more ambiguous than most. Those of you who are amicably disposed may even have called it general, in the old style, rather than ambiguous, in the new. The word "rhetoric" has for a long time served for both the study of the art of persuasion and for the art itself; Aristotle's *Rhetoric,* uppercase, is still unsurpassed, but take away the capital letter and Aristotle's rhetoric is often very bad indeed, at least as we view it. In the second sense rhetoric has never had a real quantitative revival because it has always thrived; but in the first sense we seem to be in the midst of a revival of rhetoric unmatched in the twentieth century. Unfortunately, in spite of some very good work, there are signs that it may prove a very shoddy revival indeed, with no more lasting effect than the rhetorically oriented "communications" movement of a decade ago, unless we take thought about precisely what we are doing.

What is it that we are reviving? As applied to the art of

Slightly revised from an address delivered to the annual meeting of the Modern Language Association in 1964. Reprinted with permission from *PMLA,* vol. 80, no. 2 (1965).

speaking and writing, rhetoric today can refer to anything from mere ornamental figures tacked on or subtracted from a composition to the whole range of all possible ways, verbal and nonverbal, to change men's minds; as systematic study, rhetoric may refer to anything from a pointless classification of those ornamental figures to a whole philosophy of man as a logos-possessing animal. What is worse, one cannot predict, even now after nearly a decade of revived respectability, whether the term will be used to refer to something good or something bad. In publications for freshmen it has recently been an O.K.-term. Yet it is still used in ways that might well deter us from calling ourselves "professors of rhetoric." Listen to Malcolm Muggeridge, in a recent *Esquire* article: "Like a man in a dark place without a lantern, Churchill in his war memoirs has to fall back on shouting—that is, rhetoric, which is a factor of power rather than of understanding. If the Sermon on the Mount had been expressed rhetorically it would have made little impact, and that only at the moment of delivery. . . . Churchill's rhetoric, like Henry V's in Shakespeare's play, was essential for war purposes, but proves increasingly disastrous as a literary style."

Here, as in much of current usage, rhetoric is still bombast, mere propaganda, perhaps necessary for the affairs of men but necessarily tainted, anti-literary. Obviously I did not come here to plead for a revival of such stuff. But I might well have come to describe how it feels to live in an age dominated by it. A case could be made for the claim that we live in the most rhetorical age of all time, if by rhetoric we mean whatever men do to change each other's minds without giving good reasons for change. I have in mind not only our fantabulous annual expenditures on advertising and public relations and political campaigns, though these alone might brand us, quantitatively, as the most rhetorical age of all time. I am thinking even more about how image building and propaganda have come to dominate fields where traditionally one could expect to find not blandishment or trickery but either solid action or genuine argument. The hand that used to guide the plow now pens the Agricultural Association Press Release. The warrior's sword is now either a typewriter or, if still in fact a destructive weapon, one that is wielded not so much to win battles as to change men's minds. The whole affair in South Vietnam, as President Johnson has said, is carried on in order to prevent Peking and Hanoi "from *thinking* that their current policy of military force will pay dividends" [my italics]. Our nuclear deterrent power is not discussed much any more in terms of its superior strength—nobody doubts that—but in terms of its "credibility." But surely credibility is a rhetorical term. We ask not whether our weapons will destroy you but whether you *believe* that they will destroy you.[1]

I could go on through almost every part of our lives and show a similar reliance on suasion rather than "substance." In journalism we find traditional notions of news accuracy replaced more and more, especially in the news magazines, by standards of rhetorical effectiveness; in place of the facts we are titillated and aroused by weekly collections of little short stories, rhetorically organized to sell an editorial point of view. Or again, our notions of personal worth, once decided by such hard substantive matters as moral virtue, or family history, or money in the bank, are now settled rhetorically. The new annual publication, *Celebrity Register,* as Daniel Boorstin has pointed out, says of itself: "We think we have a better yardstick than the *Social Register,* or *Who's Who,* or any such book. . . . It's impossible to list accurately the success or value of men; but you *can* judge a man as a celebrity—all you have to do is weigh his press clippings." *Who's Who* is more pretentious, but it is, finally, not much different. Its criterion is announced under the exalted phrase, "subjectivity of reference," which, after long puzzlement, I take to mean simply the number of times people are likely to want to look you up.

More significant to us here, perhaps, is the transformation of intellectual disciplines to "merely rhetorical" uses—to continue for a moment with the inadequate notion of rhetoric as something divorced from genuine argument. I have a strong conviction, difficult to prove, that standards of controversy in history,

1. Five and a half years later, Johnson and President Nixon are still talking the same language. Johnson said, on the day after the invasion of Cambodia, "The president's problem is the same as mine was, to get Hanoi to listen."

philosophy, and literary criticism—to name only three—have become less and less substantive throughout this century; irrelevant blandishment, name-calling, sheer one-upmanship have increased, while solid argument has diminished—sometimes to the point of disappearing altogether.[2] There are, of course, splendid exceptions in all disciplines; if there were not, the disciplines would themselves disappear. But I invite you to examine your favorite journal—even if it is one of those few that have tried to maintain serious standards—and count the number of solid *reasons offered* as compared with irrelevant ploys like guilt-by-association, old-hatism, and so's-your-old-thesis-chairman. Wherever one looks one is likely to find, in place of a coherent effort to move from evidence to conclusions, an outpouring of what one of my colleagues calls a mere rhetoric of conclusions. Controversy is conducted as if all strong effects were equally valuable; to shock or simply to win are more important than the discovery of truth. I announce no secrets here, of course; many of our most prominent controversialists have

2. Critical comments by two of my friends have made me think that this claim is not only difficult to prove but quite probably mistaken. Mr. Ronald Crane suggests that it reflects plain ignorance of just how low controversy sank in previous centuries. "Have you read the attacks on Bentley?" Mr. Laurence Lerner reminds me of the standards, if they can be called that, of political controversy in the seventeenth century. And I remind myself, now, of what public debate could be like in nineteenth-century England and America.

Clearly the sweeping historical claims that run throughout this first section of my talk are in no way demonstrated by my examples. They might, in fact, be taken as illustrations of the very thing I am claiming to oppose: the use of mere assertion (the more extreme the better) in place of careful argument. Fortunately my argument that we need more and better rhetorical theorizing does not depend on the extreme claim that we are the *most* rhetorical age: it is enough that our lives are permeated by rhetoric, good or bad, and nobody doubts that.

I still suspect, *pace* Mr. Crane, that we are *quantitatively* the most rhetorical age in history—and not only in the undeniable sense that more men are living by rhetoric than ever before. Surely the *proportion* of rhetorical activities to nonrhetorical (like plowing, shearing, or building) is higher now than ever before. But this modified claim, a radical retreat from my original assertions, may be unimportant, and it is certainly one that would be hard to prove (Crane: "Can you think of any previous age with as much pure science or pure music? These two are *less* rhetorical than ever before").

explicitly repudiated reason in the name of rhetorical effects like shock or outrage.

In short, it is not difficult to find signs that we are a rhetorical age, if we mean by that—once again—an age in which men try to change each other's minds without giving good reasons for change. I know of no past culture where power was so persistently thought of as power to manipulate men's minds; where beauty was so persistently tested by mere popularity or salability; where the truth of propositions was so persistently judged by whether this or that group accepts them; where notions of human greatness were so persistently reduced to the question of fame or "national luminosity"; where, finally, educational goals and methods were so persistently reduced to the notion of conditioning or of imposing already formed ideas or practices upon an infinitely malleable material.

I might very well, then, have come to plead for a further revival of rhetorical studies in order to protect ourselves and our students from rhetoric as a bad thing. Many popular prophets have in fact, like David Riesman in his portrayal of the other-directed man, implored us to find a mode of guidance for our lives somewhat more substantive than a perpetually operating radar set turned to receive rhetorical directions from other members of the lonely crowd.

But I have played too long with a definition that I don't believe in. Rhetoric can mean good things, too. All of the critics who have taken part in the revival of rhetorical studies that began in the mid-fifties have defined the term in ways that would require us to speak of "*bad* rhetoric" when we refer to the perversions I have just described. The definition of *good* rhetoric, or of rhetoric in general, good *and* bad, varies from critic to critic. But beneath the differences there is general agreement that to engage with one's fellow men in acts of mutual persuasion is a noble thing when it becomes mutual inquiry. Indeed, none of the corruptions found in our rhetorical time would even be possible in a society which had not also laid itself open to the great virtues of moral and intellectual suasion when properly used. Consider once again, for example, my summary description of our rhetorical age. One can easily translate it, proposition by proposition, into a description of a kind of utopia. Supposing I could say of our society the following: I can think of no previous society in which questions of political power were so persistently referred to the people for consultation and decision; where questions of beauty were so often decided not by arbitrary rules imposed by an elite but by reference to a genuine capacity of art works to please those who experience them; where questions of truth were so often tested by debate rather than settled by decree; where notions of human greatness were so consistently determined not by fiat of an hereditary aristocracy or plutocracy but by reference to standards testable on the popular pulse; where, finally, educational goals and methods were tested so constantly against practical experience, and where it was unfailingly assumed that, since all men are educable—that is, subject to good rhetoric—there is no limit to the good that can be done through improving the rhetoric of education. Would not such a society—fully as rhetorical as the earlier one—be a noble thing indeed? All of the evils of a rhetorical age are thus corruptions of tendencies that might be ennobling, or at least liberating. Or, to put it again in terms of Riesman's radar set owned by the other-directed man, everything depends on how the radar set is aimed and on the quality of the messages received. An other-directed society might be an ideal society if the "others" were in fact bearers of truth, goodness, and beauty.

Why is it, then, that so much of what we see about us, so much that is done in the name of advertising, of news reporting, of political campaigning, of education, is so cheap, so obviously aimed at persuasion without justification? If I thought I could get away with it here, I might intone an answer something like this: the bad rhetoric of our rhetorical time can be blamed on our almost total failure to develop good rhetorical theory adequate to our needs. I could not get away with such oversimplification, because you are all aware of how little can be changed, directly, by *any* theory, good or bad. But let me try a statement slightly less forceful and perhaps more useful to us: of all the causes of our rhetorical shoddiness, the only one that you and I have much chance of doing anything about is our shoddy rhetorical theory and our shoddier teaching of rhetoric. To our students not majoring in English, we have offered a collection of high school and freshman textbooks that, with few exceptions, are as shameful as any of the ills they purport to cure. To our majors, graduate and undergraduate, we have offered even less: at most universities a student still cannot undertake serious rhetorical study even if he wants to, for lack of teachers, courses, or library facilities.

Finally, what have we offered to the public? That the American public wants rhetorical assistance in an age of rhetoric is shown by the almost incredible success of a popular rhetorician like Rudolf Flesch. Flesch's plausible half-truths about achieving an interesting style by using short words, short sentences, and a personal tone are dangerous, but it is hard to think of what guide to recommend to a literate adult in their place. If someone asks me for works that will help him in reading poetry, I can suggest dozens of respectable books, some of them very good indeed. But if I am asked for guidance in distinguishing good controversial argument from bad, or in constructing a really powerful argument on one's own, or even in constructing an effective—not just a passable—staff report, what do I say? Where, in all of our textbooks about how to write, do we send an intelligent adult for guidance in the true arts of transferring ideas, motives, intentions from his mind to other men's minds?

Please don't try to fob me off with the title of your favorite freshman text, or with Strunk and White. There are some good guides to aid us on the road to literacy, and there are handbooks aplenty. But we must be quite clear about what is needed, and it is not to be found in works designed, for the most part, for semi-literates. What is needed can be seen clearly if we ask where I might turn, in the available rhetorics, for help in improving this talk. I can get help in improving my diction and sentence structure, help of a general kind, from most freshman texts. But where is the theory, where are the practical rules for ensuring that this talk will not only grab you, as the Madison Avenue rhetoricians say, but keep you grabbed and send you away determined to behave differently?

Most of the rhetorical advice I find, even in texts that go beyond simple formulae for correctness, is entirely general. Be brief. Be clear. Be forceful. Revise carefully. Use short words. Such advice is not plainly wrong. It can even be useful. But since it is general, it gives me no help in deciding what arguments might appeal to you, sitting out there in all your particularity on a particular occasion. What appeals are available to me? What order should I give them? Brevity, clarity, unity, coherence, emphasis—none of these will be worth a brass farthing unless somehow I have managed to invent an organized chain of arguments about *this* subject for *this* audience that will bridge the gap between what you believed when you came and what I want you to believe when you depart. But you will look a long while in the available modern rhetorics before you will find much that could possibly help me in this central task.[3]

I do find considerable help about such matters in Aristotle and the many traditional rhetorics fathered by him. They all tell me to look to my arguments and to make sure that there is at least a semblance of genuine connection between them and my conclusions. More important, they tell me that what will *be* a semblance of sound connection can be decided only by considering my audience, and they all give me, by implication, some notion of what a large gathering of more-or-less-middle-aged and thoroughly fatigued teachers of language and literature will demand or allow, as a ratio of real proof to other, incidental appeals. They all suggest ways of handling emotional appeals and those essential but usually disguised claims that I am a citizen of good standing in the world of letters. I find it interesting, incidentally, that with all our modern passion for inventing new studies with proper labels we do not even have words in our language for the sciences of invention and arrangement or for the study of emotional and ethical appeal. With all our new grammars and new stylistics, with our proxemics and tagmemics, surely it is time for someone to make himself a professor of inventionics or arrangementistics.

---

3. I am happy to be able to say that there is a good deal more available in 1970 than there was in 1964. I have been especially helped by the works of Chaim Perelman and by the new journal, *Philosophy and Rhetoric*.

The traditional rhetorics had terms for such matters, and they can still give us more help than most of us suspect. We would be in much better condition if everyone now reviving rhetoric took at least the trouble to learn one traditional rhetoric thoroughly.

But it would be naive to think that reviving Aristotle or Quintilian or Campbell or Whately could solve our problems if only we studied them carefully. For one thing, the age of rhetoric has invented forms of persuasion that earlier ages knew not of. Much, perhaps most, of our rhetoric occurs in informal situations; we need a rhetoric of the symposium, of the conference room—I would hope somewhat more respectable intellectually than what is now offered the public under terms like "group dynamics" and "conference techniques."

What is more, we cannot take for granted, as most traditional rhetoricians felt that *they* could, a systematic coverage by other teachers of logic and dialectic. Our students are not trained, as they could assume of their students, in the analysis of serious argument. Whether we choose to extend the term rhetoric to include the whole art of meaningful discourse or confine it to nonbelletristic, obviously persuasive forms, or confine it even further to the paralogical elements in such persuasive forms, we must find some place in our revived rhetorical studies for training in how to build arguments that coerce, by their cogency, the agreement of all or most of those who will attend to them. Traditional logics and grammars will help us here, but I suspect that modern logics and semantics and grammars will prove indispensable. The revival, here again, must do more than echo the past.

But the main reason for not depending on the revival of earlier rhetorics is simply that none of them can possibly give us the comprehensive rhetorical theory we seek. Living in a new kind of rhetorical age, surrounded by, indeed practicing daily, forms of persuasion their authors never dreamed of, we inevitably hunger for a theory that will do justice to *our* manifold rhetorical experiences, and we do not find that the categories used by earlier theorists quite do the job. I can illustrate this point by asking if you have not felt impatient, so far in my

talk, by my omission of the rhetoric of literature. I have talked
as if the whole problem were that of finding a theory of rhetoric
for the teaching of composition. But you and I are groping for
much more than that, as we work at reviving this old, magical
term. Why have some of the greatest theorists of our time—
men like Richard McKeon and Kenneth Burke—found themselves trying to construct unified rhetorical views of all the
verbal arts? Obviously I cannot answer this rhetorical question
about rhetoric in our time, but I can suggest an answer by asking another: Why do we find ourselves gathered here engaged
in rhetoric about rhetoric and literature? Whatever answer we
give must include, I think, a recognition that we are a rhetorical
age in a sense far more profound than the one I began with.
We believe in mutual persuasion as a way of life; we live from
conference to conference. More significantly, the intellectual
inquiries of our time, even at their most responsible level, have
tended to be inquiries that can best be called rhetorical. In
philosophy we do not begin with metaphysical questions and
pursue "being" and "substance" to the bitter end; rather, we
begin with existentialist commitment, induced by rhetorical
works in philosophical garb, or we analyze the uses of language.
We *do* philosophy on each other, rather than pursue truth as
if it were a thing to be obtained. In literary criticism, similarly,
we have constructed innumerable semantics and rhetorics and
stylistics and linguistics. Even our histories tend to be histories
of linguistic or rhetorical fashion. New sciences like cybernetics
are invented to unite all human inquiry under one science of
information. Even the so-called hard sciences are discussed in
terms of information theory. Last month a new interdepart-
mental committee was formed at Chicago, to supervise information studies—I assume that they will be studying the rhetoric of
genes, atoms, and computers.

To try to deal with such a profusion of sciences of communication with traditional theories would be folly. We hunger, or
at least I hunger, for a comprehensive view of the arts and
sciences of man, a view at least as comprehensive, say, as the two
radically different but equally thoroughgoing views of Plato
and Aristotle. What we have instead is a logomachy, a rhetorical

babel about forms of rhetoric. And the warring factions wage their battles without generals and without having had their basic infantry training.

It is time now for me to come out from behind that feeble metaphor and make my main plea quite openly. My rhetorical point to a group of rhetoricians is twofold: first, that in a rhetorical age rhetorical studies should have a major, respected place in the training of all teachers at all levels; and secondly, that in such an age, specialization in rhetorical studies of all kinds, narrow and broad, should carry at least as much professional respectability as literary history or as literary criticism in nonrhetorical modes. Whether we restore the old chairs of rhetoric by name or not, chairs like my own Pullman Professorship ought to exist in every department, to provide visible proof that to dirty one's hands in rhetorical studies is not a sure way to professional oblivion.

If I had made such a plea for a genuine revival of advanced rhetorical studies ten years ago, I would have had to base my appeal almost entirely on your sense of duty: "The condition of our writing courses demands that we sacrifice ourselves by doing the unpopular thing." But in 1964 one can indulge in that appeal dear to the hearts of all rhetoricians, namely: "Here for once duty and profit and pleasure are reconciled." The fashionable demand for rhetorical studies is such that even the worst textbook profits from the word rhetoric in the title. (I speak from experience: whatever the faults or merits of *The Rhetoric of Fiction,* it has profited factitiously from my having used a fad term, quite unwittingly, in the title. I learned last month of a teacher who had ordered it as the basic text for his freshman composition course!) If, as I am assuming, you want to do serious intellectual work without undue penalties from society, and if—like most of us—you want your work to have some relevance to the real needs of society, you need neither blush nor tighten your belt when you turn from belles lettres to rhetoric.

To those of you who feel that your present research is trivial though respected, I should say: drop that study of Phineas Fletcher or of Suckling's imitators and take up the great rhetorical theorists and the great rhetoricians who helped to mold our age. Those of you, on the other hand, who are doing seemingly nonrhetorical literary study that you know to be not in the least trivial can find both fun and profit in discovering what happens if you grasp your subject by a rhetorician's handle. You might in the process even discover how to transform the current dangerous clamor for "relevance" into an asset: rhetoric at its best has always been the art of revealing connections—"relevancies"—that other men have longed for but ignored.

CENSORSHIP AND
THE VALUES OF FICTION

To the teacher, any attempt by outsiders to censor teaching materials is self-evidently wrong. To the censor, it is self-evident that a responsible society must supervise what is taught to its children. Little wonder, then, that attacks on censorship, like defenses of responsible supervision of materials, too often assume what they set out to prove: addressed to those who are already converted, they may be useful for inspiriting the troops, but far too often they do nothing to breach the enemy's line.

To convert any "enemy," we must show him not simply that respectability or tradition or the National Council of Teachers of English are against him but that he is wrong, wrong according to his own fundamental standards. To tell him that he is wrong according to *our* standards gets us nowhere, though it may be great fun; the problem is to find, somewhere among *his* standards, at least one that is violated by what he proposes to do.

In dealing with censors, as with other enemies, it may very well be that the enemy is in fact so far beyond reason that there is no possible point of contact. But if we assume, as I think we

First printed in *English Journal*, March 1964. Reprinted by permission of National Council of Teachers of English.

must, that at least some of the would-be censors are men of
goodwill whose values, at certain points, coincide with ours,
then we must work at the extremely difficult task of showing
them that even according to their own values, the effort to
censor is misguided.

The sources for such points of contact—and hence of real
rather than merely self-comforting arguments—are many.
Most censors want to preserve some form of society in which
they can exercise their own freedom; we can argue, following
Mill and many others, that the kind of society the censor *really*
wants cannot be maintained if his kind of censorship prevails.
Similarly, most censors respect and seek to further the "truth" as
they see it, and some of them can be shaken by arguing, with
Milton and others, that truth flourishes best when ideas can
compete freely. Or again, many censors, irrational as they may
seem to us, respect consistency and would like to think of themselves as reasonable; they can be shaken, sometimes, by showing
the inevitable irrationalities and stupidities committed by any
society that attempts to censor.

Every teacher in America today owes it to himself to have
ready, either in his mind or in his files, a portfolio of these and
other arguments against censorship, fleshed out, of course, with
the details that alone can make them convincing. He can never
know when the censors will move in his direction, nor can he
know in advance which of his supply of arguments will be
effective in a given crisis. But he can know that unless he has
thought the issues through, he is likely, when the attack comes,
to stand tongue-tied. Of course he may go under anyway, no
matter how well-prepared his defense, if the censor will not
listen to his reasons; one should have no illusions about the
easy triumph of freedom or truth, in any market place, open or
closed. But even if the censor wins, there should be some comfort in knowing that one has at least said what can be said for
the free teacher, freely choosing his own materials.

Since many censorship drives begin with attacks on specific
works, an important and often neglected section of one's "Freedom Portfolio" ought to deal with some such heading as "The
Moral Quality of Individual Works." Though censorship cases

are seldom fought without some appeal to general political and social arguments that apply to all cases, they would more often be won if, at the first threat of attack on any one work, the teacher had ready a battery of specific defenses.

What is usually offered, in place of such specific arguments, is a standard collection of highly general claims, already known to the censor, about the moral value of literature. There is good reason why such claims do not convince. For one thing, some literature is *not* moral, and there is even much good—that is, clever—literature which is quite obviously at odds with any moral values the censor can be expected to care about. For another, most literature, even of the most obviously moral kind, is potentially harmful to *somebody*, as Thomas Hardy pointed out in defense of *Tess of the D'Urbervilles*. The censors are thus always on safe ground, from their own point of view, so long as we talk about all literature, or even all "good" literature. Even the most ridiculous attacks—say those on *Robin Hood*— have this much validity: it is *conceivable* that such a work might alter a child's beliefs, and if we admit this, we must also admit that the alteration might be "for the worse," according to the censor's values. The child who reads *Robin Hood* might decide to rob from the rich and give to the poor, or he might even decide to support a progressive income tax. We do no service to our cause if we pretend, as some have done, that literature cannot have such effects because it does not deal with beliefs. Any literary work that we really read will play upon our basic beliefs, and even though fundamental changes of belief pro- duced by novels may be rarer among mature readers than among novices, it would be foolish to pretend that they do not occur. If the change is "for the worse," from the censor's point of view, then the work has done harm, and it should be banned.

In contrast to our general claims, the censor usually has some specific danger in mind which is directly and literally related to something he has seen in the text. He has found profanity or obscenity or depravity, and we tell him that the book will, like all "good books," do the students good. In Austin, Texas, a pastor who was testifying in a hearing against *Andersonville* read aloud a long sequence of cuss words, excerpted from widely

separated bits of the novel. The committee was quite properly
horrified. The book they "read" was a bad book by any criterion,
and certainly it would be a bad book to teach. But the horrifying
fact about the episode[1] is not that the committee members were
offended by what they had heard but that none of them had
enough gumption to read so much as a single page of the real
book straight through. It would do no good to say to such com-
mitteemen, when the preacher was finished, that *Andersonville*
is really a highly moral work; the "book" which they experienced was not. Similarly it does no good to say to the censor of
The Catcher in the Rye that it is really "calling for a good world
in which people can *connect*—a key word in twentieth-century
writing."[2] One can picture the reactions of the irate parent who
has discovered the obscenities in *Catcher*, as he reads the following defense of the morality of fiction-in-general:

When the student learns to see great books, classic or contemporary,
as metaphors for the whole of human experience, the study of literature contributes in a unique way to this understanding of these
traditions. They help him to discover who he is and where he is going.
  An abstraction may have little emotional impact. But the dramatization of an abstraction, of concepts and values, offers us something
we can grasp. We begin to feel and understand the abstraction.[3]

Now here is something for the parent really to worry about:
if *Catcher* is on his mind, he will think that we teachers are
treating its profanity and obscenity as standing for "the whole
of human experience," suitable to help his child "to understand
who he is and where he is going"! It is surely no comfort to tell
him that literature, by dramatizing the experience of profanity
and obscenity, makes it have more emotional impact.

  The obscene phrase that Holden tries to erase from the school

1. As reported in Jack Nelson and Gene Roberts, Jr., *The Censors and the
Schools,* (Boston, 1963), pp. 136–37.
2, This phrasing was in an early draft of the excellent NCTE pamphlet,
The Students' Right to Read (1962). Every teacher should own and use this
pamphlet, but it does not, even in the revised form, show the censor why
we misguided teachers are so thoroughly convinced that immoral books are
moral books.
3. *The Students' Right to Read,* p. 11.

walls toward the end of *Catcher* is concrete, literal, visible; our "defenses of poesie" tend to be abstract, metaphoric, intangible. We must somehow make them seem to the censor as real as the abuses he has found, but to do so will never be easy. To be concrete and specific about the moral values even of a short poem is terribly difficult, and the precise inferences through which a good reader constructs his reading of a complete novel are so complex that it is no wonder we draw back from the effort to describe them. Yet it is only by learning to follow such processes for himself—that is, by learning how to read—that the censor can discover what we really mean by the morality or immorality of a work. Unless those who wield educational power know at first hand what we mean when we say that a literary work can be moral even though many of its elements are to them objectionable, the other defenses against censorship may finally fail.

I have a frequently recurring fantasy in which I am called before a censorship committee and asked to justify my teaching of such-and-such a book. As hero of my own dream, I see myself starting on page one of whatever book is attacked and reading aloud, with commentary and discussion, page by page, day by day, until the censors either lynch me or confess to a conversion.

A pipedream, clearly. And the one I use for substitute is not much less fantastic. An irate committeeman comes to me (I am a very young instructor in a highly vulnerable school district), and he threatens to have me fired for teaching *The Catcher in the Rye* (or *Huckleberry Finn*, or *Catch-22*—one can of course mold one's daydreams to suit current events). I look him boldly in the eye and I ask him one question: "Will you, before you fire me, do me one last favor? Will you read carefully a little statement I have made about the teaching of this book, and then reread the book?" And since it is fantasy, he says, "Well, I don't see why not. I want to be reasonable." And away he goes, bearing my neatly-typed manuscript and my marked copy of *Catcher*. Some hours later he comes back, offers his humble apologies for what he calls his "foolish mistake," and returns my manuscript. Here it is.

WHAT TO DO WITH A LITERARY WORK BEFORE DECIDING TO CENSOR IT

Let us begin by assuming that we ought to censor all books that we think are immoral. Learned men have offered many arguments against this assumption (you might want to take a look at Milton's *Areopagitica*, John Stuart Mill's *On Liberty*, or the NCTE pamphlet, *The Students' Right to Read*, a copy of which I can lend you), but other learned and wise men, like Plato and Tolstoy, have accepted it, and we can do the same—at least for a time. What should determine whether a book is among those we want to censor?

The question will not arise, of course, unless you have found, as in *Catcher*, something objectionable. There you have found such things as teenagers speaking profanities, the phrase "Fuck you"—repeated!—and a schoolboy's visit to a prostitute. It must seem to you that I am being merely perverse when I say that such a book is really highly moral, when "read properly." Yet I mean something quite real and concrete by this claim. Unfortunately, to see fully what I mean you would need to sit in my classroom every day, throughout the time we spend trying to learn how to read *Catcher* "properly." I know that you cannot spend the time that would be required for this experience, and the principal probably wouldn't allow it even if you could. But there are certain things you can do, on your own, to discover what a "proper reading" of this book might be.

The big job is to relate the seemingly offensive passages to the context provided by the whole work. To say this is not, as you might think, merely a trick to sidestep the true issues. We all relate literary parts to their contexts all the time, almost without thinking about it. If someone told us that a book talked openly about nakedness, we might, if we are worried by pornography, begin to worry. But we are not troubled to read "I was a stranger, and ye took me in: Naked, and ye clothed me: I was sick, and ye visited me." The context has transformed both the word "naked" and the concept of nakedness to obviously moral uses. Similarly, when we read about the woman "taken in

adultery," caught "in the very act," we do not ask that the reading be changed to something less specific. Not only do we take
for granted the piety of the Bible—something we do not and
cannot do for *Catcher*—but the immediate context in John viii
quite evidently requires a forceful statement of the nature of
the sin that is being forgiven. If you doubt this, try substituting
some lesser sin—say gossiping—for adultery in the passage, or
some euphemism like "caught flirting with another woman's
husband."

When we read the many other specific and colorful accounts
of sexual abuses that the Bible contains—of seduction, incest,
sodomy, and rape—we do not put the Bible on the list of
banned books, because we know that the context requires an
honest treatment of man's vices, and that it at the same time
changes the very effect of naming them. Though we might
question the wisdom of teaching particular sections of the Bible
to children of a particular age, we would never think of firing a
teacher simply for "teaching the Bible." We would want at the
very least to know what the teacher was doing with it. We know
the context, in this case, and consequently we know there is at
least one book with many bad things in it that is still a good
book.

It is exactly this same claim that we teachers want to make
about a book like *Catcher in the Rye* (though few of us would
want to go as far as one theologian who has called it a piece of
"modern scripture"). But since the claim is much harder to
substantiate with a long work like a novel, I want to begin with
a look at how the process of transformation works in a short
simple poem. Any poem with possibly offensive elements would
do, but I have chosen a highly secular one that is likely to
offend in several ways: "ygUDuh," by e. e. cummings.

      ygUDuh

          ydoan
          yunnuhstan

          ydoan o
          yunnuhstan dem
          yguduh ged

            yunnuhstan dem doidee
            yguduh ged riduh
            ydoan o nudn
    LISN bud LISN

                dem
                gud
                am

                lidl yelluh bas
                tuds weer goin

    duhSIVILEYEzum

This poem may very well seem unintelligible to you on first
reading. I've seen a class of high school seniors flounder with it
—until I asked one of them to read it aloud. But then they
worked out something like the following "translation" (though
there was finally some unresolved debate about whether it is
spoken by one speaker or two):

            You've got to
                You don't
                Do you understand?
                You don't know
                Do you understand those
                You've got to get
                Do you understand? Those dirty
                You've got to get rid of
                You don't know anything
            LISTEN, Bud, LISTEN
                Those
                God
                damn
                little yellow bas-
                tards, we're going
            To CIVILIZE them.

   Now that the poem is out in the open, as it were (though
limping badly), it obviously offers several possible kinds of
offense. We can imagine, first of all, a National Association for
the Advancement of Yellow People rising in protest against
the offending phrase "yellow bastards," just as the NAACP of
Brooklyn had *Huckleberry Finn* banned because it refers to
Jim constantly as Nigger Jim. What right has a poet to use such

language, degrading a whole people? Even though the poem was obviously written in wartime, when tempers ran high, that is no excuse for descending to such abuse.

"The context of the whole poem" provides an answer to this imaginary protest. Does Cummings, the poet, call the Japanese "yellow bastards"? Obviously not. There is a speaker, drama- tized for our literary observation, a speaker whose tongue bewrayeth him, with every half-word that speweth out of his mouth. It is this speaker from whom the whole content of our paraphrase comes: he it is who would take those yellow bastards and civilize them. What *Cummings* says, of course, is provided only by inference from the way in which the statement is con- veyed. The speaker provides, in the many signs of his brutish inarticulateness, evidence that Cummings is as greatly opposed to his foolish bigotry as the president of the NAAYP might be. And of course, the poet expects us to take pleasure in the comic contrast between the speaker's lack of civilization and his bold program.

If the members of the NAAYP still felt dissatisfied with our effort to place the line in its dramatic context, claiming that they simply would prefer not to see such language in print, we could only ask, "Would you prefer that bigots who hate your group be portrayed more politely, hence more favorably, and hence more deceptively?" It is clear that as the poem stands, the more crudely the bigot is portrayed the stronger the indictment. Is it not likely that a student subjected to this poem in a litera- ture course would come out of his experience *more* sensitive to the issue of bigotry, and *less* willing to accept the crudities of bigots than before?

Other readers, as you may have noticed in your censorship hearings, will object to the profanity. But again we see that the "poem" is no more profane than it is bigoted; it is the speaker who is profane. The purist may still say that he does not want profanity presented even as part of an indictment, but I have not noticed that censorship hearings have been marked by the censors' reluctance to speak the words they object to.

Though the steps we have taken so far with this poem by no means exhaust what the good teacher would want to bring out in discussing it, they show very well what the good censor will want to do before carrying out his job.

1. He will refuse to draw any conclusions whatever from any element of a work taken out of its context. This means that he will read the whole work.

2. He will not be satisfied with one reading. When a work is assigned and discussed in class, it receives several "readings," sometimes quite literally and always in the sense that first impressions are modified by sustained reflection. As a class progresses, a poem, play, or novel is traversed by the alert student again and again. What the censor should be interested in is what the student will get after such reflective rereading, not the errors he might fall into if he read the work without the teacher's encouragement to thoughtful rereading. But of course this means that the censor himself must go through the same process. Any censor who rejected "ygUDuh" on one reading would be a very foolish censor indeed.

3. The true values of a work—the real moral center which we may or may not want to rule out of our children's experience —cannot usually be identified with the expressed values of any one character. What we might call the *author's* values, the *norms* according to which he *places* his characters' values, are always more complex than those of any one of the characters he invents. To censor the Bible because Satan plays a prominent and sometimes even dominant and persuasive role would be absurd. It is equally absurd to censor any book for expressed values which are, for the proper reader, repudiated by the author's implied criticism.

If these three points apply to a short minor poem like "ygUDuh," they are even more applicable to the more complex reading tasks presented by long fiction.

The degree of difficulty varies, of course, depending on the reader and the work. It is easy for most readers to recognize, for example, that Mark Twain does not himself use the word "nigger" in *Huckleberry Finn*. "We blowed out a cylinder-head," says Huck. "Good gracious!" says Aunt Sally. "Anybody hurt?" "No'm. Killed a nigger." The whole point of this episode, coming as it does long after Huck has been forced by experience to recognize the nobility of "nigger Jim," is that even Huck cannot resist thinking as he has been taught to think. Huck here not only uses the word nigger, but reduces "niggers" to less than human standing.[4] But it is not hard—at least for a white man—to see that Mark Twain is far from making the same mistake; indeed, he would have no point in relating the episode except to show a lapse from his own values.

A Negro[5] reader is given a more difficult task. To place the offensive word or concept into its transforming context requires a kind of dispassionate attentiveness that his own involvement with words like "nigger" may easily destroy. The word sets off responses which, though appropriate to most occasions when it is used, are totally inappropriate to the very special use that Mark Twain has made of it. It is likely that every reader sooner or later encounters books that he misreads in exactly this way. And it is highly unlikely that we will ever discover our own errors of this kind, because the very nature of our fault, with its strong emotional charge, keeps us from listening to those who might set us straight.

With all of this as background, suppose we turn now to your objections to *The Catcher in the Rye*. You said that you objected to the printing of the obscene phrase that Holden tries to erase. But in the light of your objections to the book, it is surely strange to find that you and Holden have the same feelings about this phrase: you would both like to get rid of it.

It drove me damn near crazy. I thought how Phoebe and all the other little kids would see it, and how they'd wonder what the hell it meant, and then finally some dirty kid would tell them—all cockeyed, naturally—what it meant, and how they'd all *think* about it and maybe even *worry* about it for a couple of days. I kept wanting to kill whoever'd written it.

4. A possible alternative reading would see Huck as himself master of the ironies here. Since he is author of his own anecdote, he may be thought of as choosing a moral language which he knows will be convincing to his auditor. I do not read it this way, but to do so would not affect my point.

5. Note, 1970: No doubt if I were writing this today I would say "Black" instead of "Negro"; but most "Negro" readers *then* would have felt insulted had I written "Black." A striking instance of how complicated a "context" can be!

Holden could hardly be more strongly opposed to the phrase; it is significant, surely, that throughout the scene from which this passage is taken, the tone is entirely serious—there is none of the clowning that marks Holden's behavior in many other passages. But this immediate context cannot in itself be decisive. Though it is unequivocal about Holden's serious repudiation of the phrase which *you* repudiate, the *author* after all does print the phrase and not some euphemism, and this surely suggests that he is not so seriously offended by the phrase, in itself, as you and Holden are.

Clearly we are driven to thinking about what kind of character the author has created for us, in his lost wild boy. What kind of person is it who, a moment later, concludes that his effort to wipe out the obscenities of the world is "hopeless, anyway," because they are unlimited.

You said this afternoon that you found him to be a terrible person. But supposing we begin from the other direction and ask ourselves why young readers find him, as they do (I have yet to find an exception), so entirely sympathetic. When I ask my adolescent students why they like Holden so much, they usually say, "Because he is so real" or "Because he is so honest." But it takes no very deep reading to find many additional virtues that win them to him, virtues that you and I must admire. It is true that his honesty, or rather his generally unsuccessful but valiant attempt at honesty, is striking. But a far stronger magnet for the reader's affections is his tremendous capacity for love, expressed in deeds that are extraordinarily selfless. The book opens, for example, with his visit, extremely distasteful to him, to the sick and aging history teacher. Holden knows that the old man loves him and needs him, just as he needs the love of the old man; it is out of real feeling that he subjects himself to the sights and smells of age and illness. The moral sensitivity revealed in this scene is maintained through the book. Again and again Holden reveals himself—often in direct contradiction of his own claims—to be far more sensitive than most of us to the feelings of others. He "feels sorry" for all the outsiders, and he hates the big shots who, like the Headmaster, allot their attentions according to social importance and try to shut out

those who are fat, pimply, poor, or corny. He has genuine
affection even for the Ackleys and Stradlaters ("I sort of *miss*
everybody I told about"), and he is extraordinarily generous,
not only with his possessions (almost everything he owns is on
loan to some other boy) but with himself (he is the only boy who
thinks of including the impossible Ackley in the trip to the
movies). Though he often hurts others, he never does so in-
tentionally ("I was sorry as hell I'd kidded her. Some people
you shouldn't kid, even if they deserve it.") His heroes are those
who are able to love unselfishly—Christ, Mr. Antolini, his
sister—or those who, like James Castle, show moral courage.
His enemies are those who deliberately inflict pain—for example, the boys who drive Castle to suicide.

A full catalog of his virtues and good works would be unfair
to the book, because it would suggest a solemn kind of sermon-
izing very different from the special *Catcher* brand of affection-
ate comedy. But it is important to us in talking about possible
censorship of the book to see its seeming immoralities in the
context of Holden's deep morality.

The virtue most pertinent to the obscene phrase is of course
Holden's struggle for purity. The soiled realities of the "phony"
world that surrounds him in his school and in the city are
constantly contrasted in his mind with the possible ideal world
that has not been plastered with obscenities. His worrying
about what Stradlater has done to Jane, his fight with Stradlater, his inability to carry through with the prostitute because
he "feels sorry" for her, his lecture to himself about the crudities
he watches through the hotel windows, his effort to explain to
Luce that promiscuity destroys love—these are all, like his
effort to erase the obscenity, part of his struggle to find "a place
that's nice and peaceful," a world that is "nice and white."
Though he himself soils, with his fevered imagination, the pure
gesture of Antolini, revealing how helplessly embedded he is in
another kind of world altogether, his ideal remains something
like the world of the nuns, or the world of a Christ who will not
condemn even Judas to eternal damnation. He is troubled, you
will remember, when one of the nuns talks about *Romeo and
Juliet,* because that play "gets pretty sexy in some parts, and

she was a nun and all." Nuns ought to live in the pure, sexless, sinless, trouble-free world of his ideal, just as his sister ought to live in a world unsullied by nasty scrawlings on stairway walls.

All of this—the deep Christian charity and the search for an ideal purity—is symbolized in his own mind by the desire to be a catcher in the rye. He wants to save little children from falling, even though he himself, as he comes to realize, is a child who needs to be saved. The effort to erase the words is thus an ultimate, desperate manifestation of his central motive. Though it is a futile gesture, since the world will never in this respect or any other conform fully to Holden's ideal of purity, it is produced by the very qualities in his character which make it possible for him to accept his sister's love at the end, give up his mad scheme of going west, and allow himself to be saved by love. It is clear that he is, for his sister, what she has become for him: a kind of catcher in the rye. Though he cannot protect her from knowledge of the world, though he cannot, as he would like, put her under a glass museum case and save her from the ravages of the sordid, time-bound world, he can at least offer her the love that comes naturally to him. He does so and she is "saved." Which is of course why he is ecstatically happy at the end.

Now none of this is buried very deep in the novel. I've not had to probe any mystical world of symbols or literary trickery to find it out; it is all evident in the actions and words of Holden himself, and it is grasped intuitively, I have found, by most teen-age readers. Their misreadings are caused, in fact, by carrying this line too far: they often overlook Holden's deficiencies. So strong is the persuasive power of his obvious virtues (obvious to them) that they overlook his limitations of understanding and his destructive weaknesses: they take him at his word. They tend to overlook the strong and unanswerable criticism offered by his sister ("You don't like *any*thing that's happening") and by Antolini, who tries to teach him how to grow up ("The mark of the immature man is that he wants to die nobly for a cause, while the mark of the mature man is that he wants to live humbly for one"). They also overlook the author's many subtle contrasts between what Holden says and

what he does. In learning to read these and other built-in criticisms, students can learn to criticize their own immaturities.
They learn that such a book has been read only when they have
seen Holden's almost saint-like capacity for love and com-
passion in the light of his urge to destroy the world, and even
himself, because it cannot live up to his dreams.

I am aware that what I have said does not "prove" that
Catcher is harmless. I'm sure there are some young people who
might be harmed by it, just as reading the Bible has been known
to work great harm on young idealists given to fanaticism. I
have not even "proved" that the book can be beneficial. Only
your own reading can convince you of that; again I find myself
wishing that you could reread the work with us, in class. But
perhaps you will return to it now and try once more, moving
from page 1 to page 277, thinking about Holden's moral life
as you go.

I know I do not have to ask you (the dream continues) for
your decision. As a man of honor, you can only have carried out
our little experiment to the letter, and the book is now cleared
of all suspicion. I should not be surprised if your experience
has also made you wonder about other books you have suspected
in the past.

You may have guessed by now that I have been inching my
way all this while toward a repudiation of our original assumption. Is there really a place for *any* censorship other than the
teacher's careful choice? The skill required to decide whether a
work is suited for a particular teaching moment is so great that
only the gifted teacher, with his knowledge of how his teaching
aims relate to materials chosen for students at a given stage of
development, can be trusted to exercise it.

Such a teacher can be trusted even when he chooses to teach
works that reveal themselves, under the closest reading, to be
immoral to the core. Let us suppose that you have performed
the kind of reading I have described on a given work, say
Peyton Place or one of Mickey Spillane's thrillers, and you find
that it does not, as with *Catcher*, have any defense to offer for
itself: it is immoral no matter how one looks at it. So you go
to the teacher to insist that the book be removed from the

reading list. You should not be surprised if the teacher replies: "Oh, yes, I quite agree with you. *Peyton Place* is inherently an immoral work; there are, in fact, far worse things in it than the few sexual offenses you object to. Read carelessly by high school students, it could do tremendous harm—like other books of the same kind. That's why I insist on spending some time, in my advanced sections, on this particular kind of shoddiness. I find that most of my students have read the juicier sections on their own, anyway. By placing those pornographic bits back into the shoddy context from which they have been torn, the student soon comes to treat Metalious' commercial sensationalism with the contempt it deserves."

So you see, sir (the drama has by now shifted, dream-like, from manuscript to real-life drama, and I am hearty, confident, even slightly patronizing as I fling one arm across his shoulder), the only person who can conduct the fight for good literature is the person who has some chance of knowing what he is doing: the sensitive, experienced teacher. He it is who. . . .

Dreams of wish fulfillment always end with a rude awakening. My dream ends with the admission that even with the best of luck my argument about *Catcher* would do no more than shake a censor's confidence in his own judgment. Wide awake, I know that many censors will only scoff at any efforts we may make to reason about the issues of censorship. But as I write these final lines, in South Africa, in August 1963, I do not doubt for a moment that even an ineffectual defense of freedom is better than no defense at all.

THE UNCRITICAL AMERICAN
OR,
NOBODY'S FROM MISSOURI
ANY MORE

In Memoriam, P. A. Christensen

I

My family were almost all passionately committed to education. They were schoolteachers, most of them, and they believed in the righteousness of collecting academic degrees. Their church had taught them that man cannot be saved in ignorance, that the glory of God is intelligence, and that any right-living man can become a god of his own world by learning—over aeons— how to do it. Yet they were deeply suspicious of that chief product of genuine education, the critical intelligence. The very words "criticism" and "critical" were anathema through-out my adolescence, when I was first discovering the pleasures of critical probing. "Anybody can criticize," my mother would say to me, in rebuke, even as she struggled toward her bachelor's degree, won at age forty-six, and her master's, at fifty-six. "If you only wouldn't stir things up so much," she would say, while encouraging me in what she liked to call my progress toward the Ph.D. There was never the slightest doubt in any-one's mind that to move toward higher and higher degrees

Revised from an address given to the teachers of English at Asilomar, Cali-fornia, 1969.

was to *progress;* yet whenever I tried to apply anything important that I learned from my best teachers—whenever, that is, I
tried really to think about everyday matters like politics or
church belief or the Boy Scout movement, it was, "There you
go, criticizing again!"

I don't suppose you'll be surprised when I say that in this
ambivalence toward education and its fruits my family was
very much like the whole of this nation today. Never before has
a country spent so much of its substance on education; everyone pursues degrees like merit badges, and it is quite clear that
the kingdom of heaven is closed to drop-outs, no matter what
we heretics may say. And yet few of us seem willing to accept the
educated behavior that ought to result from formal education.
Few graduates of our high schools or colleges seem able to apply
their minds in an educated way to the world around them; few
of them threaten anyone with a genuinely critical judgment. I
don't know whether we are a more credulous generation than
our fathers, but it surely must be true that in proportion to the
amount of time and money we spend ostensibly educating each
other we are the most credulous, gullible, superstitious people
of all time.[1]

Since if this is true it is a pretty serious indictment of all of
us teachers, I'll want to give some documentation about it as we
go along. But first I should make clear that I am not simply
repeating that old charge men often make against those who
believe what to them are foolish or outlandish beliefs. It is
easy to whip together a collection of all of the nonsense *other*
men believe, label it something like *The Anatomy of Nonsense*
or *The Prevalence of Nonsense* or *Scientific Fads and Fallacies*
or *Science is a Sacred Cow* or *Strange Beliefs of Mankind* or
The Age of Credulity or *Bouvard et Pecuchet* or *This Believing
World*—and you've got a very amusing book. Such collections

---

1. The reader may notice that once again I am struggling, as in *The Revival
of Rhetoric* (p. 38), to generalize about our rhetorical situation without
exaggerating for effect. Again I hear Ronald Crane, now deceased, saying,
"What's your evidence?" But on this point I think I have enough to satisfy
even Ronald Crane.

of stupidities, such *sottisiers,* usually say more about the collector than about those he describes. Each such book I have seen has succumbed to the temptation of making the beliefs seem more outlandish than they ever were in their original form, in order to make the collection more amusing or startling. But when I describe our time as a credulous time, I am not thinking of our many crazy beliefs so much as of the *way* we believe them; not what we believe but how. Even if every one of us in this room knew the ten most insidious errors of our time, and set out to spend the rest of our lives correcting them, we could not hope to make an appreciable difference in the Total Error Count, our TEC, before we die; ten errors will spring up for every one we kill, and what is more, we will ourselves manufacture errors even as we try to communicate our beautiful list of truths. But if you and I could learn to think for ourselves, and if in our lifetimes we helped a few of our fellows to do the same, our troubled country might someday notice the difference.

The test is, then: What process has been gone through by the believer before he has made up his mind? An educated man in this sense is one who requires of himself certain kinds of mental activity before he will accept an idea, follow a leader, embrace a plan of action, or embark on a way of life. He will certainly make use in his cogitations of promptings from the heart and gut, but knowing as he does that these organs are the devil's favorites, he will reserve a special scrutiny for all beliefs that carry with them slogans like "In your heart you know he's right." He will never forget that like all other men, he lives in error. There is no way to avoid it, in any society, and especially in one like ours that employs a huge corps of professional deceivers who work full time to maximize, as it were, our TEC quotient. But knowing how inescapably he shares the common lot, he will know one thing that is not common: how to match the degree of his conviction to the quality of his reasons. He will labor to believe only when belief is warranted and to doubt only when doubt is warranted, and he will thus labor to master the processes of thought that yield warrantable belief or doubt.

II

When we shift our concern in this way from *what* is believed to *how* it is believed, it is easy to see that our problem is not simply one of a too easy affirmation. We do have many round-heeled folk whose minds are easily seduced, and we have polite old-fashioned words for them: they are credulous or they are gullible or they are superstitious. The words for those who fail in the opposite direction are not so clear. Some of them we call cynical, or skeptical; we might coin a word *substitious*. Young people often try to simulate education by moving from superstition to substition. After all, if I don't commit myself to anything or anybody, nobody can accuse me of naive commitment. But once they have found some sort of commitment, they accuse those who refuse to follow them of being "overly analytical," of spoiling the world by intellectualizing it. College students often accuse faculty and administrators of using reason to postpone commitment and action, or substituting study and scholarship for the truths of the heart.

As soon as we look behind the epithets used by believers and doubters against each other, I think it becomes clear that to be genuinely critical—to judge on the basis of thought—is to have no easily predictable relationship with belief or doubt, with yes or no, with joining or splitting. The critical mind does not know in advance which side it will come out on, and the surest sign that a man has given up thinking is to find that the *yes*es and *no*s flow in predictable, general patterns. Someone said that the trouble with President Johnson is that you can't even rely on the *opposite* of what he says. The joke was intended initially against Johnson. But it bounces back finally against the teller. Like the rest of us, he wants a neat formula for belief: my enemy is *for* it, so I know where *I* stand.

It is clear, then, that it will do no good to indict a "nation of sheep" and try to turn them into a nation of mules. A blind confidence in negation is as credulous, as uncritical, as a blind confidence in affirmation. In fact the two forms of blindness are very closely related and easily lead into each other: mankind cannot endure very much uncritical doubt for long, and it is not surprising that men who have learned that nothing can be proved soon feel licensed to believe anything they damn please. If no convictions can be finally supported by reason, then why not succumb to the will to believe something, anything, rather than operate in a belief vacuum?

It is scarcely surprising, then, that all about us we see social and religious solutions being invented and embraced as lightly as one might choose a breakfast food. For some it is the John Birch Society—a group whose works are clearly going to affect your life and mine with increasingly disastrous results in the next few years. For others it is left-wing groups showing equal carelessness about fact and an open contempt for any effort to think things through. For some it is new religions whose claims are embraced without even a pretence at thought; for others it is one or another of the pseudo-psycho-religions, claiming to cure the soul with nudity or vegetables or group therapy sessions or orgone boxes or omphalic worship or standing on your head. Nothing has surprised me more than the recent revival, among would-be intellectuals, of interest in astrology. Astrology has always had its believers, but now one finds adherents cropping up everywhere—not just in reactionary bastions like the Living Theater but among students in major colleges and universities. I don't have time to give here my neat little refutation of the claims of astrology, but needless to say they are not decisive for anyone who has already decided to believe. What is interesting—for those of us who are interested in that sort of thing—is the comic flimsiness of the evidence offered *for* astrology—or for astroprojection or flying-saucerism or whatever. No doubt each of these and innumerable other beliefs *work,* as we say, for some believers. Miraculous cures occur in most new religions, and they are not to be scoffed at, especially when they are performed by the devil himself. Even those curious half-religions that spring up around academic subjects have the power to heal loneliness or boredom: if Bacon or Marlowe really wrote Shakespeare's plays, life may be interesting after all. And if you ask for evidence, you are at best a spoilsport and more likely an enemy of the Light.

We seem to be approaching a glorious age when everyman

will be entitled to his own cult, as a birthright. Can we wonder that a man as intelligent as Malcolm X should require decades to see through Fard's myth of Yacob when his white brothers, with university degrees, were preaching Velikovsky's myth of the earth's history or Egyptian numerology or what not? I know men who talk as if they would give their lives for this or that totally conjectural theory about who killed Kennedy or King or Kennedy, or about a currency standard that will save the world, or about how the Jews are conspiring for world mastery. Most of us seem convinced that commitment is so valuable that even a commitment to madness is better than apathy. Somehow we have failed to teach those who have passed through our schools—and all of these credulous folk have done so—that commitment is admirable only when it is to admirable causes. When a member of the California state board of education, George A. Brown, commits himself to a pernicious campaign of censorship, his commitment is a pathetic thing because it is uncritical. No doubt he has the best of intentions, as we say. He believes that he is serving truth and virtue (or so one can assume). But even the most elementary critical ability —what one would hope for from an average eighth grader— would have shown him that truth and virtue are not served by cutting swear words out of short stories. Mr. Brown wants Hugh Hefner's story deleted from a text because Hefner's Playboy philosophy is objectionable. I happen to think the Playboy philosophy is one of the silliest bits of intellectual pretension ever to catch the American mind and heart, and its popularity illustrates my thesis about uncritical Americans. But did none of us teachers ever try to teach Mr. Brown that this method of combatting Hefner's story is first undemocratic, second irrelevant, third totally ineffective, and fourth unnecessary? Mr. Brown is, I'm afraid, closer than he would think to the current mood of many college students who believe, or seem to, not only that truth can be discovered intuitively (and it can be) but that it is tested that way as well. The motto seems to be, If you feel it's true, it's true. Well, I was brought up with this notion, which was used by every religious denomination, including my own, to demonstrate its superior truth. One man who lived not far

from my home *felt* in his heart that God had commanded him
to kill his wife, and he did. Last spring two other men acted,
apparently, on the truths of the self-righteous heart and assas-
sinated what they took to be enemies of their countries.

But I have been coming dangerously close to the very error
I warned against—listing foolish beliefs as if in themselves they
provided proof of our uncritical habits. But they do not. For all
I really *know,* some of these beliefs may turn back against me
ultimately, by proving to be true. Though I think that to have
so many contradictory beliefs points to our mass credulity, to
me a more convincing kind of evidence is found when we look
at how men proceed when they attempt to persuade each other.

Every argument (whether openly argumentative or disguised
as journalism or literature) will betray the author's picture of
the educational level of his readers, and it will do so far more
profoundly than in the simple choice of vocabulary that is sometimes tested by the news media when they want to discover
whether they are writing over everyone's heads. The picture of
the reader will be made most revealingly at those many points
at which the writer ceases to push his argument, believing that
he has found an assertion which the reader will take either as
self-evident fact or as self-evident principle or assumption. If
an author tells me that I should vote for Wallace because the
Supreme Court has gone too far too fast in its decision on race
relations, he has told me not only something about himself but
something about his picture of me; if another author tells me I
should vote for Wallace because it is good to get the racists out
into the open—period—he has told me something of his picture
of my natural assumptions and natural critical expectations.
And I submit that the reader implicitly portrayed by what gets
addressed to the American public these days, in general journals
of left, right, and center, is one that ought to insult us all.

Take as an example an article on "The Good Things in
America Today" in *U.S. News & World Report.* It was published just after the Democratic convention of 1968, when
perhaps more people than ever before were calling America
"sick," and though it was thinly disguised as a "report," it
argued quite openly, from the title on, that "the nation's

strengths are . . . great and varied," that "the United States today is not the 'sick giant' so often portrayed by critics—but a strong and powerful nation, one that continues to be the envy of the world at large." Now I think a case might be made for this position, but it would not be an *easy* case. If it were made with care, by someone who took the trouble to look first at the arguments for our being a sick society, it would induce thought on both sides, and it might even lead to some ideas about how to capitalize on our strengths and reduce our weaknesses. But how do you suppose *U.S. News & World Report* handles the case?

The article reveals in every detail that the anonymous author assumes a reader fat for the kill—not only already in agreement, or very nearly so, but unaware of any possible counterarguments and totally indifferent to all demands for coherence of argument or precision and relevance of factual evidence. The editors of *U.S. News & World Report* see their readers as prosperous white businessmen—and there's nothing especially wrong in that. But that they should see them as ignorant, uncritical, complacent white businessmen is disturbing, since it seems likely that most of the readers are formally educated, as we say—not just high school graduates but college trained.

The first three arguments for the thesis of health appear under the boldface heading "So much for so many": (1) "Never, in the past, has a society offered so much prosperity to so many of its people." The reader presumably can be counted on to remind himself that he shares in this prosperity, and he needs no proof that his material prosperity is a sign of national health. Yet it takes only a moment's thought to show that nobody who has claimed that the nation is sick has denied our material prosperity—not in this sense. (2) "Far from being a sick society, Americans in the majority are showing themselves to be strong and morally responsible." It feels good to be told that you look strong and morally responsible, especially when others have been nagging at you about how peaked you look. The only evidence given, therefore, at this point, is that Americans "are spending billions to erase poverty in the nation—and more billions to help other nations." Again this would not be denied, as a bare fact, by the critics, and the reader is expected to say to himself, "Actually I'm generous to a fault—all that money down the drain, and all we get for it is criticism!" The evidence for strength is our "nuclear defense system . . . that is providing security for much of the world. American troops drove Communist invaders out of South Korea, kept the peace in Lebanon and staved off a Communist take-over in South Vietnam." Again it is revealing that the author stops at this point; these are thought to be self-evidently good things, as signs of our strength. The reader is postulated as someone so uncritical that he will not know or will forget that for most of those who call the country sick, the undeclared war in Vietnam is one symptom of the disease.

Next we turn to culture, and we learn that "the 'American way of life' is turning up everywhere"—the two pieces of evidence offered are that young people in Communist countries "are playing 'rock' music" and that in France the "light luncheon favored by American businessmen is making heavy inroads on the Parisian cuisine"!

And so we go on through this cheerful, mindless landscape. There are, of course, some arguments in the piece that might be taken seriously by critics as well as by the pre-sold: for example, professors might be impressed by the assertion that "university presses, alone, have multiplied sales five times since 1948." But the interesting revelations come from all those arguments that will seem absurd, or at best incomplete, from *any* other point of view except that of the "uncritical American." Some arguments are so curious that it is hard not to suspect that the editors are joking: "Similarly, a French philosopher noted: 'To make life simpler in an increasingly complicated world is an American art.' That art is making it possible, as one instance, for Americans to dial a number on the telephone and hear a prayer, a short sermon, the latest baseball scores, a lecture on alcoholism, or arguments against committing suicide." One can imagine exactly the same list used by the proponents of the view that America is sick, since Americans cannot distinguish the important from the trivial and do not see the difference between "dialing a prayer" and praying. But such imaginings are not assumed to be within the capacity of the reader of this piece.

One good way, then, to discern the reader whose uncritical biases are being played to, is to ask, "Where do the arguments stop? What is thought to need no proof?" Another way is to look at what lines of argument are most heavily emphasized and what played down or ignored. In this piece, economic power abroad and prosperity at home ("for the majority") are dwelt on lovingly: "America's economic power, far from declining, is pushing ahead to even more dominance in the world." "Predictions are heard that U.S. industry on that continent [Europe] soon will become the world's third-largest economic power—after America itself and Soviet Russia." When poverty is mentioned, it is "what passes for poverty," and it is "seen by many foreigners as an acceptable standard of living." There is no mention of reports of widespread starvation and malnutrition in America. When black America is discussed, it is almost entirely in terms of the increased prosperity of those above the poverty line: "Since 1960, the number of Negro families earning more than $7,000 a year has more than doubled. Median income of the Negro family has gone up from $3,233 in 1960 to $4,900."

Even when the article finally returns for a second try at cultural matters like education, books, and music, the emphasis is statistical and economic. It is assumed that there is no reason to meet arguments against the *quality* of education, so long as we have more people in college and high school than other nations. Nothing need be said about the *quality* of the books we produce, so long as the "dollar volume" of book sales has doubled in ten years. When religion is mentioned, again statistics are decisive: "45 per cent of all Americans" attend church during a typical week; "97 per cent of adult Americans" believe in the existence of God.

No such analysis as we are undertaking here can tell us whether the conclusions of the writer are true; all we can say is that the reasons offered could be persuasive only for a reader with certain very strong and very obvious prejudgments and certain very dangerous habits of mind. He believes in economic and military power as ends in themselves; he is impressed by quantities rather than qualities; he enjoys personal prosperity and power and does not want to think about them; he wants to see himself and his country as moral and generous and "cultured" (but he doesn't care too much about the details); and he is terribly eager to be convinced that things are getting better all the time. The boldface headings of the sections taken by themselves reveal these biases almost in schematic form: "So much for so many; Succor to world; Story of progress; Rise from poverty; Production miracle; A rugged dollar; America's head start; Passion for education; Europe surpassed; Book-buying people; Wide map for culture; How Americans really feel; Steady, undramatic lives; Money ignored; Courage rewarded." (The evidence about the praiseworthy indifference to money— college youngsters work in slums and in camps for under- privileged children—is especially interesting in view of the contrasting evidence throughout the article that the readers of this magazine are not the least inclined to ignore money).

Bad as this is, I must remind you again that no analysis of this kind, even if prolonged indefinitely, can establish the falsehood either of the general case or of the particular claims used to support it. All it can lead to is an assessment of the adequacy of the *case made* to the *conclusions.* And when the case made is as feeble as this one, we can only infer that the assumed reader is by no conceivable stretch of our definition an educated man. It is hard to deduce whether the author is con- sciously playing down to a least common critical denominator or is himself unaware of how shoddy his case is. If he is aware—and there is plenty of evidence that the writers of such articles in the weekly media frequently are—then we have proof of a moral as well as an intellectual problem; his cynicism is a direct threat to us all. If he is unaware, then we have just one more un- educated man on our collective conscience: if he or any of his presumed readers ever studied under any of us, and we tell him now that he is pathetically unqualified for making his way in the world, can we English teachers honestly claim to have done all that might have been done for him, before it was too late?

Anyone who once starts thinking about these matters will find examples in almost every journal, left, right, and center. I could have spent time, for example, on an incredibly empty

piece in *Ramparts,* a panegyric on District Attorney Garrison
in which the evidence supporting him and his conspiracy theory
is chiefly assertions about the stupidity and wickedness of
Garrison's enemies and about his own courage and liberality of
viewpoint. Or I could have used examples from SDS literature,
in which unproved assumptions about depraved America and
its revolutionary situation are offered fully as uncritically as
anything I have quoted. I could have used the opening pages of
Mark Lane's *Rush to Judgment* or the lines of so-called argument in any one of dozens of pieces of literary criticism *in my
files* (as the other McCarthy used to say). Or I could have used
the advertisements of intellectual journals. I especially like the
ad of a new journal, the *Marshall McLuhan Newsletter,* which
will cost fifty dollars a year and which promises to get itself into
my hands in as "little as 72 hours after Mr. McLuhan has written it." Its service will include, the ad says, not only detecting
changes in American society "the minute they occur—but following them, monitoring them, checking their feed-back to
evaluation potential and consequences at every stage. This is
not (like a book) merely a snapshot of the present; it is a radar-
fix on its every movement. . . ." Here is prophecy hot off the
mountaintop, available for only fifty dollars a year, and cheap
at the price. The only reasons for subscribing, stated or implied,
are that the stuff will be new, up-to-date, fresh from the oven,
and that it will thus put you ahead of other men if you read it. I
tremble as I wonder whether any of my former students will fall
for that ad.

None of what I have said today gets us very far in the positive
task of deciding how we should think and how we should act.
What are the *valid* processes by which an educated man tests
whether he should believe or doubt? Where *does* truth come
from? Doesn't it often come intuitively, and are we not all
dependent, as Pascal said, on truths of the heart that reason
does not recognize? And if that is so, aren't we right back where
we started?

Well, I hope not, not if we can become aware of the temptations and make it a major task of our lives to learn how to combat them. I certainly cannot claim to know any simple formulae

for the processes of heart and mind that will carry you and your students through fraud and greed and folly to sound beliefs and effective action. But I am convinced both that the task of becoming educated is more difficult than ever before and that, in spite of what some people are saying, it is still both possible and relevant. You cannot solve all of life's problems by learning to think, but you can't solve any of them without it. You can't avoid mistakes by determining to combat the new credulity, but you will make many more if you simply swim with the tide. Learning to think for yourself will of course get you into kinds of trouble that simply accepting slogans and clichés will often avoid. It may, in fact, lead to imprisonment and even death if our society should finally, like many societies past and present, corrupt itself to the point of denying us the right to free thought.

In the next few years the uncritical Americans are going to come out of the woodwork in battle array, and in increasing numbers. In their very existence they are an indictment of American education and by implication of the English teachers who have failed to educate them. In their attack on us, however, they may show more clearly than some of us have seen what the nature of our vocation is. We are committed to the awakening of minds, to the sharpening of the critical intelligence, to the creation of critical Americans. There is no profession nobler than this—if we practice it honestly and well. And there is no profession which so clearly has the future of America in its hands. If that frightens us a little, it ought to, even as we remember for our comfort Socrates' discovery that it is better for a man to die than to stop thinking.

Part

OF
THE RATIONAL
PERSUASION

Keep reason under its own control.
—Marcus Aurelius

OF THE
RATIONAL PERSUASION

One of my philosopher friends claims that when I try to philosophize it is a shameless form of revenge on modern philosophy. If trained philosophers still worked on ethical and social and educational problems in ways accessible to a literate public, amateurs like me would not have a chance.

Amateur is certainly the word—with both good and bad connotations. I have loved philosophy ever since I devoured, at fifteen, that abominable book by Will Durant, *The Story of Philosophy*. And I have been flailing about for more than twenty years (including one glorious year financed by the Ford Foundation "reading philosophy on my own"), trying to convince myself and my students that skepticism and nihilism, like dogmatism and fanaticism, are finally unreasonable—not just unpleasant to other people but genuinely indefensible on intellectual grounds.

The world has not noticeably surrendered to the force of my arguments, which are usually borrowed and always a bit underdeveloped by the standards of contemporary philosophy: the arguments of a rhetorician. I believe that meaningful argument is possible about even the subtlest of human choices; a reasonable rhetoric is possible on any important subject. Fifteen years ago this seemed a more old-fashioned faith among philosophers than it does now; the Wittgenstein who had seemed to claim that we can only "remain silent" about the values we care for most is now less fashionable, even among followers of Wittgenstein. But my gropings still have a distinctly eighteenth-century air. It is in the Age of Reason, or at the latest in Coleridge, that I find my sources, when they are not classical— men who not only believe in a rational persuasion but who can be said to be *of* the rational persuasion: their religion and their reasonings are inseparable.

I know, or think I know, that it makes a real difference how men argue and what they argue; I know, or think I know, that the difference would not be finally real if the cosmos itself did not issue the command to us: Be Reasonable. The command is of course muted and garbled, like all messages from the oracle. Living in an age when the quarrels among philosophers themselves have been especially destructive of faith in reason, I have surely been a poorer listener than I might have been in other places and times. But I have no doubt whatever that the most important moments of my life—except for moments of love and music—have been when genuine philosophers have cleared away the background noise and enabled me to do a little direct listening.

KNOWLEDGE AND OPINION

Since this is obviously my last chance at you seniors, I was tempted to wrap up in one bundle all of my present opinions about politics, art, education, science, the old alma mater—indeed, about everything—and set you straight once and for all. I even went so far as to write out my five most important opinions—a five-minute statement of each opinion. It was a beautiful job, written in lovely professional style, with unity, coherence, and emphasis—but I had to give it up. On reading it over, I saw that even if you picked up all five of my conclusions—conclusions that to me represent years of what I sometimes like to call intellectual struggle—they would be worthless to you. Even if you imbibed them in something like the unadulterated form in which I poured them out (which, judging from my experience with examination books, is unlikely), even if you held to them throughout life as "something I learned at college," our time here would have been wasted.

Let me try to explain why I resisted the temptation—one that

Originally given as the Senior Recognition address at Earlham College, 1956. Reprinted with permission from *Journal of General Education,* January, 1957.

will *not* be resisted by many a convocation speaker this spring—to add a few more sterling opinions to the no doubt impressive list you have compiled during the last twenty-one years or so.

I

I should make clear at once that I am not calling my opinions worthless simply because, transferred to your mind, they would prove to be fleeting. It is true, truer than many of you may yet realize, that all of our opinions are shamefully fleeting. If you doubt me, try reconstructing what you believed four years ago and then compare those beliefs with your present enlightened views. Since I have a somewhat longer time-span available, I can achieve even more impressive results looking back to my freshman year. In 1939 I remember being taught in my freshman chemistry course, for example, the opinion that the atom consisted of a nucleus made up of protons and electrons and a group of planetary electrons. Protons and electrons were tiny charged material particles. Even then, had I known, this picture was already outmoded, and by now most of what I memorized has been revised. Or, again, in 1939 in my freshman English course I learned that the eighteenth century was a dry, passionless time when men were interested only in empty formalism and that the romantics restored emotion to its proper sphere. I did not know that this view had already been shown to be completely misleading twenty-five years before—the new scholarly conclusions had not yet trickled down as opinions to college English texts. Nor did I foresee that fifteen years later I would consider this dry, formalistic period to be one of the most interesting periods in English literature.

In 1939, finally, I learned that the universe was millions of years old, perhaps hundreds of millions of years old. Arguing with my fundamentalist friends at Brigham Young University, I can remember shouting, "But it's been proved!" Since then, of course, I have followed meekly after the scientists, revising upward to one billion, then to two billion, then four billion, and now six billion—the last I heard.

II

Yes, your opinions will change—I hope—but that is not what I am talking about. Much more important is that even your unchanging opinions are in no sense true for you unless you know their intellectual bases, unless you know, in a nonhistorical sense, where they came from. And we know where they came from only if we can reconstruct the reasons for believing them in the first place. Indeed, to know the reasons for believing an opinion makes it something more than a mere opinion: it makes of it an idea, and only a body of ideas can give us knowledge. Everybody has opinions, but only the man who can think for himself, or at the very least reconstruct the living process of thought pioneered by others, has ideas.

Opinions are almost always proved to be false. In the long run they are, by their very nature, likely to be discarded—just as my completely thoughtless view of the atom has been shown to be false as I have accepted another thoughtless view of the atom which will in turn be shown, I can be sure, to be false when another view is popularized, and so on. But ideas, in the sense in which I am using the term here, are seldom shown to have been false though they may prove to have been inadequate. Democritus, for example, thought about the problem of constant change and came up with the idea that nothing could account for all this shifting world but the existence of invisible atoms changing about into an unlimited variety of combinations but themselves remaining unchanged. His atomic theory, however inadequate by modern standards, was an idea, in my sense. Given the facts he had to deal with, the assumptions under which he necessarily worked, and the purposes he had in mind, his conclusions follow just as vitally today as they did more than two thousand years ago. And the basic problem he wrestled with—whether the fundamental particles of matter themselves remain unchanged—is still plaguing the physicists and philosophers.

Similarly, the romantics who originated the cliché that the eighteenth century was a drab time when the human spirit was in fetters, were not themselves dealing in clichés; they had an *idea* not only of what they wanted to get *away from* but also of what they wanted to *move toward*. They saw something that was truly lacking in the eighteenth century. Though they over-looked a lot that was just as truly there, they cannot be said to have been flatly wrong. Given what they knew at first hand of classicism gone to seed, and given their own psychological inter-ests, they were right to revolt. But when *we* come along and pick up from some textbook the opinion, more than a hundred years late, that the eighteenth century was only those things which the romantics revolted against, we are espousing positive untruths. We do not have an idea of our own, made up of living thought processes that really answer questions important to us, but only an opinion, torn from the only context that ever gave it meaning.

If you will think back over most of the textbooks you have used in college in the light of what has been said so far, you will see why they are so deadly dull: they are full, for the most part, of opinions rather than of ideas. In the study of literature, for example, of what conceivable use to you is another person's opinion about a book you have not yourself read? For all pur-poses except tea talk the opinions of others about a book are positively dangerous, unless you have read the book and can thus rebuild or incorporate the opinions into genuine ideas of your own. Similarly, of what conceivable use can it be to any-one to learn from a philosophy text that the realists believed that universals really exist and the nominalists believed that they really do not. These two conclusions, surrounded in their original form by hard thinking which made them genuine ideas —and I would even argue *true* ideas—for those who held them, can be read in a textbook, memorized for an examination, and even used in conversation—in some circles. But in themselves they are no more related to ideas than my opinion about the carburetor is related to the actual functioning of an automobile. I have a verbal opinion that the carburetor is the place where gasoline is mixed with air. I memorized this opinion once and confirmed it yesterday by looking into a dictionary. It is useful for my talk today, but you would be foolish indeed to ask me to repair your carburetor on the grounds that I have a "true" idea about its function.

A final example of the difference between an idea and an opinion: If you are a science major, you very likely believe by now that $E=mc^2$. I have known science majors who would go to the stake as readily for $E=mc^2$ as St. Joan went for her voices, though I have never found one yet who professed to be able to reconstruct Einstein's reasoning in support of this interesting proposition. It might be asked whether $E=mc^2$ is true. I would argue that as it is stated and believed by most of us, or as a student explained it to me once this year ("Mass and energy are really the same thing—only different") it is neither true nor false but simply meaningless, no truer, essentially, than the statements "matter is spirit" or $M=ec^2$.[1] A student could memorize it, and memorize definitions for the terms it contains, and still be talking meaninglessly if he said, "It is true," unless he understood the extremely complicated and limited area of discourse in which it can be made to apply. We can all assume, of course, that it is *not* only an opinion to someone who really understands what goes on in Einsteinian physics. We can assume that it is true, for its purposes and in its world, just as Newton's laws are still true, for their purposes and for their world. For us these are assumptions, opinions about opinions. But, for Einstein, $E=mc^2$ was not an isolated conclusion, to be voted upon or promulgated or fought over aside from the context of his scientific reasoning. It was a part of a system of thinking, and it was thus a tool for further thinking, producing consequences for that further thinking.

In short, insofar as you hold your opinions about any subject in isolation from the thinking processes which produced those opinions, they are never true, even if they are very popular or in the vanguard of "current thought." Whether you have been taught Keynesian or classical economics, Freudian, gestalt, or behaviorist psychology, Aristotelian or Crocean aesthetics, Euclidean or non-Euclidean geometry, Christian or utilitarian ethics, classical or quantum physics, what you know is not

1. As a piece of men's room graffiti at the University of Chicago has it, "$E=Mc^3$—by slow light!" (1969 note).

knowledge at all unless you know how it was derived from the raw data of the subject matter.

III

All this can be put another way by saying that all truth *is* in one sense relative. Some of you have heard me previously try to refute relativism, and before you jump on me for inconsistency, let me hasten to make clear that I am not agreeing with "real" relativists who argue that there is no absolute truth. I am not saying, "Anything you *think* is true is true for *you*," or "Anything *I* think is is true for *me*." I am not saying, "Since all men are fallible, no man is more entitled to claim truth than any other man." And I am not doing anything so obvious as calling attention to the fact that different people in different cultures believe in different truths. I *am* saying that the truth of any conclusion, any proposition, is partially relative to the world of discourse in which it is formulated. The universe presents us with what William James called a "blooming, buzzing confusion"—a reality, in other words, richer than any one of us can encompass. We choose to abstract from what looks like hopeless confusion small worlds of discourse for the purpose of dealing with particular problems. We could not deal with the world intellectually at all if we did not do this. But the price we pay for it is that we never can get more than a partial view, even at our best. And most of us operate not at our best, on the level of living ideas, but at our worst, on the level of isolated opinions.

I should like to illustrate all this by supposing that I now moved away from the podium here and socked the dean on the nose. I rather suspect that we would all immediately become more aware than we usually are of blooming, buzzing confusion. This confusion would inevitably raise problems in your minds —problems that could be solved either by offering ready-made opinions about the action or by a genuine investigation of it. Without investigation, you could all go away from the assembly arguing vociferously, plastering the college opinion board with opinions, ignoring each other's arguments, shouting louder and louder until finally dinner time made you forget this, as it has in the past made you forget more important problems.

But now suppose we had a few men in the audience who wanted to get at the truth of the situation—professors most likely. Would *they* not be able to come to some agreement about it, and then pass along the correct opinion to the student body and resolve all the confusion? I have not really made myself clear today unless you see that the answer must be "No." Even the most highly trained observers could not come to the same conclusions about this action. Yet this failure to agree does not at all mean that none of them, or, on the other hand, that only one of them, has the truth. Different investigators would be interested in different aspects of my action. Professor Hobbs, interested in ethics, might very well be most concerned with whether I was morally right to do what I did. He would then formulate his general principles concerning personal violence and, by examining the particular circumstances, try to decide whether the moral principles applied to my case. Suppose that he learned of a long-standing feud between the dean and me. He might then offer the tentative conclusion that merely being on the stand together with the dean proved intolerable to me and that my action was an expression of hatred and thus, although understandable, nevertheless wicked.

Then Professor Trueblood, also interested in ethics but convinced for some reason that I would not do a wantonly wicked thing, at least not without provocation, investigates further and discovers that the dean has been pelting me with spitballs throughout my speech. He could then explore the problems of revenge and retaliation as they relate to *his* principles of right and wrong. He might come up with the conclusion, "I think it was not wrong, but it was certainly unwise for the speaker to strike the dean." It is obvious that a third person, overhearing these two, would get nowhere merely comparing their conclusions and announcing that the philosophy department of this college is split wide open over the moral quality of my action. The two professors are not talking about the same facts, nor are they asking precisely the same questions.

Professor Van Dyke, as a physicist, has meanwhile been exploring the situation from a totally different point of view. He has noticed that, in falling, the dean's head described a much wider arc than would normally be expected, considering his height and weight and the normal acceleration of gravity, 32 feet per second per second. Though he has not yet solved the problem, he is overheard to say, "There's something wrong about that whole affair." Students overhearing him conclude that he is agreeing with Professor Hobbs that *I* was wrong

While Professor Van Dyke is making a careful drawing of the lines of force, Professor Grohsmeyer has been investigating *his* idea of why the whole thing occurred as it did—asking, as psychologist, what looks like the same question as the others asked but what is actually a question in a totally different world of discourse. It is perhaps by now needless to say that, even if he conducts the soundest, most sensitive, most penetrating psychological investigation of my neuroses, of my childhood traumas, of my present frustrations, and discovers the full psychological truth of the matter, his formulation of it, though perhaps true enough, will bear no relationship to that offered by the previous investigators.

Meanwhile Professor Strong is studying my adrenalin output. Professor Stinneford is using my case as one instance among a rising number of professorial outbreaks, resulting in part from low salaries and financial worry. Finally, Professor Root writes a poem about it all, and he is heard to murmur, "It was beautiful, beautiful. How *good* to see something dramatically *right* on our stage for a change."

Now the point is that all these conclusions might be true, if the investigations were carried on properly, but obviously they are true only in light of the questions raised, the subject matter considered relevant, and the assumptions and methods used by the investigators. You cannot answer ethical questions by studying blood pressure, though you may use words like "good" and "right" in talking about it. You cannot predict the weather by studying economics. You cannot discover how to live wisely and well by investigating cellular structure, any more than you can determine the composition of the atom by studying Shakespeare. Each investigator may grasp something of reality, but he imposes something *on* reality as well, and his conclusions must be read in the light of the limitations he has inevitably imposed.

IV

As a test of this interrelationship of conclusions and the purposes and thinking processes which produce them, we can look for a moment at the seemingly contradictory pronouncements, "All truth is relative" and "Truth is absolute." I have already suggested that when most people defend either of these propositions, they are merely uttering received opinions, isolated conclusions, which cannot be said to be either true or false; they do not belong in a context of defined terms, first principles, and reasoning processes. On the other hand, there are some men who really mean something when they say, "All truth is relative." If you press them further, they may very well say something not too much different from what I have said today: "If you define truth as 'man's formulations of truth,' and if you mean by 'relative' something like 'dependent on a finite vision which can't under any circumstances comprehend the whole of things,' then obviously 'all truth is relative.'" Each man, in attempting to formulate truth, imposes something of his own vision upon it and in a sense changes it in the process.

The result is that human formulations are never permanently or exhaustively valid. Even such statements as "The world is flat" can be either true or false, depending on one's definitions and purposes. The world *is* flat for most of our practical purposes, and if you do not believe me, try, when you leave this college and enter the "real world," to build your buildings, cross your streets, butter your bread, and pursue your brides, taking into careful account at each step the world's quite irrelevant curvature. On the other hand, the statement that the "the world is round," true enough for men who want to sail the ocean or aim guided missiles, would prove dreadfully deceptive if acted upon literally by an astronomer. Even such obvious and eternal truths as that two plus two equals four require redefinition and restatement in some contexts for some purposes.

Very few of those who claim that truth is relative take the trouble, however, to think through in this way what they mean; they are thus usually unable to see any sense in the other view —that "truth is absolute." Yet if we define truth not as man's formulations of reality but as the basic principles of reality itself—the fundamental laws which make the world what it is and man what he is, whether discovered by man or not— then clearly truth is universal and absolute in the sense that it depends on neither times nor circumstances nor man's formulations for its existence as truth. Though truth in this sense— which has sometimes been considered one aspect of God's nature—presents itself to us in an unlimited number of perspectives, to say this is far from saying that truth is relative to our own private, subjective preferences. It is relative only to the world of discourse we have chosen to operate in, and within that world, whatever it is, there are always rigorous standards which dictate decisions as to truth or falsehood. It would take another, longer talk to substantiate this claim. But I hope that most of you have experienced something of what I mean by it in learning to meet the standards of proof in your major field.

V

Let me reformulate the whole problem of ideas and opinions one more time. As I look around at you seniors—those of you who have any interest at all in what you have learned—too many of you seem to be either dogmatists, relativists, or eclectics. The dogmatists of course do not need to look further for truth, because they have it already. Their only problem is how to use propaganda, or shouting, or force—the three main persuasive devices of our time—to convince their opponents.

The relativists do not need to look further, because whatever happens to look good to them now is "relatively speaking" as true as anything else they are likely to find. And the eclectics, who think that there is a "little truth and a little falsehood in all," while they do have the advantage of thinking that there is some point in trying to learn more, are doomed to find nothing but the shifting sands of isolated opinions no matter how far they look.

There are a few of you, however, for whom man's search for truth will be forever meaningful. Unlike the relativist, you believe in truth and in the possibility of men's fighting through to some meaningful glimpse of it; and yet, unlike the dogmatist, you have begun to realize how difficult it is to catch it as it flies. You have learned that, while in one sense the universe is simple, simpler than it looks—what the philosophers call "one"—in another sense, and from man's point of view, it is always more complex than we ever realize. You have learned that to the man who is willing to pay the price of hard work and hard thought, *ideas* will come. And you know, or are beginning to learn, that to the man satisfied with a hodgepodge of scattered and isolated *opinions,* even the little truth that his opinions might have is practically worthless.

Having rejected other positions, I am tempted—my second major temptation of the day—to give a label to my own. I might, indeed, have concluded the preceding paragraph with the resounding climax, "You who have learned these things are the true pluralists." All of you could then have left the hall today carrying the opinion that I am not a dogmatist, not a relativist, not an eclectic, but a pluralist. There is only one trouble with that. While the statement "I am a pluralist," as a conclusion to this talk today, fitted thus into its proper context, is true, as soon as it becomes your opinion and is carried into other contexts, it ceases to be true.

In the first place, some of you have no doubt not been listening very carefully, and you will unquestionably go through life convinced that a pluralist is someone who slugs deans. Second, the word *pluralist* means so many different things in so many different contexts that your opinion of me as a pluralist is worthless, unless you can reconstruct for yourselves what "He advocated pluralism" means in this context. In other contexts it might mean "He advocates belief in two or more gods" or "He believes not in a *uni*verse but in a *pluri*verse" or "He is a follower of William James, or of David Daiches" or "He says we should all have more than one wife." As an opinion, a conclusion wrenched from its context, it is, in other words, of no use to you; it will not justify your having spent thirty minutes picking it up. As an idea, applied actively to your other ideas and opinions, it might provide you with a tool for intellectual growth and at the same time a weapon for defending yourselves against the attacks on reason so characteristic of our time.

THE ONTOLOGICAL PROOF

The debate about the ontological proof—the proof that says we can infer God's existence from the idea we have of him—is an old one, one of the oldest in the history of philosophy. Eminent and respected philosophers, men of unquestioned intellectual integrity, have taken positions on both sides of the question. Whenever we find old pros in disagreement, we should exercise a good deal of caution. If men like Anselm, Aquinas, Descartes, Spinoza, Kant, and Bradley have disagreed, we should all think carefully about what we are doing and about what possible hope we have of obtaining any profit from the debate. We cannot hope to out-think Aquinas or Spinoza, and if they disagreed fundamentally about a matter of this kind, what point is there in our going over their ground only to conclude that philosophers cannot agree? How can we do more than go through the age-old controversy, repeating the arguments that have always been offered on both sides of this question?

The debate about the ontological proof cannot be resolved

Opening statement in a debate held for a philosophy seminar at Earlham College, about 1960.

simply by asking the philosophers to define their terms. If we ask them to define what they mean by God, by proof, by ontological, and by exist, we immediately find ourselves in a sinkhole of confusion: the very methods of definition, the very notions of how one breaks a semantic deadlock, are themselves the product of philosophical presuppositions. "Define your terms," one philosopher shouts at another, meaning "Give me an unequivocal, permanent delineation of the absolute confines of this term in our future uses of it." The other philosopher, believing that life is much too fluid to be fixed in a definition of that kind, may try hard to define his terms, but at heart he will be ready to shift his definition whenever it becomes necessary to suit a new context. They may discuss together for a long time, thinking that they are talking about the same thing, only to discover finally that even when they defined their terms their notions of definition and proof were so different as to make agreement impossible.

On the other hand, history offers many examples of philosophers who *have* resolved disputes by careful effort to understand each other. And most of us have had the experience of changing our minds about the validity of a particular doctrine once we come to understand it. The ontological proof played a very important part in my own thinking in this regard. I had learned certain standards of proof which I thought I could rely on, and according to them the ontological proof was obviously nonsense. For anyone to pretend that the *existence of an idea of perfect Being in his mind* presupposed the *existence of the object the idea represented* was really exasperating to me: it was so obvious that the desire to believe was overriding the desire to show intellectual integrity. What's more, I had read Kant's cogent refutation, and respecting Kant as I did then (and do now), I felt that I had ample support for my own common-sense rejection of the palpable nonsense of ontologism. Nothing can be proved by synthetic, a priori, proofs, Kant had taught me, and to prove the *existence* of God on a priori grounds would be precisely to claim a synthetic, a priori, proof. Once I had fixed Kant's heading in my mind—"The Impossibility of Ontological Proof"—I was faced with a clear problem: I must either believe

Kant on the one hand or Anselm and Descartes and Spinoza on the other. I could not carry on a flirtation with the ontological proof without threatening infidelity to Kant. And since Kant seemed so clearly on the side of common sense in this instance, I rested comfortably in his camp, though I was careful, since at the time I considered myself to be an atheist, to part company with Kant at those points where he made it clear that he believed in God for other reasons, even though he had disproved the traditional proofs.

My conversion to what I hardly dare call the truth came only when I became convinced that in philosophy a kind of bigamy is legal. As long as I had to choose between Kant and Anselm, I had to choose Kant. But when I began to suspect that they were both talking about different Gods, using different methods for different purposes, I was ripe for my moment of illumination, which came in reading Anselm (and Richard McKeon's commentary on him) after having steeped myself in Plato for some weeks.

You all will remember that Plato held the outlandish doctrine that ideas are real, that they exist independently of your mind and mine. He not only held the doctrine, he built one of the two or three greatest philosophies on it. That ideas are not and cannot have independent existence has, of course, been proved again and again throughout philosophical history, and yet foolish Platonists go on believing that ideas are real in this sense and claiming that the refutation doesn't talk about what they mean at all. Grimsley Hobbs and I were originally to debate tonight the problem of whether or in what sense universals exist. Our debate will, I suspect, be closely related to that other, unheld debate, since the ontological proof rests on the belief that ideas are things.

Everyone admits, of course, that an idea in my head is real, *in a sense*. It exists as a thought, as a mental process. But Plato means much more than this. Ideas exist, for him, quite independently of our discovery of them. Note that I say discovery, not invention; true ideas are not invented by us, but discovered; they have always been lying in wait, as it were, for our apprehension, and when we are dead and gone, when the final bomb destroys the last man, the ideas will be exactly where they always were, not in any *place*, but everywhere, operating throughout the universe or ready to operate when the conditions are ripe.

Consider a favorite example of all the ontologists: the triangle. In the natural world man has found no precise triangles, but he found objects close enough to triangularity to suggest geometrical investigation. Finally he came to draw so-called perfect right-angle triangles, and yet he always knew that the triangles he drew were not perfect. If I draw a right-angle triangle with even the most refined instrument, its largest angle will not be precisely equal to the sum of the other two angles: my lines must occupy enough space to throw my measurements and calculations off if they are sufficiently refined. But of course I don't calculate with this *drawn* triangle at all; I calculate with a perfect triangle, a triangle in my mind, imperfectly represented on paper. In this perfect triangle the largest angle *does* equal precisely the sum of the other two.

I use it, I calculate with it, yet where does this triangle exist? Not on the paper, but in my head, we say. But not only in my head, surely. You have all followed my discussion here, so I can assume that triangularity as a perfect conception exists in your heads, too. But if that is so, if (as Augustine is so fond of pointing out) we hold the idea of triangularity *in common* rather than having it as the peculiar property of any one of us, we are forced to the conclusion that we did not make it but found it. But found it where? We have never sensed it, never derived it from the natural world. It is a pure idea, one of the eternal characteristics of the unseen universe that underlies and orders the visible world. When that last bomb destroys the last man and the last triangle, plane triangularity will still be exactly where it always was, everywhere and nowhere. If other worlds and other rational creatures exist in the universe, we can be sure that the concept of a right angle on a plane surface will always include the characteristics we have described. New kinds of triangles have been discovered, of course, on other than plane surfaces, with weird characteristics. But they do not affect our problem in the least. Presumably the number of ideas—

such as triangularity—that man may discover is, as Spinoza says in different language, limited not by *their* nature but by our *own*.

You will notice that in going this far we have already found ourselves presupposing that there is some connection between our ideas as we think them and *things* as they really are. But the *things* with which we are concerned when we claim that our ideas relate to them are not sensible objects like tables, chairs, or drawing-board triangles. They are those more real because more permanent things that lie back of this visible world. My idea of triangle has a closer relationship with eternal triangularity than it has with the triangle I draw in geometry class. There is thus a real relationship between idea and *thing,* since in fact ideas both in my head and as eternal characteristics of the universe are real *things.*

The ontological proof rests absolutely on this recognition of the thingness of ideas, as existing in a real sense independent of the human mind. All refutations of it that I know of finally rest on a denial that ideas are real, in this sense, because, as I hope to show, once we admit that ideas *are* real, the ontological proof becomes unassailable.

Where does triangularity exist? Everywhere and nowhere, I have said. It is an eternal element or possible patterning in the ordering of extension, of space. But the question immediately arises: is it self-subsistent or does it fall under some larger, more extensive concept which determines its nature? Obviously the latter: it is *one* of the ways in which extension works. It has interesting relationships, for example, with the way a circle works. Compared with the totality of Euclid's *Elements,* it is a very "imperfect" idea, and Euclid's *Elements,* compared with what we *now* know about the possibilities of geometry, is itself radically imperfect. Are our present ideas of geometry still imperfect? I suspect that no one here thinks that we know now all that we may someday know about geometry. *But why do we think that this is so?* Obviously because we think that there is something more to be known. But *where does this something more exist?*

Think hard about this. What is this "something more" that

we expect to learn, and where does it now exist? Do its parts relate meaningfully to each other? All of us assume that they do —that's what makes further inquiry meaningful for us. But where does the *principle of interrelation* exist? Everywhere (and nowhere), and it is God, that is, Supreme Being.

I have just used, in somewhat disguised form, the ontological proof for the existence of God, my own version of it. You will note that the God I have proved by it is, you might say, merely the perfect geometer; he has no other qualities at this point, but he contains all that will ever be truly known about extension, whether plane, curved, rubbery, or whatever. He has no personality as yet—and it should be noted that none of the ontological proofs has ever claimed to prove God as a thing like a human being, with personality like human personality. They claim only to prove order and power, supreme order and power: in my case, an ordering of all geometrical concepts.

It is obvious, I think, that the same operation can be carried out with any set of ideas we have which give order to our experience. I observe—or rather Newton observed—that planets and objects on earth could be described in similar mathematical formulae: he discovered, as we say, the law of gravitation. Einstein went beyond it and found that the law was applicable only in certain situations; another set of equations had to be devised which would take into account what Newton discovered and what Einstein knew. Now *where* were Einstein's equations—say $E = mc^2$—before Einstein discovered them? Everywhere, and nowhere: if the equations prove ultimately second, they will be found everywhere, yet they *exist* in the usual sense of the word, nowhere.

Are our present ideas of physical law throughout the universe still imperfect? I suspect that everyone here thinks that they are —in other words, our minds, as the philosophers used to say, are inevitably driven forward from the imperfect to the notion of the more nearly perfect, and finally to perfection itself. We believe that there is something more to be known about physics; and that something more must inevitably subsume, when it is discovered, the less nearly perfect laws discovered by Einstein. But where does this something more exist? Why do we assume that it is there to be discovered at all? Simply because we cannot resist living in the conviction that it is there; we cannot resist the ontological proof, in spite of ourselves.

We can go on to less mathematical matters. If we think of power, we are driven sooner or later to think of supreme power. Is there some power stronger than the H-bomb? Obviously. Than the most powerful action yet observed? Obviously. Does it work according to the supreme law we just talked about? Obviously, because that's what the supreme law is—how the supreme power works.

Similarly, if we think of love, we are driven sooner or later to think of supreme Love. Even if we think of things that exist, so long as we recognize that ideas really exist, we are forced to think of supreme existence, the Supreme Being. And the very thought of such extreme forms of each category of being, and of being itself, is itself the "proof" that such supreme forms exist— not, of course, as particular triangles or tables exist, but as triangularity and table-ness exist, eternal and immutable and not available to our senses: we can never look upon the face of God and live.

There are two standard objections to this proof which we have already, I feel, implicitly answered, but which should be treated directly. The first is that we haven't proved anything, but merely reaffirmed our faith. This is in one sense a sound claim. We have not proved the existence of God in the same form that I can prove that if you prick a man he will bleed. There is no logical pattern, no syllogism leading from self-evident premises to undeniable conclusions. What we have really done, in a way, is to point out to ourselves what we believed already. As I'm sure Grimsley will say, we have been tautological, even circular, in a sense, because the significant thing about this proof is that it proves a God which almost everyone believes in before the proof begins. This is why most of those who have held to it have so blandly assumed that only the fool can deny in his heart that God is, and even the fool when he denies is unconsciously affirming. The God that is proved here is the total ordering and power in the universe, the very nature of order itself, and just as in more literal phi-

losophies the law of noncontradiction, itself unprovable, is
always taken as self-evident, so in analogical philosophies God
himself comes to seem self-evident. In fact, there is to me a firm
connection between the self-evidency of the law of noncontradiction and the ontological proof. At least I can move easily
from the law of noncontradiction to the proof. If the law holds,
if it is really something that exists (and I am unable to treat it
as if it were only a human construct, since, like Aristotle, I find
that I cannot imagine two houses, say, occupying the same space
at the same time, and I cannot believe that my failure to so
imagine is merely the product of my own mental limitations)—
if the law holds not only in my mind but, like other ideas, in
fundamental reality, then I have already begun an ontological
proof based on it. It is part of the nature of God, and my mind
cannot resist the ascent to whatever supreme law includes in its
scope the law of noncontradiction. But this is a digression. The
point is, we can admit that the proof is really only following out
the implications of what we already believe; it is still a "proof"
nevertheless, because the fool *can* deny, before he recognizes his
own foolishness, what he ought to see self-evidently: that he is
part of an order the supremity of which he cannot deny. Proof
in this context is thus defined as any mental process that will
produce conviction in every man who understands it.

The second objection, repeated with boring regularity, is that
if we can infer God from our thought of him, we should be
able to infer other things from our thought of *them*. But this
has been explicitly denied by every philosopher who has used
the ontological proof. We are not proving the existence of contingent things with this proof, as Spinoza reminds us again and
again. We are proving the existence of those things which are
ideas, and there can be only one supreme and necessary one
among those. Insofar as the ontological proof is confined to the
proof of perfect, necessary being, it can apply to only one thing
in the universe, God himself, because only in his nature is
existence presupposed in the very idea of him. I can no more
think of a supreme physical law that doesn't work to organize
all laws—that is, does not exist—than I can think of a square
circle. If it *doesn't* work, if it is merely a figment of my wild

imagination, then it is not a supreme law. Yet willy-nilly I cannot avoid thinking of a supreme law: as Einstein says, he cannot believe that God dices with the universe; and he devotes his life, partly under the guidance of Spinoza and largely motivated, as I see it, by the ontological proof for the existence of supremity, to finding the really basic formulations that will come nearer to explaining the whole.

Perhaps it is now clear how I have achieved my bigamous union with both Kant and Anselm. I can accept with no reservations Kant's refutation of the ontological proof *as he sees it.* You cannot prove the existence of the kind of God in which he is interested by the ontological proof as he understands it. "All the alleged examples" (of the kind I have used above), he says, "are taken from *judgments,* not from *things* and their existence. But the unconditioned necessity of judgments is not the same as an absolute necessity of things." Fine, I agree completely, since Kant makes it quite clear that he is talking about existence in an entirely different sense from mine. (He uses, for example, the concept of 100 thalers as contrasted with 100 "really existing" thalers) . There are no synthetic, a priori, propositions, so long as one defines things in the way Kant defines them; any proposition truly declaring existence in his sense must be either analytic or a posteriori. But if *ideas exist* outside my mind (and they do) then the existence of the supreme fountainhead of all ideas, the totality, the supreme coherence of all the "nature" or "working" of the universe, of all the power and knowledge and love, must exist.

Each philosopher who has used the ontological proof has shown his sense that his proof was, in fact, self-evident, and I find myself tempted to fall into the same tone here, to say, "If you don't see it, you're just not looking." Anselm, in answering Gaunilon's claim that there is an analogy between the idea of a being greater than all other beings and the idea of an island more excellent than all other islands, and that one could be proved just as effectively as the other, cries: "But I call on your *faith* and *conscience* to attest that this is most false." Descartes claims that simply because we cannot avoid having a clear and distinct idea of supreme being, it must exist. Both men may seem terribly naive, talking of faith and conscience and strong conviction as if such personal attitudes could settle philosophical disputes. Spinoza concludes his proof with the claim: "This, I think, will be evident to every moderately attentive reader." But if these men are naive, it is only in expecting their readers to be moderately attentive and respectful of what the context says about the proof. Wrenched out of context, their proofs become ridiculous and naive. And yet in every philosophy, even in those which contain the most cogent refutation of the ontological proof, the eternal things, the ideas, on which the proof is based and which it explores and explicates, find *some* position. They may be sneaked in the back door, while the sign on the front porch claims that only hard facts are admitted here. But in one form or another, all philosophizing depends on a faith in supreme reason, and a supreme reason which has its own mode of being, related to but not confined to reason as we human beings experience it. The only way to refute the God proved by the ontological proof is either to ignore him or to use him unconsciously in an effort to deny his existence. To paraphrase Anselm and scripture once again, only the fool can say that there is no God, and he contradicts his own beliefs when he says it.

HOW NOT TO USE ARISTOTLE
THE *POETICS*

A few years ago at Earlham College, Eliseo Vivas visited us to
give a lecture on the "Nature of Literature." He began something like this: "Perhaps the least perceptive of all the influential theories about art is that of Aristotle, who taught that
artists imitated, or copied, nature. Now it is obvious that no
artist simply copies nature; he always transforms it as he repre-
sents it, and it is thus hard to see how anyone could ever take
Aristotle's doctrine seriously, or how anyone who advanced it
could possibly have earned a reputation as a great critic." He
then went on to say that what the artist really does is construct
"constitutive symbols." In the question period, when I tried to
press him about what is symbolized by art, his answer came
astonishingly close to what I had always thought Aristotle
meant when he said that the artist makes imitations. But when
I tried to show that Vivas had distorted Aristotle, he dismissed
my question curtly: "If imitation doesn't mean copying, then
why did Aristotle use the word?"

In this interesting semantic maneuver you may already have

Lecture to students in Humanities II at the University of Chicago, 1963.

recognized a first misuse of Aristotle; it consists of treating him as a primitive, useful only as a springboard into the higher truths of our more sophisticated times. It is a procedure now hallowed by long and distinguished usage, especially in the innumerable accounts of how Aristotle was tossed, along with those cannon balls of varying weight, over the edge of the Tower of Pisa.

The fact is that there is no subject on which it is safe to dismiss Aristotle lightly. The *Poetics,* like all his other works and like any other document ever written by anyone, *is* necessarily a limited document; it is full of conclusions that apply, if at all, only to a small number of Greek plays, and of assertions that seem nonsensical on first encounter. But it is a highly delicate barometer for measuring a reader's diligence and sensitivity. Nothing reveals a critic's superficiality so quickly as a hasty, contemptuous reference to primitive notions like the catharsis of pity and fear or the observation that a tragedy has a beginning, middle, and end. Aristotle may prove wrong in more ways than I have yet discovered. But I should be very much surprised if anyone who had read him carefully concluded that he is sophomoric, superficial, or irrelevant.

But I shall say no more of his opponents. The fact is that most of the abuse of Aristotle has come from those who profess to follow him. Because his methods are so rich and his doctrines so diversified, he has inevitably given birth to a great many partial dogmas, based on the reduction of his whole approach to one or another of its aspects. It is in general the resulting dogmatisms that have aroused—quite rightly—hostility against Aristotelian*ism.* For every Aquinas or McKeon, able to preserve something like the breadth of vision and incisiveness of method that Aristotle himself had, his works have spawned hundreds of enthusiastic defenders of this or that doctrine which, when taken out of context, becomes at best a half truth and at worst a positive falsehood.[1]

1. Revising in 1969, I should note that the best introduction I know to this subject is Elder Olson, *Aristotle's* Poetics *and English Literature* (Chicago: University of Chicago Press, 1965).

I shall not try to trace the history of such reductions; I'm not qualified for the job, even if I felt that it was what we should spend our time doing. For the purposes of using the *Poetics* without abusing it, an analysis of the various modern reductions will prove more valuable. Just to prove my loyalty to "the Philosopher," as men called him in earlier times, I'll organize the various dogmas as Aristotle himself might do, according to the "four causes," as they are reflected in the first six chapters of the *Poetics,* and in the four-part definition of tragedy that is gathered together in chapter 6.

I

First, dogmas about the *structure* of literature, what Aristotle calls the *object imitated,* constituting the *formal cause* of the literary work (you will soon learn not to be troubled by that word *cause;* it doesn't mean quite what we mean by cause, though it includes that meaning). In dealing with structure, Aristotelian critics have departed from Aristotle in at least two main directions. The first distortion—what might be called the heresy of structure if that word heresy had not been so badly overworked in recent decades—is the tendency to think that abstract structure is an end in itself, that to construct a series of nicely articulated parts, a neat, unified package, is sufficient for the artist, and that to discern whether or not the package is neat is sufficient for the critic. The most notorious expression of this view was the passionate pursuit of the "unities" of neoclassicism, the unities of place, time, and action. You will no doubt know that Aristotle says nothing about unity of place, and very little about unity of time—certainly he does not say that the action *must* take place in twenty-four hours, as some neoclassical critics thought. What is less often understood, even today, is that Aristotle never talks even about unity of action, by far the most important of the three, as an end in itself, as a sufficient achievement for the artist, or as something which, if properly achieved, will excuse the artist for other failures. Unity of action is a means to the end of realizing the full effects of the plot. Though it will yield a kind of pleasure in itself, since a skillfully articulated whole does give pleasure, this is not the end of literary art, or at least not the end of tragedy as he knew it.

You may be aware that many modern aestheticians consider pleasure in the contemplation of abstract artistic qualities (such as unity or fused complexity) the only truly *aesthetic* pleasure; all the other pleasures that literature can yield are thought to be impurities, perhaps necessary impurities, since words inevitably suggest emotion-charged characters and events and ideas, but impurities nonetheless. Perhaps few of these pure aestheticians think of themselves as Aristotelians. But there are plenty of his avowed followers who have gone almost as far in making structure the end of art, in complete divorce from considerations of achieved effects on the proper spectator. Whenever you find someone objecting to an inconsistency in the time scheme of *Othello,* without asking what the inconsistency *does* to the overall tragic effect of the play; whenever you find someone objecting to a play or novel because it doesn't "hold together," or praising it because of its magnificent unity—without referring this blame or praise to an achieved artistic intention, a realized effect upon the proper reader or spectator—you can suspect that he is a victim of this form of pseudo-Aristotelianism. One of the most amusing examples of structuralism run wild can be seen in the *Finnegans Wake* idolators, who will say that it is a great novel because it has the most complex structure of any novel yet written, even while they admit that no reader has yet discerned what that structure really is. One can't be sure that *Finnegans Wake* is *not* a great novel; perhaps someday readers will discover that the complex structure they now dream of and quarrel about is a realizable structure, an experienced structure. I doubt it, but it may happen. Until then, each new intricacy discovered, each new pattern of allusions and cross references, reveals precisely nothing more than that: a new intricacy. And the artistic question that Aristotle would want to ask is, if I may translate the original Greek, So what? To what effect? Why?

The second abuse of structure relates closely to what I'm going to say about *effects* a little later and is much less popular now than in former centuries, so I'll mention it only briefly and move along. It is the notion that certain specific structures are sacrosanct, that all authors ought to imitate such-and-such objects only, with this kind of "beginning," that kind of "middle," and another kind of "end," being sure to throw in a bit of "reversal" here and "discovery" there. Again this abuse was far more common in the neoclassical period than it is now, at least in forms explicitly attributable to Aristotle. But in the twentieth century the distortion has crept upon us in reverse, as the notion that certain *non*structures are superior to careful planning and composition. To be artistic, works should not be plotted; there should be no resounding conclusions, no enticing beginnings, no tell-tale signs of planning. You may have heard of the French novel by Marc Saporta, called *Composition no. 1*. One reviewer complained that when he opened the covers the unbound sheets fell all over the floor, but it turned out not to matter, because the instructions were to shuffle the cards and read in whatever order came up. Obviously, in an age when such a work can be published, whether seriously or as a joke, we are in no danger of being bound to any single, tight canon of OK-structures. But we may be threatened by the belief that structurelessness is best, since "life is like that." Incidentally, I think Aristotle would have been pleased by the reviewer's response. He repudiated the experiment because the results were monotonous; he didn't say that M. Saporta ought to write novels with good old-fashioned plots, but rather that unfortunately no matter how one shuffled the cards they were boring.

Let's turn now to the "final cause," the end or effect or purpose. Some of what I've said might be taken to suggest that all one need do to be a good follower of Aristotle is relate everything to its effect. There is a sense, I believe, in which this is so. The question that was constantly on Aristotle's lips was, Why? What is the function? What is the purpose? The end, the final cause, is everything.

All right, then. What we should do is ask of a literary work, Does it hit me hard? We can find many critics, good and bad, arguing in this way, from the Romans on down. Molière, for example, said again and again that anything is forgiven the dramatist if he gets his effect. Poe's theory of composition seems to make effect absolutely primary, the bigger the thrill the better the work. Many popular handbooks on "how to write fiction that will sell" assume the same primacy of effect, *any* effect.

Well, if the *final* cause is, as we say, supreme, and if in drama the final cause is the effect, what is there to worry about in this simple development of Aristotle's functional approach?

In the first place it easily confuses simple *strength* of emotional effect with the notion of powerful effects achieved by means that themselves give artistic pleasure. The effects of good literature are, as Aristotle knew very well, extremely complex. Though it is true that a great tragedy will produce pity and fear, it produces them not as they might be produced by a documentary movie, say, showing little children being devoured alive by lions, or by a newsreel shot of a terrible earthquake. Any third-rate amateur movie maker could move your pity and fear more powerfully than the greatest art, if he happened to be on the scene in Vietnam, or if he had enough skill to give the illusion of actuality. Another example: the sound of a fingernail scratching on felt will give me gooseflesh much more reliably and powerfully than the most effectively goosefleshy art I know. Similarly, the smell of a long-dead chicken will nauseate me more devastatingly than Sartre's *La nausée*. Turning to comedy, there are undoubtedly more laughs per minute in a first-rate vaudeville act, or even in a good TV comedy or variety show, than in Molière's *Tartuffe*. Even when the laughs are not canned, the audience probably laughs more at its favorite comic than any audience ever laughed at *The Silent Woman* or at Falstaff's antics in *Henry IV*. Unless we want to say that the TV comics, clever as they are, turn out week by week a better art than the great classics, we must moderate the notion that intensity of effect can be used as a simple test. Though we can easily say that if there is no intense effect—given a reader or spectator sufficiently alert and well-trained to receive it—the work must be condemned, the presence of strong effect is not in itself an adequate test of quality.

An explanation of this can be seen by considering the second error implicit in the notion that emotional impact is all: treating effects as they come from discrete moments, particularly from the final punch scene. I've even heard beginners with the *Poetics* argue that since effect is obviously the *final* cause in the definition, the effect we must look for is the maximum final effect, the greatest punch in the closing scenes.

But to argue in this way is absurd because it obscures the very distinction between the shaped experiences offered by art and the often more intense but less organized experiences offered by life itself. Pity and fear, in the tragedies considered by Aristotle, are not emotions arrived at *finally*, at the moment when disaster strikes. In any good tragedy, there is a structure of rising pity and rising fear. Pity and fear are shorthand terms for the structure of the thought and emotion embodied in the play. Similarly, catharsis is not something that is achieved in one glorious moment tacked onto the end of the play, though there are many plays in which, as in Shakespeare's tragedies, there are final scenes which draw to a conclusion the manifold ameliorations and transformations of pity and fear which run throughout the play and which distinguish it from any experience of pity and fear in real life.

A corollary of this is that in any good novel or play there must be many moments when the immediate emotional impact is relatively subdued. There is, in other words, a *structure* of effects in all great art, and we can see immediately, when it is put in this way, that the "heresy" of structuralism is the converse of the "heresy" of self-sufficient effect. The one tries to elevate structure into an abstract, architectural edifice, divorced from the effects of each part in relation to the effect of the whole; the other tries to measure effects with a psychic voltmeter, quite aside from our intellectual and emotional awareness of the *ordering* of effects that takes place in any structure of human actions.

The worst form of the voltmeter approach is of course the reduction of literature to a kind of rhetoric, on the assumption that if literature is to be tested by effects, then we must study particular audiences and see what sorts of effects please different men. Those of you who know the *Rhetoric* of Aristotle will recognize that this is not far from the procedure there: the student of rhetoric, like the rhetorician himself, must know the differences among men and how to appeal to them, how to use metaphors that will please labor union leaders and southern senators, how to create rapport between a Catholic candidate and the Protestant voters, or between a college president and the students. No good speaker would give the same speech to two radically different groups, and much of his attention in preparing a speech will be not on the subject matter but on how to arrange and doctor it to suit the special audience. Perhaps the strongest so-called Aristotelian tradition in criticism was the Horatian, which to a large degree turned the study of literature into a rhetorical study of this kind. Instead of emphasizing the creation of beautiful art works that will, because they are of such-and-such a kind made in such-and-such a way, affect men of good judgment and normal sensitivity in a given way, "poetic" questions became rhetorical: How can men manipulate such-and-such an audience into being powerfully moved?

In the twentieth century this emphasis has split into two very interesting extremes. On the one hand we have had an intensification of the rhetorical reduction in the hands of commercial hacks, reaching its extreme in the construction of audience reaction machines of various kinds, including one that will pre-test novels before publication. On the other, serious authors have reacted to this commercialism by claiming that true artists should ignore the audience—even that hypothetical, ideal audience of normal men presupposed by the *Poetics*—and write for themselves alone. One amusing development of this reaction is that some authors and critics have developed a kind of unacknowledged reverse commercialism which is just as much geared to particular audiences as is the rankest best seller. I once heard the owner and editor of a small avant-garde publishing house say that there is no widely read fiction or poetry that is any good, because (and this was his only reason) if it *is* widely read it can't be any good. And he went on to name two or three poets who he used to think were pretty good, when *he* published them in editions of 200 copies, but now he knew that they were not, because they were published by the *Evergreen Review* people. And he concluded with a grand generalization: "The poet who thinks of himself as trying to communicate is lost." The truth would rather seem to be that all art has a rhetorical dimension in the sense that every art work is capable of communicating itself to *some* audience. I am convinced that criticism in our time has been partially vitiated by faulty convictions about an ideal purity, a freedom from this rhetorical dimension. But it may also be true that art in our time is still more strongly threatened by the first rhetorical reduction, the danger symbolized by the TV executive ordering that a good line must be deleted because they'll never understand it in South Bend.

We might summarize all this by saying that the least Aristotelian thing you can do is to separate considerations of structure from considerations of effect. As we turn now to the efficient cause, to talk about what Aristotle calls manner and what most modern critics would call technique, we find that the same summary applies: the abuse of technical study is the separation of technical rules from considerations of structure and effect; its salvation lies in a constant reference back, through the question *why,* to ends and to the literary structures that realize those ends. The history of criticism is strewn with the corpses of dogmas about technique that died slow painful deaths as critics discovered that though the dogmas were useful in looking at some structures, they didn't apply at all to others. In drama there were such rules as those governing *liaison des scènes*—never allow the stage to be empty at the end of a scene, but always join scenes with a steady, "natural" flow of group after group. In poetry there have been innumerable rules of prosody, and so on. But the rules I'm acquainted with best are those in favor of dramatic, objective narration in fiction. These rules stem originally from Aristotle's distinction between dramatic and narrative manners; his few comments indicate that the poet should appear as little as possible in his own person, because that is not the imitative way, and that choral commentary is better when it is integrated into the action. The collection of rules against "telling" and in favor of "showing" has grown and grown until now a novelist who took them seriously might find himself doing what M. Saporta has done in the novel

I mentioned earlier: construct a loose collection of dramatic scenes, leaving to the reader the whole job of building meaningful coherence.

Wouldn't Aristotle be happy about that, you may ask, because someone has at last seen the full value of his rules about the superiority of drama, with no poet visible at all? But of course Aristotle had better sense than that. Though technical experimentation may be interesting to the literary historian, what the critic finally cares about is what the intelligent reader cares about: works that do whatever they set out to do so well that they excite our admiration. If the result of following a technical rule out to the bitter end is boredom, monotony, flatness, then scrap the point-of-voyeurism and find something that will work for real results.

As I come to the fourth cause, the material, the "means of imitation," language, my organization becomes anticlimactic for the moment. Unfortunately for my presentation, all of the contemporary dangers and abuses of language and metaphor and symbol seem to have little or nothing to do with Aristotle. Prominent current dogmas about style come for the most part as reductions of Coleridge, Kant, and Croce. Nobody is likely to misuse Aristotle on this subject, because almost everybody ignores the few hints for a theory of style that he gives in the *Poetics*.

End of anticlimax.

II

I've now dutifully made my way once through the four "causes," as they serve to distinguish *aspects of literary works,* and in doing so, I've inevitably been neglecting the application of the same causes to *aspects of Aristotle's activity as critic.* Any human action and any human product can be viewed in these four crosslights; obviously the critic who analyzes the object, manner, means, and end of tragedy can himself be described according to the structure, method, material, and purpose of his critical endeavors. But I shall resist the temptation to go through all four again, concluding with only a note on Aristotle's method and two standard perversions of it.

The two points about method may seem contradictory to some of you. They are that the two surest ways to misuse Aristotle are, first, to use him piecemeal, a bit here and a bit there, as we have seen in some of the examples above, and second, to apply him wholesale, constructing as clear a picture as possible of his total system and then applying it to the world of art.

The first use is perhaps the mort frequent these days. Many contemporaries pride themselves on being what they call inductive or empirical or undoctrinaire or pluralistic; the last thing they want is a deductive total system. To such people, Aristotle inevitably seems overly systematic, even dogmatic.

Much as such critics may impress us with their flexibility and freedom from dogma, their approach is likely to be deadly when they try to make use of Aristotle. They are likely to pick out fragments of what he has to say, making use of whatever happens to seem attractive. The result is that none of the terms or doctrines that they make use of means what it means in the distinctive context of Aristotle's argument. When the notion of "plot" is wrenched from its context, for example, it becomes possible for a critic to show how foolish Aristotle was to think that plot was more important than character. Everybody knows that character development is much more interesting than plot —until the thought occurs that any *development* must be *plotted*. Similar refutations of what Aristotle never meant can be based on almost anything he seems to say. But even the friendliest critics are likely to produce disaster if they apply his doctrines indiscriminately. When any of the specific statements is applied to any form other than certain kinds of Greek tragedy, nonsense is likely to result. I have seen the claim, for example, that Fielding violates Aristotle's dictum about the best kind of recognition scene when he uses a strawberry mark for the recognition in *Joseph Andrews*. But we have almost nothing from Aristotle on comedy, and nothing whatever on what Fielding called the comic epic in prose; there is no reason to think that Aristotle would say the same thing about recognition scenes in comedy as he says about those in tragedy. I find it hard to discover a single normative statement in the *Poetics* about any one of the parts of tragedy that is not misleading or even downright false if applied to any but a very small number of tragedies—*Othello* is perhaps the best of these few—written since his time.

Perhaps even more deadly is the direction some critics take in the effort to avoid the piecemeal, eclectic approach, the direction of making him into a system-builder who proceeds by deducing from first principles the conclusions that ought to hold in the real world. One critic, in trying to reconstruct what Aristotle would have said about comedy, proceeded by a process that might be called reverse deduction: wherever the *Poetics* says one thing about tragedy, he said the opposite about comedy, since comedy is obviously the opposite of tragedy! Other critics have too often used the few hints at classification in the *Poetics* to suggest the construction of vast charts of possible literary forms, not only the four types of tragedy (or is it sixteen?), but also the "thirty-six plot forms," the ten basic archetypes of the novel, and so on. I'm not sure whether Aristotle would be as distressed with such procedures as I am, but I am quite sure that for most purposes nothing is accomplished in this direction. If the piecemeal approach leaves one limping from work to work, pitifully dependent on the accidental intuitions of the moment and the more or less inapplicable concepts provided by Aristotle, the a priori approach is likely to ignore actual works altogether, or to force them brutally into molds that they were never designed to fit. It is an approach that crops up, of course, in many contexts in which Aristotle is never mentioned. The Freudian who sees sexual symbolism in all literary works, the myth critic who sees a sacrificial king or the Dying God under every bush, are likely to accuse Aristotelians of being deductive and arbitrary, but their depredations take exactly the same logical shape as those of the Aristotelian who tries to fit all serious works into the tight frame of the *Poetics*.[2]

2. At this point the original lecture included a section on the limitations and powers of Aristotle's methods, omitted here. Most of the points are touched on in the next lecture, given five years later. Perhaps I should make explicit what I think is obvious throughout, that in everything I say about this subject I am greatly indebted to Richard McKeon, Ronald Crane, and Elder Olson.

The *method,* not any one of Aristotle's conclusions, is what is decisive. In using the *Poetics* as I deal with a given work, say *Tristram Shandy* (that great non-Aristotelian, loose-jointed, improbable, untragic work), I find very little use for what Aristotle *says* in the *Poetics.* But I find much use for what he *does;* that is, I find his essentially inductive search into a work's intentions, according to a four-cause analysis leading to a discrimination of the functional parts of the work (seldom the same parts as those he lists for tragedy), leading then to an assured grasp of what it is that constitutes the "soul" of this work comparable to the plot that is the soul of tragedy—I find this inductive search endlessly fruitful. Working on *Tristram Shandy* or *Ulysses,* one will, in short, be most Aristotelian when he sounds least like Aristotle, when he surrenders to *this* formed experience of a kind that Aristotle never dreamed of, and tries to answer the fundamental questions about the artistry of the work.

Perhaps I can illustrate this concluding point best by telling of an assignment given about fifteen years ago by Professor Ronald Crane. He taught a mean course; that is, he would stand for no nonsense, and he often led students to accuse him of dogmatism. But it did not take long to see that he in no sense idolized Aristotle. He might, in fact, have been accused of undermining him—and in a way that I found wonderfully stimulating. The assignment that I'm thinking of went something like this. "In what ways would Aristotle have been forced to revise or extend the *Poetics* if he had known *Macbeth?*" If you must use the *Poetics,* and I hope that some of you will find that you can't sidestep it, *that* is the way to do it. Or, if what you prefer to do is abuse Aristotle, the surest way is to fiddle with that question until it reads like this: "What elements do you find in *Macbeth* that do not accord with what Aristotle says about tragedy?"

HOW TO USE ARISTOTLE

One good test of whether you are dead on your feet is to look at something you wrote six months ago, or a year ago, or six years ago, and see whether it embarrasses you. All genuine students are shocked when as sophomores they read their freshman essays. If they *remain* genuine students, they will be shocked as seniors when they discover how sophistical their sophomoric sophistication was. And so on through life? Unfortunately there comes a time for everyman, sooner or later, usually very early, when the reverse process sets in. When Swift reread his *Tale of a Tub,* in his later years, he is supposed to have exclaimed, "Good God, what genius . . ."—a most poignant confession of envy for his younger self.

I mention this because I want to depend in this lecture on a lecture called "How *Not* to Use Aristotle," first given to a humanities class nearly five years ago. Since it's that old, I *ought* to find more wrong with it now than I do. But I'm afraid that like Huck Finn looking at the book *Tom Sawyer* I must say it told the truth, mainly, though with some stretchers. It seems

Lecture to Liberal Arts I, a freshman course at the University of Chicago, winter 1968.

unduly abstract and a bit dull, but the message still seems to me sound. Clearly I've not grown enough in the last five years.

That lecture was given on the assumption that its hearers had been tempted by the cold but seductive kaleidoscope offered by Aristotle, and I thought that my job was to warn them against the insidious dogmatic reductions that Aristotle can be made to support. But I found, of course, that the lecture was entirely misdirected: talking to students who hadn't the slightest inclination to become Aristotelians, it was absurd to warn them against becoming the *wrong* kind of Aristotelians.

Today I shall be trying to show what Aristotle can do—trying in effect to produce Aristotelians so dogmatic that they need the warning of the first lecture. If you are taking this course seriously, and if the course works from week to week, you will find that each philosopher as we come to him has so much to say for himself that you cannot imagine how he could be resisted. My point today says of Aristotle what Mr. Denneny's brilliant lecture mistakenly said of Kierkegaard: seek no further, the saving truth lies here. But of course the salvation I'm talking about is a far less glorious thing than being saved from Kierkegaard's despair. It is simply the salvation from talking nonsense about literature.

Mr. Denneny's lecture is a good place to begin, because he said some very harsh things about the Stagyrite, the Philosopher, the Master of them that know. He accused him, among other things, of pushing a life of dull contentment, of fat middle-class complacency. I think that what Denneny said about Aristotle, in Kierkegaard's name, *is* almost precisely what Kierkegaard himself would say, and I think that I could show why it is a brutal distortion of what Aristotle is talking about. But instead of defending Aristotle's picture of virtue and happiness, it should be more profitable to consider for a few moments why Kierkegaard-Denneny, because of their choice of method and problem, inevitably come out at such cross-purposes with Aristotle.

Kierkegaard-Denneny (or K-D as I shall from now on affectionately call them) are radically dialectical in method, in the sense that everything in their thought depends on a basic polarity that is more important to them than anything else. There are, in other words, only two positions on their moral chart, the saved and the despairing, and their intellectual chart is identical with their moral and spiritual chart. The task of thought, in K-D's view, is to be *edifying,* which means simply to move as many souls as possible from one position on the two-position board to the other position, from despair to faith. You will note that K-D found it easy, beginning with this intellectual chart and holding to this intellectual purpose, to dismiss Plato, Freud, and Aristotle: each of them can be seen, to no one's surprise, to have only two positions on *his* chart too, and then it can be easily shown that they are the *wrong* positions.

Note that once you are committed to dealing with the world as thesis and counterthesis (with a possible synthesis) , everything can serve as evidence for your view. It matters little that Aristotle, for example, never saw himself as reducible to two terms; our dialectic enables us to see that he *was really* only working in pairs, but he just didn't realize it. It matters little that men in general do not divide simply into those living in "despair" and those living in "faith"; *we* see the truth about their souls better than they themselves, and we can tell the happy young maiden, "You are in despair," with as much confidence as Christ showed when he said, "He who is not for me is against me." Every kind of human life, every conceivable fact, can be fitted into one side or another of our pair and then used as evidence for our contention. Remember what Mr. Sinaiko said: *Everything is by definition locatable* on the simple chart somewhere.

An Aristotelian's first objection to such procedures, then, is that they oversimplify the world of fact in fantastic ways, and thus claim proof for themselves when all they have done is slice up a cake. Unfortunately this general objection is not much use in itself; the dichotomizer has only to say, "You're another" —that is, "You are trying to complicate what is after all very simple. All of your intellectual complications are simply an effort to conceal from yourself that you are living in despair."

But I think with the oversimplification come other costs that are more troublesome. With any philosophical or political or critical system that covers the world with two or three concepts, one is almost certainly tempted to deal with that world at a level of abstraction that is not only remote from experience but also temptingly aloof from the harsh corrections which such experience can give to concept-jugglers.

We see such harsh effects most clearly whenever war or warlike conditions lead us to place all men, all concepts, all actions, into two groups—those that are for us and those that are against us. Of course our terminology is skillfully adapted to conceal from us how far our abstractions are from the concrete reality of persons, feelings, facts. A cartoon I saw last week showed an air force general saying, "I can't see the objections to spraying people with napalm if it makes the world a better place to live in." In the world of abstractions in which we fight this war, phrases like "making the world a better place to live in" or "defending the free world" or "fighting world communism" neatly divide all men into two kinds, those for us and those against us, and in the service of the phrases individual men and the qualities of individual actions are forgotten. And of course such polarities produce in others a comparable response. Those of us who oppose the Vietnam catastrophe become tempted to think that all men are of only two kinds, and if someone is not clearly for us he must be against us. A protester last week accosted the wife of a university trustee as she was leaving a dinner at which Vice-President Humphrey spoke, saying, "Do *you* have a son in Vietnam?" Then, looking at her elderly figure, he said: "Oh, I see you couldn't possibly have a son!" I can easily imagine the reply that he would make if he heard me say that the world was by his cruel statement made a worse place in which to live; he would say that the feelings of an elderly woman do not matter as compared with the horrors of the war. But the decision to balance her feelings against napalm was not forced on him. He *chose* to assume that any banquet at which Humphrey spoke must taint everyone who attended it, and he chose to assume that insulting her would somehow improve the world. He thus turned a real woman with real feelings into an abstraction. I happen to know that the woman has openly opposed the war, but that's incidental. What is important is that he had committed what Sartre calls the greatest sin, turning actuality, the real living, feeling, woman, into an abstraction.

History is full of atrocities committed in the name of abstract terms like freedom and salvation. The Albigensian crusaders are said to have hacked at the defenseless folks of southern France shouting, "Kill all; let God save the innocent." Why not? There were only two kinds of people, the saved and the damned. History is also full of sudden awakenings, when contact with real persons and things breaks through abstractions. An ex-Communist I met in London in 1957 said to a meeting of Communists and ex-Communists who were troubled about the Hungarian affair, "I don't know what I am going to do, now that I can no longer support the Party. But one thing I do know: I'm never again going to deliberately hurt any individual human being in the name of Party abstractions." Compare that statement with the reported statement of one of the protesters who broke up the meeting of newspaper editors in Washington: "If you don't like what we're doing, you're against life and for death." He was being strictly logical—*if* there are only two kinds of people and two kinds of ideas, his kind and the others. When enough people in any society come to think that a given abstraction—whether party, nation, idea of progress, or solution to the war—is worth killing for, then of course either war or civil war results. War, genocide, silencing by forceful picketing, drafting draft protesters—these are all expressions of the notion that all men and all ideas can be divided into two kinds according to two opposing abstractions.

Another objection to dialectical juggling of concepts is that it often leads men to a kind of Utopianism that cannot help finally producing disillusionment. If we begin by asking what it means to be saved, absolutely, sure enough we discover that just about everybody is damned; if we begin by demanding a perfect society, we must end despairing of *any* real society. If we insist that a university must be either perfect or damned, we shall of course damn all universities, but especially those that seem to come closest to having a chance for perfecting themselves: they are most obviously betraying their possibilities.

Finally, thinking by juggling abstractions constantly invites

one to use analogies that distort or ignore the concrete actualities of things and persons and works of art. We can see this
most clearly when the abstractions and polarities are exhibited
by someone distant from our own thinking. When Nazi censors
divided books and plays and movies and poems and verbal expressions into those that were *echt-Deutsch* and those that were
non-Aryan, the fact that all art was being analogized to political oratory or pamphleteering was obvious to almost everyone
outside Germany. But it is not quite so easy to see what has gone
wrong when Freud is forced, by *his* simple triad, to treat all
art according to an analogy with neurosis-induced dreams; or
when some sociologists reduce art to social expression; or when
some philosophers and religious critics reduce art to its truth
value; or when some historians reduce art to its role as product
of historical antecedents.

It's easy—one more time round—to see what has gone wrong
when the small-town censor attacks *Catcher in the Rye*, reducing its fictional value to his simple pairing: moral public utterance v. immoral public utterance. It may not be quite so easy
to see what has gone wrong when the subtle, literate critic writes
a history of American fiction under a similarly constricting pair
of concepts—the garden (of innocence) and the machine (of
corruption). His analogy of fiction to scripture may enable him
to say some interesting things about America and its novels, but
the individual works in such a treatment may be treated as
brutally as individual soldiers are treated in the dialectic of
war, or as the frightened cries of individual children are treated
in the Air Corps statistics on "public annoyance levels due to
sonic boom."

Now if there were no alternative to the juggling of polarities
or triads, listing all of these dangers and temptations would be
rather pointless. If the battle lies, as K-D seem to suggest,
between one set of pairings and some other set of pairings, we
would be forced either to struggle on to find the right set or to
become relativists. K-D chose the former alternative, with the
hope that men would be driven to a faith that will transcend
despair; but I suspect that the effect of such an emphasis for
many moderns is to heighten despair. If I must make the choice

offered me by K-D, between despair and a faith that is announced as "absurd," indeed as infinitely irrational, I know where I'll come out every time.

Similarly, if there is no way of thinking about the Vietnam war other than to face the choice between U.S. violence and the violence of the most militant protesters, then of course we are doomed to choose our abstractions and forget the human beings who will be hurt by our choice. Full-scale wars force this kind of abstraction upon us, and we may soon come to a place in this particular half-war when no other ways are available. But the question for today is whether, in thinking about less gruesomely pressing matters, you want to fall into the same kind of distorting abstraction-mongering.

Before you do, let me try to show that there *are* other possibilities. We can choose, if we wish, to deal with the world in an entirely different way. Instead of playing with pairs of concepts inevitably distant from existence, we can become "existentialists" at least in the sense of attempting to deal with the world's problems quite literally for what they are. Instead of dividing the world into real forms and unreal matter, for example, we can look at the real things around us and try to find ways of dealing with them, intellectually and practically. Instead of dividing each man into body and soul, or id, ego, and super-ego, or dividing all men into the despairing and the faithful, we can choose to look at the things that men in fact can do, the actual problems they face, the consequences of various kinds of action, and the capabilities of various aspects of their unified being. Instead, finally, of trying to deal with art under abstract aesthetic or moral categories, forcing it to serve the state or salvation or the fulfillment of intellectual patterns, we can simply ask of each work, quite literally, in strict repudiation of all analogy, *What is it?* Your Christian, your Communist, your aesthetician can ask "What is *art?*" and they may turn up some interesting and even valuable talk on their way. But meanwhile the problem of what *this* work of art is, *as distinct from all the others,* remains unsolved, as does the problem of how I might improve it or make a better one like it.

To shift our attention in this way to another sort of intellectual work entirely is not, let me hasten to say, to surrender all questions of value to the dichotomizers. The man who, like Aristotle, decides to study a great many actual political constitutions rather than write a Utopia does not surrender thereby his right to judge the success or failure of constitutions; and the man who, like Aristotle, chooses to look at how particular plays and kinds of plays are made rather than writing a treatise on ideal beauty does not surrender his right to judge the difference between good and bad plays. But he does embrace, with what might almost be called loving eagerness, the concrete actualities as they are, in contrast to abstract ideals that never could exist on land or sea. Just as there is no point in talking of friendship and love of all mankind if you *just cannot stand* your roommate, there is no point in dealing with Art with a capital A unless you mean by it *this, this,* and *this* particular work of art. There is an old joke that says, If you want to know whether to go downtown, ask Plato; but if you want to know how to *get* downtown, ask Aristotle. It's a misleading joke, because Aristotle will be quite willing to deal with the bigger questions, too, in the proper time and place. But meanwhile it remains true that if you want to know how to get downtown, if you want to know how to write a tragedy (not a Thing of Beauty or a Work of Art but a particular tragedy) or how to judge one, the *Poetics* will show you how you might do it well.

Let me dramatize just how radically *particular* is the criticism that results, in contrast with what our other three men (Plato, Freud, and Kierkegaard) might attempt, by turning to a particular story, Joyce's "Clay."

Of what possible use is Aristotle to anyone who would like to say something worth saying about a story like "Clay"? I must admit, first, that he's not much use at all to anyone who wants to answer any of the following questions:

1. What was the creative process of Joyce as he wrote "Clay," or how does "Clay" express Joyce's own psyche?

2. How does "Clay" express the society of its time?

3. Is "Clay" true to life?

4. Is it moral for an author to write about such helpless creatures as Maria, and even to make fun of them?

5. How does "Clay" represent the literature of its time?

Aristotle may be of *indirect* help in answering some of these questions, by helping us to answer first his own kind of question. But in contrast with all of these general questions, Aristotle, the lover of the particular, will demand, if you take him seriously, that you *come to know the thing as it is,* "Clay" in all its individual quality; this must mean that you come to know it as something unique—even though it shares qualities with many other works. You will come to know it not by analogy with what it resembles—after all, with a little imagination I can prove that it resembles everything else in the universe, from Christ-myth to jet engines—but rather *literally,* in its differences from everything else that is. You will, if you take him seriously, come to know the works you love for what they are, and not for what they can do as illustrations for your pet ideas or as evidence for your political party or church or for your lecture on Aristotle. If you come to know "Clay," goaded by Aristotle, you will know *how it works,* which is to know why its parts are as they are in relation to the effect of the whole. You will not be satisfied even with the sensitive and convincing reading of the ending of the story that was given by Mr. Frese last week, illustrating as it did his thesis about the way language and the use of language is treated in *all* the stories of *Dubliners.* Under Aristotle's tutelage you will be satisfied only with coming to know the life and soul of *this* story, what makes it a unique artistic event even while it resembles other stories in *Dubliners* and other stories of its time and of our time.

Aristotle would not, unlike Mr. Frese, see the story as saying something about language, or as a statement or illustration of a general thesis, but rather as a shaping of human experience, Maria's experience, with its inescapable emotional overtones and meanings—inescapable for those readers sensitive enough to see that experience as Joyce intends. Though the story includes meanings of the kind Mr. Frese outlined, it is not essentially a communication of meanings—to say that it is a communication would be to analogize it to the essay or the philosophical pamphlet. Rather it is—*what it is,* a representation, a shaping, an imitation of a human action that is (rather) serious, of a certain (very slight) magnitude complete in itself, in language with pleasurable accessories; revealing the helpless, sad triviality of a woman who passes from mild hopefulness through mild disappointments to mild and unconscious realization of her final hopelessness; in a narrative manner bound rigorously to the limited consciousness of the main character; all serving to heighten the reader's pity relieved by the wonder of truth revealed: here is the pitiful (or painfully absurd) reality of this kind of life.

No honest student of Aristotle will be content, in talking of any story, until he has wrestled with all the four questions which I just now touched on in that definition: the shape of the thing (the what), the style (the *in* what), the manner (the *by* what) and the effect (the *for* what or why). Until one can state with some confidence that this story is *doing* such-and-such (in this case, working toward a realization of the pathos of Marianess in the world), by means of such-and-such a shape of event, conveyed in such-and-such language, with such-and-such narrative technique, one really has no ground to stand on in saying anything about its quality or about the quality of any of its parts. When I *have* gone through all this, I am ready to look Joyce in the eye and say: "By God, man, you did it!" (or, "What a botched job!"). I am ready, further, to apply Aristotle's twin tests of transposability and expungability of the parts; in this story I find that absolutely nothing can be cut without my regretting it (strictly speaking, there are no "episodes," only "incidents"), and I find nothing that can be reordered without harm. Of course the fact that *I* find nothing to change doesn't mean that I am right. But it tells me all that I can ever hope to know, without relying on other critics, about what a beautifully achieved story it is. Though I cannot, when I am through, talk with Joyce as an equal, I can hope to talk with some precision on his own wavelength:

"What I liked was the way in which you managed to convey, from the opening line, Maria's helpless little anticipation of a mildly pleasant evening, and her fear that Joe will drink too much, and then how you made everything lead at the end to her sad choice of the clay (death) and her mistake with that song, Joe drinking heavily all the while, her own soul unconsciously baring itself, baring the hurt resulting from all of the little insults you have scattered through her evening. I see exactly why you have her stand in front of the mirror, looking 'with quaint affection at the diminutive body' and finding it a 'nice tidy little body.' I would never have managed that so well myself, try as I would, but I see why you've done it, and it's great, man. And I see why she must be ugly, and dwell in her own mind on the ugliness of her nose almost meeting her chin, and why she must be so simpleminded. And I see why almost nobody says anything in the story (except as Maria hears it and reports it), making the long outburst of Maria's song seem much more of a climax. And I see why the wry comedy of all the fools and knaves Maria meets is appropriate to her pathos: 'and his [Joe's] eyes filled up so much with tears [of sentiment] that he could not find what he was looking for and in the end he had to ask his wife to tell him where the corkscrew was.' Joe, as Maria has promised us earlier, 'was so different when he took any drink.' Oh, the wrenching of it, the human wrenching of it, all these lost lives, these Dubliners . . .!"

We can be grateful that Joyce knew enough to keep all such rhetorical outbursts purged from his story. As Aristotle says, the poet is poet primarily through his imitative power, and he should intrude into his stories no more than is "necessary." In this story no intrusions by the author are necessary, except for the two titles, which in a sense tell us that here is a lump of significant, death-bound "clay" from among his "Dubliners."

We can see that Joyce's poem is something totally foreign to anything Aristotle could have imagined. The characters are far below the intelligence and general sensitivity that the average reader will attribute to himself, and Aristotle would never have dreamed that someone like Maria could be endowed with noncomic poetic power. He was quite right, though, about the impossibility of making a great tragedy out of such stuff: even the genius of Joyce could never make a complex tragedy out of Maria—though presumably he might manage something in the "tragedy of pathos." What we have, however, is not tragedy of any kind mentioned by Aristotle; it is rather a new thing under the sun, quite new—at least in English—when Joyce did it: a prose-poem of pathetic self-revelation—or some such thing.

You will notice that as I have proceeded, in my brief effort to attend to the unique work in its highly particular kind, I have inevitably touched on other matters, like Joyce's genius, or the history of tragedy, or the novelty of this kind of thing historically. These are not my subject, as "poetic" critic, but if I ever chose to become biographer of Joyce and tried to assess his genius, as an Aristotelian critic I would have no doubt about where to find my primary data: not in Joyce's statements about genius, not in psychological probings into his so-called creative process, not in abstract theorizing about the nature of art or creativity, but in "Clay," the finished work, the achievement in "Clay," and in the other works considered in *their* uniqueness. And similarly, if I wanted to write a history of the short story, it is hard to believe that my history would be relevant to what counts unless it were based on hundreds of reconstructions of this kind. Most histories of the short story, needless to say, like histories of the other arts, are not based on this kind of particularity and complexity; they trace some one interesting aspect—narrative manner or this or that stylistic trick, like stream of consciousness, or some quirk of subject matter, like the rise of laundry maids and their kind in modern fiction, or this or that pair of themes. Seldom do they trace the rise and fall of essential forms, sought for in the particular unions of form and matter that particular works amount to.

Meanwhile you may want to insist again that there are many questions that Aristotle's approach will not answer: questions about the spirit of tragedy through the ages, questions about how to rise from despair to faith, questions about how to use art to attack your enemies, questions about which modes of art should be given to children at which ages to educate their souls—these and many others are either ignored by him or are treated briefly in other contexts. To anyone who does not care about what makes a great story great, what he says must seem boring and irrelevant. To anyone who prefers to dwell steadily on the level of abstract ideas, debating forever questions like whether the spirit of tragedy is dead in our time, or whether the novel is dead, or whether the new media have killed the message, his stuff will seem initially pedestrian and literal-minded. But, you know, there is no better cure for despair than rousing oneself and joining a great artist in his particular creative acts; there is no better proof of man's nobility than seeing a bit of it really work in a great piece of art; there is no more satisfactory proof of the existence of the good, the true, and the beautiful, than experiencing their fusion in the unique, particular achievement of a story like "Clay."

For those who manage, unlike K-D, to use moderation in their choice of question—for those who would rather solve solvable problems than juggle abstractions for purposes of warfare or evangelism, the concrete things of this world—the absurd, threatening, despair-ridden but art-filled world—can prove a thing of immeasurable interest and reward. If it is an existentialist choice you are looking for (goaded on by that prophet Denneny), why not choose an "existentialist" who really believed in the glory of existing things?

PLURALISM AND ITS RIVALS

Everyone here today has just lived through a scandalous period in the university's history. No doubt each of us would describe the scandal differently, but for the purposes of this course perhaps the most humiliating side to the affair has been the way in which so many faculty and students have, as the old-fashioned expression goes, lost their heads. I have sometimes felt, during the past six weeks, as if I were surrounded by colleagues, old and young, who were deliberately repudiating all they ever knew about trying to use their heads. I'm sure that you can think of plenty of examples of blind, uncritical, even stupid credulity. Haven't you encountered a fantastic amount of just plain gullibility lately? But now ask yourselves honestly: weren't the examples you just thought of committed by people who were not on your side, whatever that was? Am I right? The uncritical distortions that strike me most are usually committed by my enemies. I am not so impressed by the follies of my friends, and when the unscholarly credulity is exhibited by

Final lecture to Liberal Arts I, winter 1969. Students had read works of Aristotle, Plato, Freud, and Nietzsche earlier in the academic quarter. A sixteen-day sit-in occurred in February.

myself, it becomes for some reason excusable, even in the rare
cases when I am forced to admit that I *have* been credulous. My
enemies are *gullible,* if they are not actually liars; the average
man (committing exactly the same offense) is *uncritical;* my
friends are sometimes inclined, quite forgivably, to *leap before
they look;* and I—I am so loyal to my own noble principles that
I occasionally, just once in a blue moon, overlook a minor fact
or two.

But let me give you two examples, one from each "side," as
we have tragically learned to say. A faculty member said to me
two Saturdays ago, "Have you heard that 'they' have threatened
again to destroy the university?" "No, I haven't." "Well, Professor X told me that they've issued a new set of demands,
saying that if we don't meet the demands by Tuesday, they'll
burn the place down, or something like that." A few moments
later another faculty member told me the same thing, also derived from Professor X. The source of this rumor was that
mocking phrase in the leaflet, "will in and of itself constitute
grounds for further militant action"! Example two: On the second day of the sit-in, when the students opposing it were trying
to hold a meeting in Mandel Hall, a student asked to make an
announcement: "I've just learned from one of the marshalls
[of the students in the building] that the Ellis Avenue exit has
been closed, and that men who look like they're dressed in
Chicago city police uniforms are stationed inside." A gasp went
through the audience and many students left in excitement.
The young man then came down into the hall, sat down beside
me, and whispered, "Mr. Booth, is that true, what I just said?"

These two examples of intellectual irresponsibility, not to
say lack of integrity, could be multiplied indefinitely. Too
many of us have behaved as if we had never come within miles
of any educational institution, let alone one that prides itself
on a tradition of aggressive critical-mindedness, or that offers a
course like Liberal Arts I that is supposed to deal with the arts
of inquiry, argument, and proof, and with such questions as
"What is a fact?"

So, it is a scandal. Or it would be, if we had a climate of
opinion, here and elsewhere, in which acts of criminal credulity
were taken as seriously as they ought to be. But we live in a

credulous age and country. We live in a time when hundreds, perhaps thousands of people in Chicago can be convinced that President Kennedy is still alive by a letter read over the radio by a disk jockey; a country in which Attorney General Garrison can get away with his antics without providing as yet one shred of solid evidence; a country in which millions of citizens, apparently, believe that flying saucers come from outer space, while few of those citizens will bother to read Condon's scientific report on the subject; a country, in short, in which there is a credibility gap far greater than the cliché usually suggests: the real credibility gap is between conclusions and reasons for conclusions. You and I are members of a public that is increasingly a nonpublic, in Dewey's terms, not because we expect to be deceived by each other—though that would be bad enough—but because increasingly we don't even care whether we *are* deceived. Every man, in this newly levelled egalopolis, is entitled to his own brand of nonsense, and woe unto the elitist who demands evidence. I asked Mr. Lemke what he thought would happen on campus if a forceful speaker argued that he had seen the prophet Elijah return to earth in a chariot of fire. "He would find many followers," Lemke said, and I could not tell—perhaps he himself could not precisely tell—whether he was joking or not.

The scandal of the past six weeks has been that the university has entered the uncritical, credulous world with a vengeance—that too many of us have too often forgotten the special responsibilities that fall on any man who would like to claim that there is some connection between his opinions and actions, on the one hand, and defensible principles or demonstrable facts, on the other.

But what connection should it be? Isn't the very lesson we learn as we scramble our way through Aristotle, Plato, Freud, and Nietzsche, that there are many different connections, depending on who you are and what you want to do? And if that is so, who is to tell us that this or that statement, whether of fact or of principle or of connections between them and conclusions, is right or wrong? You pays your money and you takes your choice.

Since I've been adopting a moralizing tone so far, let me

continue with it and say that to me it is an intellectual disaster
of a very serious kind if any student of Liberal Arts I comes to
the end of the year believing that there is no such thing as an
error of fact, or that every man's intellectual structure is as good
as every other man's, or that there is, finally, no such thing as
validity or truth. I can't begin to show, in my remaining time,
why I think this is such an enormous disaster when it occurs—
and it does occur—but I do want to try, as I continue my sermon, to wrestle with the problems that give rise to this disaster.
The catastrophe of total skepticism would not occur—especially
it would not occur with very good students—if there were not
some plausibility about it; indeed, it is part of the purpose of
this course to dramatize and make real the reasons for skepticism
about many of our beliefs. An educated man *must* be skeptical,
and in one sense sceptical about everything; when he stops
being skeptical, he stops thinking and is no longer an educated
man. We believe this—and it is therefore not surprising that
the kind of catastrophe I have described sometimes occurs. The
alternatives to thoroughgoing skepticism are mainly two, and
they can be approached best by taking any subject and seeing
what kinds of things we can say about it.[1]

I

Suppose we take the short story I asked you all to read ("Araby,"
by James Joyce) and play with it for awhile, trying to discover
to what degree it is a "hard object," as it were, that determines
what we say about it, and to what extent it is malleable—a
different object depending on who looks at it.

The complete skeptic or relativist will say, of course, that

1. The four logical possibilities when we are faced with rival claims to
truth are: one will prove right and the others all wrong (dogmatism); all
must be untenable, known in advance to be so because truth is unobtain-
able (skepticism); each will prove partly right and partly wrong (eclecticism);
more than one (but not all) will prove true, when looked at closely, yielding
a plurality of truths (pluralism). What looks like a fifth possibility—all
will prove true—is in fact no real alternative; if all possible statements
about a subject are equally true, then truth has become meaningless and we
must end in the second position, complete skepticism. For this lecture I
have simplified the four possibilities, taken from Elder Olson, by telescoping
skepticism and eclecticism. See above, pp. 90–91.

what "Araby" seems to be it in fact is. And my first point about
the story is an obvious and important one, namely that there is a
hard resistant core of fact about "Araby" that will test what
anyone wants to say about it, regardless of his system or perspective. This core we might call precritical, because it consists
of all the elements that everyone will admit to, once his attention is called to them. Some of these matters are entirely obvious
and not worth mentioning except to make the point I'm making
now: the title, for example, is "Araby," not "A Piece of James
Joyce's Soul" or "Disestablishmentarianism in Dublin." The
books that the first-person narrator finds in the priest's belongings include a novel by Walter Scott and a detective story, not
the works of Thomas Aquinas or the New Testament. The coin
that the narrator holds "tightly in my hand" is a florin, and a
florin is worth two shillings, not five or ten; the uncle is an uncle,
not a father; and so on. Anyone whose reading of the story is
clearly based on contradictions of these facts, simple as they
are, rules himself out of court. A truly committed skeptic may
want to say that to him a florin is really a crushed bluebird,
held tightly in the boy's hand, or that the word *uncle* really
stands for paternal grandfather. To maintain the full skeptical
position that "everything depends on your point of view," he
must be willing to contradict or reject any fact I advance as
self-evident. Yet if he does reject florin *as florin* he rules himself
out of any further productive discussion of the story. Everyone
he talks with will know that he is wrong, as soon as he looks at
the page and sees the word *florin*.

When the sum of such facts is totted up, for any story, it
makes a pretty big sum. It includes not just the obvious facts
mentioned so far, but everything that all readers, regardless of
their critical presuppositions, can be presumed to admit to, once
their attention is called to it. Only less obvious than florin is, in
this story, the whole sequence of actions performed by the narrator and the other characters. It is true that as soon as I describe any *selection* from these actions, I am beginning to
impose my own special views. But my imposition is strictly
limited, at this stage, by whether what I say can be checked by
any observer.

The objective test is as strict here as it can ever be in any laboratory; either I have seen what is on the page or I have not. Admitting, then, that my *choice* of details is to some degree mine and not easily demonstrated to be Joyce's, let me describe some of the precritical facts that seem to me undeniable about this story: A narrator remembers from his boyhood (age unspecified) a house he moved to, with his aunt and uncle. What he mainly remembers about the house, besides the remaining belongings of the priest who died in the back-drawing room, is his vision of "Mangan's sister," unnamed—as he saw her, as he imagined her, as she spoke to him about a bazaar, as she looked when he promised to bring her something from the bazaar. Then he remembers his impatience to get to the bazaar, his uncle's drunken forgetfulness about his need for money, his belated trip to the bazaar, his arrival too late to enjoy anything or to buy anything even if he had had enough money left. And he remembers his emotional reaction to all this: "Gazing up into the darkness I saw myself as a creature driven and derided by vanity; and my eyes burned with anguish and anger."

This sequence is by no means exhaustive of what every genuine reader will see in this story. One could expand it until one had in effect recopied the whole story, because, at the factual level, it turns out that every sentence, every word, could be prefaced with *"It is a fact that* Joyce shows his narrator remembering that——(fill in the blank)." If we did a careful reconstruction of the facts of the story in this sense, we would have performed a first-level, commonsensical, noncritical reading of it. Such a reading would be complete only when we were reasonably sure that we had reconstructed each word and phrase in the meaning or meanings most probable in Joyce's time: Café Chantant, salver, third-class carriage, "some Freemason affair," fib, and so on.

Now, of course, it is true that even while we have been reconstructing the facts, our minds have been busy putting the so-called facts together to make inferred patterns; even the inferential process whereby you and I take a word like *f-l-o-r-i-n* and constitute the fact of two shillings, which is twenty-four pence, which means, according to the arithmetic of the story, that the boy has spent two-thirds of his cash by the time he has paid the fourpence for the tram and a shilling to get into the bazaar—even this process is elaborate indeed, and it may require some of us to use a dictionary. But we are still at the unquestionably factual level for all that, because we can say, without the shadow of a doubt, that any reader who constitutes the facts differently—arguing, say, that two pennies plus sixpence is not one-third of a florin, the boy's original cash-in-pocket, or that he really may have had lots of additional cash hidden away somewhere, for all we know—any such reader can be shown to have ignored the words on the page.

Perhaps some of you may wonder at this point why I make such a big issue out of what is, after all, quite obvious. But I ask you to remember where we began, and how far we now are from the skeptic's statement that what you see in a story is true for you if it's true for you. We have already found a supply of literally hundreds, perhaps thousands, of statements about this story that are demonstrably factual or nonfactual, and not one of them would be denied by *any* critic writing from any system—if we could get his attention long enough to have him come with us and look at the words on the page. I must admit, sorrowfully, that many publishing critics do *not* stop long enough to see what is written; I would guess that more than half of the literary criticism published would not be published if the authors took proper care with this simple, precritical, task—a task that earlier critics called the grammatical task: recovering the meanings at the indisputable level.

II

It is only now, presuming ourselves to have restored all of the words and phrases to their public meanings at the time the story was written, that we begin the task of criticism. And it is only now that we can say with any clarity that our systematic biases begin to enter inescapably. When we stop asking what are the facts about florins or about the literal description of this or that episode in the story and begin to ask, what *is* this story, as a larger fact in itself, we begin to constitute the facts according to our intellectual perspectives. Each perspective can yield its results without distorting what I have so far called the facts;

yet it will seem to yield a different set of facts from those yielded
by any other perspective. In speaking of perspectives, I am of
course using a metaphor, comparing the various modes of asking questions about the soul or about art with visual slants. I
think it is a useful metaphor, because it dramatizes for us how
a particular procedure can be limited and still be true in its
own lights.

Einstein somewhere illustrates the difference between classical physics and relativity physics by talking of a cone and of
the variety of fixed perspectives a man can have of a cone. If
he is directly above it, looking down, he will see a circle, and if
he cannot shift from his fixed perspective, he'll think that he
has the true view of the cone. If he is directly to one side, he'll
see a triangle, and he'll be convinced that the object *is* a triangle. From another angle he'll see an ellipse joined to a triangle. And so on. Einstein sees the physicist as approaching
nature with an inevitably limited perspective; it is as if he and
the cone were fixed, so that he cannot shift about, add up perspectives, and finally say, "Oh, yes, now I see *it all,* it is a *cone,*
not a circle, not a triangle, not an ellipse."

I am suggesting that our views of "Araby," like our views of
nature in Einstein's analogy, are permanently doomed to par-
tiality. Each view may still be, in its own terms, completely
valid, subject to rigorous tests imposed both by limits of mal-
leability (as it were) of the subject viewed and by the standards-
of-viewing proper to the chosen perspective. But it will be only
one of many possible views, no one of them easily tested from
any *other* perspective; in fact, each may appear wrong to anyone proceeding from any of the other perspectives.

To pursue this line further would lead us into a philosophical discussion of theories of truth—the so-called correspondence
theory, the pragmatic theory of Dewey, and so on. I'd prefer
now to turn for the rest of our time to "Araby" and to questions
about its nature and purpose. What *is* "Araby"? How do we
interpret it? What is it for? Why is it made? What does it tell
us? Any one question already moves us in the direction of a
type of interpretation, but we can run quickly through some
alternatives, in order to illustrate how different perspectives

will yield different "Arabys," without our having to say either that any old statement about "Araby" is as good as any other statement, or that we must choose one as true and reject all the others as false.

III

What is "Araby"? Why, clearly, "Araby" is an imitation or representation of a character in action, as reported by himself as an older person, long after the action occurs. Unlike the action of tragedy, the action here has no magnitude to speak of—it is a mere week, or at most a few weeks, in the life of a mere boy, and what happens to him is in itself seemingly trivial. The narrative manner (moving now from the *formal* to the *efficient* cause) is in a way more complicated than the action imitated, because the manner of telling chosen by the older speaker reflects a constant ironic light over the actions of the boy. The style (the "means," the *material* cause) is "embellished" systematically to heighten the variations of manner, sometimes revealing the tonal judgment of the maturer narrator, sometimes revealing the characteristic expressions of the boy. The story is designed (now moving to the *final* cause) to yield a special mixture of sympathy and ironic amusement.

Continuing as Aristotelians, we can note that the effect of the story is due more to the manner of telling and the diction than to any inherent effect of the incidents themselves. If the story were told in a neutral tone, one could never guess, as one can with a neutral telling of a tragic plot, what effect is intended: a young boy, living with his aunt and uncle, decides that he loves a neighbor girl; he promises to bring her a present from a bazaar, but because of circumstances beyond his control, he is unable to do so, and he ends in momentary "anguish and anger." Such material could be made into comedy, farce, burlesque, pathos, romance. But the author has chosen to heighten a mixture of sympathy and ironic criticism: the boy is made essentially sympathetic by showing everything through his vision (no special sympathetic characteristics are offered or needed), and the implied criticism of his immature romanticism is thus kept under friendly control.

For such a story one needs only the generalized sympathy and tolerant amusement that everyone feels for a suffering young romantic, a young boy who chooses his books on the basis of the yellowness of the pages; a young boy who is so much in love with love that he crouches in the dark, clasping his hands together and murmuring "O, love! O love!"; a young boy whose "body was like a harp and her words and gestures were like fingers running upon the wires." Such a young man is laughable and lovable at the same time. The first third of the story establishes him in his *blind* romanticism, in the *blind* alley, looking through the *blind*, thankful that he can see so little, with his senses *veiled*—the very opposite, incidentally, of the condition that Joyce thought characterized the true artist. Then we have the only conversation with the vaguely described, unnamed, uncharacterized girl, with the promise to bring something from the fair. The rest of the story is made up of two pages of helpless grappling with the vivid and disappointing realities of the boy's very unromantic existence; in contrast to the vague romanticisms of the opening, we see harsh detail after detail of his real world, and we then see him go to the fair, with both his cash and the evening rapidly disappearing, with the very real and threatening young lady at the bazaar stall humiliating him, and with his final realization: "Gazing up into the darkness I saw myself as a creature driven and derided by vanity [and we know that this is true enough] and my eyes burned with anguish and anger [and we know that this is excessive, romantic, adolescent, if you will, and temporary]." We do not feel anguish and anger with him; the revelation of his nature and of the tightly knit episode has given us the pleasure proper to the spectacle of such pain. There is no catharsis, of course, because we need none, having felt no deep pangs of emotion.

Once we have seen the basic structure of the story in this way, we can go on to see how skillfully Joyce has heightened his effects. A full analysis of these strokes would require at least an hour; I call your attention now only to one touch not previously mentioned: the repetition, within a page, of the key memory of the girl's romanticized appearance: "The light from the lamp opposite our door caught the white curve of her neck, lit up her hair that rested there, and, falling, lit up the hand upon the railing. It fell over one side of her dress and caught the white border of a petticoat, just visible as she stood at ease." It could be *any* girl, and a page later we read, "I may have stood there for an hour, [leaning his forehead against the cool glass] seeing nothing but the brown-clad figure cast by my imagination, touched discreetly by the lamplight at the curved neck, at the hand upon the railings and at the border below the dress." Again it is all abstractly romantic. The repetition is obviously chosen with great care, like every other detail. In this story of how the boy encounters a moment of reality through the haze of youthful romanticism, every choice contributes beautifully, in ways specifiable though not spelled out here, to the pleasure of the whole.

IV

What is "Araby"? Why, clearly, "Araby" is an imitation of a human passion, the passion of youthful romanticism, in a form that is calculated to make us sympathize with a young man who gives himself over wholly to self-indulgence in his infatuation. Though it is clear to a mature reader that the author himself does not see the world as does his young hero, it is equally obvious, in the words of our master, Plato, that this is the kind of art that will corrupt the minds of all readers who do not "possess as an antidote a knowledge of its real nature." The reader is, in fact, seduced into seeing everything through the immature eyes of the boy; as we travel through the story with him, we are required, by the terms of the story as presented, to scoff at the decent lives of normal citizens ("The other houses of the street, conscious of decent lives within them, gazed at one another with brown imperturbable faces"), and to scorn a priest because of his misguided charity. ("He had been a very charitable priest; in his will he had left all his money to institutions and the furniture of his house to his sister"). Note also that we are required to assume by this bit of satire that institutions are impersonal and thus really unworthy objects of charity as compared to one's personal relatives; if we are subtle readers, we are then required to indulge in the petty pleasure of laughing at a well-meaning but ignorant boy; if we are not subtle readers, we are sure to fall into the trap of palpitating with him in his romantic haze. Whether we read subtly or not, we are required to wallow with him in his anger and impatience with his drunken uncle, and to grovel with him as he is driven, according to his own final judgment, by vanity and anguish and anger. All in all, the deeper we go into the story the more we "water" and "harrow" our pettier emotions.

But there is something deeper here. Joyce has taken a major step, as in other early stories, toward the totally distorted view of man and his proper ends which has dominated modern literature in recent decades. In his hands we approach the view that all of man's aspirations are ridiculous, that every hero is a nonhero, that life is a drab collection of realities that contrast with ideals which are absurd. In Joyce's world there is never any redeeming depth of meaning, never any grace to give significance to the petty lives portrayed. If we now find ourselves, in the last third of this battered century, unable to conceive of any genuinely heroic action, any finally defensible ideals, any value worth pursuing with courage and wisdom and a passion for decency, it is in part because Joyce and others following him have given us a literature of pettiness: Joyce gives us the illusion that to be snubbed by a bazaar clerk when you have only eight-pence in your pocket is a significant disaster—and in doing so, he has helped to take true significance from the world of literature. His story is "an imitation of a phantasm, not of the truth"; if nobody in 1969 has any inclination to *think* about justice and victimization, if we all automatically respond with quick-triggered emotions *against* institutions and *for* any character presented as a victim, it is in part because our souls have been schooled by such brilliantly produced and essentially debasing literature. "The part of us that leads us to dwell in memory on our suffering and impells us to lamentations, and cannot get enough of that sort of thing, is the irrational and idle part of us, the associate of cowardice," and it is the part that this story caters to.

V

What is "Araby"? Why, clearly, "Araby" is an expression of the author's deepest anxieties and drives, in the form of a quest for

peace in the circle of the womb. Joyce's lifelong battle for freedom from the bonds of church, of politics, of family, and of his
own fears is dramatized in story after story; here it is given
almost perfect expression in his passionate drive to leave the
harsh realities of his adoptive home and enter the mysterious
adult world of sexual freedom. The boy is from the beginning
deeply troubled by sexual fantasies, though he does not see
them for what they are. He is consciously obsessed with Mangan's sister and what he calls her "figure"; even her name is
"like a summons" to what he calls euphemistically "all my
foolish blood." His body is like a harp, he says, and her words
and gestures were "like fingers running upon wires." He sees
her, significantly enough, as a *chalice* which he bears through
the market place, yet this holy sublimation of the sexual organ
is quite openly tainted for the boy with the detail of the "white
border of the petticoat," mentioned twice. The desirability of
escape to the fantasy-world of Araby grows upon him, and he
finally, having abandoned the essentially masturbatory inaction
of chanting "O love! O love!" begins to act. He takes a *train*—
though a slow moving one—which in a few moments brings him
to the lighted dial of a *clock*. He cannot at first find an *entrance*
into the "big hall *girdled* . . . by a gallery," most of it in darkness. In a sequence that is surprisingly Kafkaesque, he enters the
vast dark hall and finds there a young lady who rebuffs him;
instead of the safety and joy he had expected, he is forced to
linger "before her stall, though I knew my stay was useless, to
make my interest *in her wares* seem the more real." Trapped by
the closed dome instead of liberated by it, he gazes up into the
darkness and sees himself in all his frustrated impotence, the
quest for release unsuccessful. But of course Joyce has managed
to achieve for *himself* some release, as our master, Freud, has
taught us to expect of all artists: the release of a mythic projection of his own entrapment.

VI

What is "Araby"? Why, obviously, it is a manifestation of what
happened to the Apollonian and Dionysiac spirits in literature at the beginning of the twentieth century. Though the

spirit of tragedy remained buried, Joyce found a new way "to parade the images of life before us" and "to incite us to seize their ideational essence."[2] Joyce knew that if he could fix the reality of any deeply felt moment in a verbal form wrought "for its aesthetic value alone," if he could realize the intensely perceived moment, however seemingly trivial in itself, he would have freed the spirits of his readers from any concern about practical effect, about the ethical qualities of his characters or his art, and have led them into an aesthetic domain. He would have made, in other words, a literary work that was strictly analogous to music. For Joyce, a work of verbal art should display the same subtle fusion of image and concept, of individuality and universality, that music displays. It is no accident that Joyce called his poems chamber music, and it is also no accident that he called some of his literary vignettes epiphanies —for him they were moments when a divine truth was revealed in the concrete individuality of things. The "metaphysical delight" of such verbal music is a translation of "instinctive Dionysiac wisdom"—all the world of practical and illusory longings shown by the young hero—into Apollonian images, creating a fusion which can then be said to have "justified the world by transforming it into an aesthetic phenomenon." Though the result is never, in Joyce, anything spectacular enough to be called a rebirth of tragedy, it is a rebirth, from the spirit of music, of "the essential metaphysical activity of man."

VII

Any of you who have really got hold of Freud or Nietzsche will have been made uneasy, I suspect, by my last two sections. I assure you that I am uneasy about them too. But at the moment I'm not so much troubled by the pseudocritics I have created as I am by all the other voices I hear in the wings, demanding to be heard on the subject of what "Araby" is. Marx is here to claim that "Araby" is *really* a portrait of decadent middle-class values, drawn by an aesthete who, despite his clever indictment of the bourgeois boy and his absurdly class-ridden quest, never

2. Now I am quoting from Nietzsche, of course.

managed to shake off his allegiance to the romantic individualism of the artist. Another economist, considerably cruder but just as insistent, shouts that "Araby" is really a commercial object, written to be bought and sold. A literary historian enters with a bullhorn to say that "Araby" is really, along with the other stories in this volume, a crucial moment in the history of narrative technique; the subtle variations of point-of-view throughout the volume show the first signs of the full flowering of technical exploration which Joyce, above all modern novelists, brought into fiction from poetry and drama. A cultural historian says that "Araby" is really a major moment in the development of attacks on romanticism as the twentieth century began; the sardonic portrait of the empty-headed young lover could not have been painted in England before this period. A rhetorical critic sees "Araby" as an obvious piece of persuasion designed to manipulate a twentieth-century audience in a certain way. While it uses what looks like an imitation of an action, it is really best explained as a series of strokes shrewdly calculated to hit us where we live. Notice, for example, the first sentence: "North Richmond Street, being blind,"—note that!—"was a quiet street except at the hour when the Christian Brothers' School *set the boys free.*" A sociologist jumps in to say that "Araby" is really one of the most interesting signs of change in the nature of literary audiences just before World War I. Though Joyce always talked as if he were writing for an audience of one, his story shares with the work of many other young writers of the time—Virginia Woolf and E. M. Forster, for example—a confident sense that a special audience had developed that did not require blatant Dickensian effects of plot or sentiment; Joyce could by now anticipate a reader who would catch the most delicate nuances, and who would at the same time respond more to subtle criticisms of sentiment than to sentimental appeals. It was in fact this audience that was to become, in some respects, the most important influence on twentieth-century culture: the bright young men and women of London and Paris whom Ortega y Gasset refers to ten years later, in *The Dehumanization of Art,* who look for an art that "avoids living forms," who demand that "a work of art be *nothing but* a work

of art," that it be "play," that it be "ironical," and that it avoid
sham and aspire "to scrupulous portrayals of reality."

VIII

And so they rush in, view after view after view. Every conceivable field of inquiry, past and future, will have *some* view of
"Araby," and though they will not all claim that their view is
the essential view, they will all define the work as a different
fact or set of facts, depending on their purposes. And many of
them *will* insist that their view is the essential view, that
"Araby" really *is* this or that, even though it obviously falls into
the clutches of men who try to make it into other things.

Yes, but what is it *really?* Well, clearly, it is—. Now, if I finished that sentence, I would be a fraud, because my lecture
should have demonstrated by now that "Araby," despite its
commonsensical core of fact, is not an entity that defines itself
aside from the purposes and views—more or less conscious and
systematic—of those who do the defining. "Araby" is not only
what Joyce made but what other men make of it; each of us
constitutes our own "Araby." To return to Einstein's cone, it is
as if none of us had ever seen a cone except from one or another
perspective. Many of us are inclined to be dogmatists and think
that our view—say, "This is a circle" or "This is a triangle"—
is *the* view. Some of us are relativists or skeptics, who say that it
doesn't matter what view you take of the cone, since all views
are false. And what I am working toward as the concluding
section of this lecture is a kind of pluralism—the notion that
every reality, every subject, can be and will be validly grasped in
more than one way depending on the purposes and intellectual
systems of the viewers; there is a plurality of valid philosophies,
of valid approaches to literature, of valid political philosophies,
of valid pictures of the soul, of valid views of the nature and
function of art. To understand what this means for your relation to intellectual pursuits will take you many years—unless
you are a lot brighter than most of us. But there are at least two
things it does *not* mean.

First, it does not mean that *every* view is valid, or that there
are not differences of validity or usefulness among different

views. If I call a cone a tragedy, because it really is a figure that tried to make it as a sphere and failed, I will have nothing to contribute to myself or fellow investigators except a feeble joke. If I say that "Araby" is really a trumpet-blast in the eternal battle for women's rights (just think about that poor anonymous girl, dressed in brown, her petticoat showing, ignored by the world, failing to receive her present—a great silent heroine!) I have so clearly allowed my intellectual system (feminism) to impose itself blindly on the world, that all validity is gone. And even among more plausible views of the story, it is often easy to show that some are inherently flimsy or impoverished while others are more fruitful and liberating. (To say what I have just said is possible, of course, only within intellectual systems that value liberation above confinement, or richness of view over poverty, which is another way of saying that these things are very complicated.)

To discuss how one chooses among the more plausible modes of viewing would take more than another lecture. But let me just assert in one more way that though complicated such choices are not ultimately beyond us. In fact we make them successfully all the time, as our purposes, both practical and intellectual, dictate. Shall I deal with "Araby" as Aristotle or as Freud would suggest? The choice will depend on what questions I want to answer. Do I want to know how "Araby" is put together, what makes it a functioning whole? Freud tells me very little, and what he tells me is so general that it will apply to most other stories equally well. Do I want to understand the secret sources of Joyce's creative energy? The *Poetics* could not be more irrelevant to my query. Do I want to know both? Then I must learn how to pursue both, and I'll probably find that I cannot do them both at the same time. At best they'll be two separable parts of my lecture, or my book, or my life—and what's more, I'll probably find that I'll do one or the other badly. Few men have the temperament or the intellectual flexibility to operate with more than one or two intellectual systems, except in different periods of their lives—and then usually after painful conversion experiences.

But this brings us to the second point. Pluralism does not

mean that one is tongue-tied in the face of sloppy work *within any perspective*. I have given today illustrations that show how choice of a valid system does not guarantee valid statements. My Aristotelian analysis, though incomplete, was moving in the direction of a more or less adequate account of "Araby" as a *made object*. My Platonic analysis, though less nearly complete, was similarly a sympathetic and more or less serious reconstruction of what is to me a plausible though unpopular view of the morality of this story. But my Freudian description was feeble and even at points satirical, and my Nietzsche was a job performed by the lowliest *Untermensch* imaginable. None of my analyses committed the fault, so far as I know, of violating the commonsense factual encounter with the story with which I began today, so my present judgment is not made as a judgment of factual error. It is made, once the elementary level is passed, on the basis of *adequacy to the possibilities of the particular system,* when held up against *the potentialities offered to that system by the particular piece of reality examined.*

A man is lucky if he learns to use even one intellectual mode well. He is luckier if he can master more than one. He is luckiest of all, I suppose, if he can invent a new road to truth that proves fruitful to other men, or can elaborate or extend an already existing one. Many roads lead toward the heart of the city, but no one is allowed to go all the way: nobody ever looks on truth bare. Or if he does—and many mystics claim to—he will find that when he tries to report back to us ordinary mortals, his report will fall into one or another of the very limited intellectual modes available, and it will thus fail to catch more than a fraction of what is, we all must believe, *really there.*

IX

Let me conclude with a summary of the four forms of behavior that I would consider scandalous if I saw them exhibited in any kind of controversy among graduates of Liberal Arts I. The first is our uncritical behavior of the past two weeks: it is credulity, gullibility, readiness to be intellectually seduced by the latest comer or loudest shouter without checking the facts. The second disaster would be two of you quarrelling together about whether Freud or Aristotle "is right." This is the disaster of dogmatism, and it can be exhibited only by men who have not yet discovered that systems answering different questions for different purposes using different methods cannot be placed in direct opposition. The third scandal would be any one of you deciding to refuse credence to *any* view because "they all cancel each other out." Since such skepticism about all systems is intolerable, those who espouse it almost always move quickly to one or another form of dogmatism, usually a highly solipsistic and self-destructive kind: if none of the great philosophies is true, then anything I come up with that happens to appeal to me is as good as anything else. From this point of view it is no accident, as the Marxists used to say, that the current student generation, more threatened than earlier generations by plausible reasons for skepticism, seems to flit from dogmatism to dogmatism. I know a recent graduate of Princeton who has moved in four years from a form of scientism through Freudianism, Marxism, and Maoism to espousing the so-called philosophy of Ayn Rand. I'm afraid he'll be a prime candidate for any openly fascistic movement that promises him some sort of final intellectual peace in a dogma imposed by an elite—and the reason is simply that he has never yet paused long enough on any one system to make it work for him.

While I would not quite claim that a fortunate exposure as a freshman to my lecture on pluralism would have saved him, a full exposure to any one of the great philosophical positions might have. But I stress the tentativeness of "might." The recent behavior of some of my colleagues, old and young, who I had thought were committed to thinking things through, has shaken my confidence that anything will save universities as a place where real intellectual differences can be freely and honestly pursued.

THE RHETORIC OF FICTION
AND THE POETICS OF FICTIONS

I

The Rhetoric of Fiction has been praised and blamed for saying many things that it does not say, and I am naturally tempted now to set everybody right about it. The invitation to reconsider my book and the responses to it is not likely to be repeated, and it would be pleasant to tick off the many misreadings, affecting the tone of those happily anonymous *TLS* reviewers who always have the last say:

Mr. X (his name is Legion) has called me a moral reactionary, because I talk about "norms." Yet Mr. X himself has shown, in his own review, that he cannot escape norms, try as he will. . . .

Mr. Y has praised me for finally providing a systematic terminology for the criticism of fiction. If he had read more closely, however, he would have discovered that I am not quite so naive as to believe in the possibility of. . . .

But even if I could make such corrections interesting, which is unlikely, I doubt very much that I could make them convincing, and they would almost certainly sound petulant. Those

Originally published in the "Second Thoughts Series" in *Novel,* Winter 1968. Reprinted with permission.

who saw the book as a quarrel with fiction, or with modern fiction, or with up-to-date morality and post-Jamesian fictional techniques are not likely to be swayed by my asserting, however passionately, that they are wrong. Any reader who can believe that the book asks novelists to return to the Victorian period, that it deplores all irony, that it requires the novelist to state his position clearly in authorial commentary, or that it implies a demand for censorship, has developed subtleties of interpretation that would keep him immune from whatever could be said in a short article.

Another tempting direction would be to revise the book instead of admonishing its readers. I could try once more on that troublesome last chapter. I could recast the section on beliefs, as Stuart Tave (and David Hume) have convinced me I should, and I might either rewrite the clumsy sections on *The Aspern Papers* and *Journey to the End of the Night* or find examples which would lead fewer readers astray. There might even be a kind of masochistic thrill in public confession and correction of stylistic horrors.

But it should be more useful, writing for a new journal like *Novel,* to resist these forms of self-indulgence and try instead to say something about where we stand, in the profession, as we try to write to each other about "the novel." Do the six years of discussion of my book suggest any reason for our failure to "get anywhere" in our criticism of fiction? I think I detect a sense of stagnation and futility in the journals, as we discover that the more we publish the less we understand. If I am right in this— if my own sense of having been more often than not misunderstood is shared by most authors who receive public comment— then many of our controversies are meaningless and much of our busy publication is fraudulent. It is fraudulent not primarily because, as nonacademics think, it is done only to get and keep our jobs, but because it pretends to be public discourse when it is really little more than self-titillation.

The reasons for any such widespread failure must lie very deep, and they may often be moral and personal; if the seven deadly sins could be conquered (I think especially of sloth, pride, and envy), a good many of our controversies would evaporate. But not all. If my experience is any guide, our failures to understand cannot be cured with simple tolerance or generosity or hard work; to me the kindly energetic critics have seemed only slightly more relevant than the cruel and the lazy. The reasons for intellectual misunderstanding on the scale exhibited in America today must finally be intellectual, and though improved habits of courtesy and mutual respect no doubt would help, they are more likely to follow on improved standards of intellectual rigor and penetration than the other way round.

Let me illustrate from my own successive difficulties with one of the most extensive critiques *The Rhetoric of Fiction* has received, "The 'Second Self' in Novel Criticism," by John Killham (*British Journal of Aesthetics,* July 1966). Both in the irrelevance of what he says of me and in the inadequacy of my first response to him, I see something like a parable of our plight.

I discovered Mr. Killham's article through a citation by another critic (in manuscript) who had made me angry by what seemed almost a deliberate effort to misrepresent. When I found Mr. Killham saying that my influence in spreading the term "second self" was pernicious; that I had completely misunderstood the relation of authors to their works and readers; that the very term "second self" must be "utterly banished and extinguished, exorcized from the house of criticism," I was of course annoyed. When I found further, in that quick first reading, that Mr. Killham had distorted what I had originally meant by the term, and had, in fact, attacked me for beliefs I had specifically repudiated, using arguments I myself had used, I was quite naturally tempted to dismiss him as not worth bothering about.

Ordinarily I would in fact have done so. But I had promised an article to *Novel,* and Mr. Killham looked to be a good springboard. So I went through the piece somewhat more carefully, though still intent only on defending myself by showing him up. Then I wrote the following "refutation":

> Mr. Killham of Keele sets out to correct my views on the "author's second self," but the views he corrects are not mine. I thought I had made a distinction among (1) the real author, (2) various forms of

narrators, "reflectors," dramatized tellers, and (3) the author implied by the totality of a work, a kind of second self that is the reader's picture of a creator responsible for the whole. Mr. Killham sets me straight by making precisely the same distinction: (1) "authors, seated at tables with pens, or typewriters, or tape recorders," (2) "the imaginary persons whom they may invent as the supposed tellers of their stories," and (3) "the idea we have of the author's literary character when we speak of reading 'Thackeray' or 'Dickens' and so on." Having thus done no more than reject my language, Mr. Killham then systematically—or so it almost seems—sets out to make a hash of disjointed and contradictory opinions in order to show the deleterious effects of the term "second self." I had written "Our sense of the implied author includes . . . the intuitive apprehension of a completed artistic whole." Within a page, Mr. Killham has translated this into the claim that I "prefer to think of a work as a person rather than a pot," and has of course dismissed my "false analogy"; and from *our sense* of the *implied author*" he has eliminated "sense of," inventing an identity I had not intended: "Thus to make the term 'second self' stand for our 'intuitive apprehension of a completed artistic whole' . . . is quite self-defeating." Yes, indeed, it would be—had I done so.

And so Mr. Killham goes on, telling me that "the sort of second self an author creates" is "produced just as inevitably by one aspiring to 'drama' or 'impersonality' as by an early novelist boldly offering to tell a tale." Precisely—as I tried to argue at length in my book. I spend about a third of my book dealing with ways in which narrators differ from their authors, and Mr. Killham hectors me for forgetting "what has been well put by Professor Kathleen Tillotson: 'The narrator . . . is a method rather than a person: indeed the "narrator" is never the author as man.' " Finally he decides that the term rhetoric is the trouble, because it means didacticism, and "no work of art, no novel, can be rightly considered rhetorical, for rhetoric is inimical to the freedom within the law a lifelike impression demands. . . . A work may attempt to teach, but only by being lifelike enough for that end: and this precludes rhetoric."

Can Mr. Killham have read so much as five pages of my book and still believe that this refutes anything I have to say? Mr. Killham's view of the invariably pejorative connotations of the word rhetoric is his own affair, and he may want to teach me a better word. But where can he and I begin in our discussion, if his notion of how to discuss leads him, whenever I use the word "rhetoric," in a sense that has a long and respectable intellectual history, to choose another meaning entirely and then blame me for the conflict between "rhetoric" and "art" that results? The deformations are indeed so frequent and so gross that I am almost tempted to guess at hidden motives. Have I attacked him somewhere, or one of his friends, without knowing it? Was he once bitten by a Chicago critic?

Having produced that much as a draft, I pulled myself up short. Could I really fall back on bias as explanation here? After all, even in his garbled report on me, there is considerable evidence, ignored in my account, that Mr. Killham has worked seriously at his job. He has read and thought a good deal about the relations of authors to their works, and much of what he says makes sense. Most important, there is no reason to believe that my defense will convince him, no matter how carefully he reads it, if the original book could not do so. What, then, has gone wrong?

Courtesy alone might at that point have dictated a decision not to talk about Mr. Killham at all. Tolerance (what some people mistakenly call pluralism) might dictate a quick run-through to find some *good* things to say about him, to balance the bad, so that he and I might continue to live together in peace. But surely only one motive can finally prove adequate to the situation: the desire to understand Mr. Killham in order to explain his misunderstanding of me in terms that might promote genuine discussion. And that motive dictated my return to his essay for a few more hours, thinking about his problem and forgetting for awhile my own.

II

What I found is that given the nature of *his* problem and given his way of taking hold of it (both of which are entirely respectable in themselves), Mr. Killham had an impossible task when he was confronted by my book. The topic of the second self is common to us both, but only as material in solving quite different problems. Mr. Killham's problem is that of reconciling what he calls the "autonomy" of a novel—a doctrine attributed to the New Critics—with his knowledge that any novel is, after all, written and read by human beings; he seeks—and he thinks that I seek—a reconciliation between the autonomous "well-wrought urn" and the world of the author's biography and psychology and intentions. In pursuing the reconciliation, he is concerned throughout with the processes of the imagination that account for how the author expresses himself in his work and yet is somehow never found directly in it. His talk is thus mostly in the expressive rather than the rhetorical mode—it is

all about how authors "express what *they* think worth expressing," about the "psychology of literary invention," about "the
attempt to find in a personal form and style a means of expressing the sense of self or inner being," about the transformation
"of an artist's personality and experience . . . by the very act of
writing."

Here, then, is an aesthetic problem seen in polar terms by a
critic who accepts some truth in both poles. A work of art can,
at one extreme, be seen as autonomous, divorced from the
author's intentions; it can, on the other hand, be seen as the expression of the author's creative powers, of a kind of enveloping
imagination, the author's creative self. Now along comes a
book which seems to attempt to solve this problem by claiming
that the author creates a "second self" which in turn works on
the reader, turning *him* into a second self. But clearly this is a
poor solution, a "too easy way of disposing of difficulties." The
better way—predictable once the problem is set up in neat
dichotomous form—is to recognize that true autonomy in a
novel comes from our recognition of its independent "sense of
life," which is, in fact, what the total creative act of the author,
with *his* sense of life, gave it. "In other words, a novel never
imitates life . . . but only depends upon our sense of life for the
creation of its autonomy." "Autonomy" and the sense of the
author's life (identical now with "the author's sense of life") are
thus reconciled in the reader's "imaginative capacity"to enter
the author's world.

Clearly there is no place, in such a synthesis of polarities, for
the second self as I described it, or for the notion of rhetoric as I
tried to develop it. It is true that Mr. Killham cannot and does
not ignore the problem of what I would call rhetoric: how the
author's vision is transmitted. He even finds it impossible to
avoid using rhetorical terms when he talks about how the author's world and the reader get together: the novel must be
"life-like enough for us to be *persuaded* to enter it, but only to
the end that we may see what the author *makes us believe* . . ."
(my italics). But though the rhetorical process (in my definition)
thus cannot be ignored, "rhetoric" must be dismissed since it is
"inimical to the freedom within the law a life-like impression
demands."

The reason it is inimical is thus found strictly in the relations of Mr. Killham's central concepts to each other. His original polarity admitted only three main positions, left, right, and center—autonomy, personal expression, and a reconciling view of their true harmony. But as in most dialectical schemes, there are good and bad versions of each polar position: harmony results from seeing the good versions and uniting them; error, from choosing the bad versions. On the expressive side, there is an incorrect way of talking about how the author imposes his creative vision—"rhetorically," "didactically," "telling" rather than expressing. It is inevitable that Mr. Killham should labor to fit me into this naughty position, inventing doctrines out of fragments of misunderstanding (for example, "the presence of a 'teller' in many novels is not a sign [as Booth believes] that all novels are pieces of the author's mind, parable-like illustrations of views he wants to make his readers accept, sophisticated specimens of 'communication' "). On the autonomous side, there is also a major corruption: the New Critics "went too far," cutting the work off from its life source. But in trying to answer the extreme partisans of autonomy, Booth has taken a false grip on the only other horn available; in building a didactic theory, turning "expression" into "rhetoric," he has left unanswered "those critics who argue for the entire independence of a work from its author's intentions."

It is easy to see that no one holding Mr. Killham's views uncritically—that is, without thinking through their implications for method—could possibly grasp my way of going about things, let alone accept it. Even if he had worked very hard to understand me, he still would have only so many places where I might fit on his implied chart of possible aesthetic views. Since it is clear that I sometimes deal with novels as in some sense autonomous, and since it is even clearer that I treat fiction as rhetoric, I must be trying awkwardly to solve the same problem *he* is trying to solve, failing in the effort at synthesis because I have used the wrong grip on each horn. If I am right in this, it is not wrongheadedness or ill-will that led him to his irrelevancies. If he had decided to become tolerant and fit me into his views, the same essential distortions would have resulted. Even if he had decided to grant the courtesy of rereading and had discovered and removed the grosser misrepresentations, the essential incompatibility of problems and methods and assumptions would have remained. In short, unless he could come to the point of enriching his repertory of possible positions, unless he could make his simple schematism more complex, he could hardly avoid reducing me to fit it.

But it is not only that my problem and method fall off his chart. Our notions of how alternative charts might work are radically different. He seems to believe that the critic should seek the one proper synthetic view of what the work of fiction *is*, and of how the author and reader relate to it. It is *either* autonomous, *or* it is an expression of the author's personality or imagination, *or* it is some subtler synthesis of the two. It is scarcely surprising, then, that when I come along believing that a novel is *both* autonomous (a concrete whole, a well-wrought urn) *and* a piece of self-expression (a lamp, a passionate cry), *and*—now moving off his chart entirely!—a work of rhetoric (a gesture, a plea to accept, an imposition by one man on another), *and* an embodiment of the social and literary forces of its times (a convention-carrying vessel, a mirror), *and* a statement of moral or philosophical truth (an argument, a philosophical dialogue, a sermon), and what not?—when I come along with such pluralistic assumptions, mostly unstated, and explore pragmatically what will turn up in one neglected mode, the rhetorical, of course he is lost. And he will remain lost unless he is willing to think about method, mine and his own.

Any novel, good or bad, "really is" many different things, and no critical language can engage it in its totality. A novel "really is" an autonomous construct, for some critical purposes, as a whole corpus of modern criticism has shown. But it is just as really the expression of the author's intentions, capabilities, and psyche; and a representation of historical realities, social, economic, political, literary; and an embodiment of world views or moral concepts that can be thought of *sub specie aeternitatis*. If I wanted to write a rhetoric of fiction, I was neither obliged nor able at the same time to write a "poetics" of fiction, analyzing some of the forms of great fiction in their autonomous purity; or a psychology of fiction, exploring the grounds of creativity in the novelist or of creative response in readers; or a sociology of fiction, tracing the history and social forms of reading publics; or a philosophy of fictional realism, testing fictional worlds against various views of the real world or against universal truths. Fragments of each of these subjects will of course appear, in distorted form, under various heads within my rhetoric. And consequently, to anyone totally committed to any other problem, it may appear that I have struggled with his problem and lost.

I did not deal with the pluralistic theory of such modes directly; that would have taken a book in itself, and besides it seemed to me to have been done already by Chicagoans like Crane, Olson, and McKeon, by M. H. Abrams in the opening of *The Mirror and the Lamp,* and in a broader sense by much of post-Kantean philosophy, with its talk about multiple languages and models and categories of perception. I wish now that I had at least tried to discuss more fully how a critical language treating fiction as rhetoric differs from or relates to other modes. To do so would have helped me, and consequently my readers, by leading me to discover my own true subject sooner than I did. The book's major fault, which I still would not quite know how to remove, lies in the confusion of focus between rhetoric as what I called "the more easily recognizable appeals to the reader" (rhetoric as overt technical maneuver) and rhetoric as the whole art of fiction, viewed in the rhetorical mode. A defense of direct forms of "telling" could be made, I think, from almost any critical position. But I tried to make it from two quite different positions, and I supported my move by stretching and contracting at will the area covered by the term rhetoric. "Even if there are permanent, universal responses embodied in the work, then, they are unlikely to move us strongly and they may be unclear—without the author's rhetoric." What does the word *embodied* in this sentence mean? According to my expanded definition of rhetoric, any act of embodiment can be treated as rhetoric. Yet the phrase, "the author's rhetoric" at the end of the sentence seems to mean simply overt rhetoric, like commentary and obvious technical manipulations. On the one hand, it means whatever the author does to make his "embodiment" clear to the reader—but the "embodiment" itself serves to do that. This circularity would never have satisfied me, I think, if I had pushed myself earlier and harder on the question of how my "rhetoric" related to other modes, and especially to poetics.

III

The book began as an attempt to show that Gordon and Tate (among many others) were radically confused about point-of-view and so-called objective narration; it was originally to be what parts of it still are, a polemical essay accepting the main premises of the various "schools of autonomy," and defending the artistic respectability of the visibly "rhetorical" elements that have been under attack at least since the time of Flaubert. It grew into a book on the rhetorical dimension of all fiction. In the original conception, the word rhetoric did not even appear. But I soon found myself using it to describe those obvious appeals to the reader which critics had attacked as inartistic excrescences. And then it took me some years to discover that it was not enough (though it was something) to accept the objectivist definitions of art and tuck the Greek chorus (as Aristotle manages to do), Iago's soliloquies, or Fielding's intrusions inside. Though I thought I could show, following Aristotle and others, that a radical purging of the author's voice need not follow from seeing fiction in its aesthetic autonomy, it became clear that a more interesting new view of the craft of fiction would come from a new definition. Despite extensive revision in the light of the new conception, the earlier book is still discernible, attempting still to answer in aesthetic terms an aesthetic question: "Is there any defense that can be offered, on aesthetic grounds, for an art full of rhetorical appeals?" Well, of course there is, and the book is in part a long footnote to what Aristotle says about "thought" and about "manner," and especially to that invitation in chapter 19 of the *Poetics* to assume about "thought" what is said of it "in our Art of Rhetoric, as it belongs more properly to that department of inquiry."

If the author is considered, in that earlier conception, as *making a concrete form,* whether an imitation of an action or a system of symbols, a well-wrought urn, it is difficult (though not impossible) to justify evidences in his work of his efforts to make it accessible to the world. If on the other hand he is thought of as *making readers,* then of course his effort is visible in every moment, and one can forget about pejorative distinctions between rhetoric and pure drama. Every stroke is in this sense rhetorical, just as in the objective view every stroke is part of the concrete form, or in the expressive view every stroke expresses the artist's psyche, and in the art-is-truth view every stroke reflects a world of values or universals which the book is "about." In this view, even the most seemingly objective, intrinsic, "autonomous" elements, including the central events, the "hardest" symbols, can be fruitfully viewed as rhetoric—that is, they can be considered *as if* aimed at an effect on the reader (because in fact they produce that effect) regardless of the aesthetic theories or the actual writing practices of the author.

Now there has seemed to be something radically confusing to some critics in this pragmatic device of trying out a definition to see what it will yield. If "rhetoric" is used to cover the whole work of art, then I surely must be saying that the work of art *is* rhetoric, and everybody knows, as Mr. Killham says, that "no work of art, no novel, can be rightly considered rhetorical." A work of art *is* either one thing or another. Have I not heard of the law of noncontradiction?

But it is rather late in the day for us to ignore in this way how our categories of perception help determine what we see. It is true that the page on which I write cannot both be in the room and not in the room at the same time. *As a physical object* it really is in the room, and there's an end on it, even for the most ardent pluralist. But *as an object of my perception* it is an unlimited number of things—scrap paper, psychological threat, material for a fire, a product of American commerce, and even something that can be both outside the room (in my imagination) and inside the room (in physical presence) at the same time.

In exactly the same way, though more deceptively, the work of art *is* many things. Some definitions of what it is are admittedly of little help to a critic trying to understand artistic qualities. If I were to argue, for example, that works of art are *really* natural products, because man is simply a product of the natural world and nature has thus produced man's novels, my redefinition would be sound enough, and it might prove useful in an argument about the nature of the universe or of God. But it will be of no use to me in dealing critically with the art of this or that work. And there are limits, very real limits: it would be hard to do much, even metaphorically, with the claim that novels are really electric fans or chicken coop roofs. Thus there are many things that art for all practical purposes is *not,* and pluralism cannot lead us to a bland tolerance of all views provided they are developed coherently. But there are also many things that any work of art *is,* and one of the things that all literary and—with especial obviousness—fictional art *is, really is,* is an action that authors and readers perform together. There need be no argument about whether this view or the view of a novel as a poetic construct is true. Both are true, and both are useful because true. If someone asks, "Yes, but which is it, really?" he will have asked a question which a pluralist (of my kind) thinks unanswerable. It is really both, or really (but not exclusively) either, just as it is really (but not exclusively) an expression of the author's personality; and so on. One is philosophically and critically naive if he spends time debating such modes of perception in absolute terms.

It is not a waste of time, however, to show how a consistent and habitual use of one definition or perspective leads critics to distort or overlook or ban elements that in other views become quite natural. A generation had come to accept without thinking that a true "poem" (including fiction) should not mean but be. With the author ruled out under the "intentional fallacy" and the audience ruled out under the "affective fallacy," with the world of ideas and beliefs ruled out under the "didactic heresy" and with narrative interest ruled out under the "heresy of plot," some doctrines of autonomy had become so desiccated that only verbal and symbolic interrelationships remained. I had been taught what still seemed to me by comparison an especially rich version of objectivist doctrine, derived from the *Poetics;* it had a way of talking about effects on readers and audiences, and it believed in the author's intentions as determinative (in a carefully limited sense) of the critic's quest. But it was objectivist nonetheless: the "poem" was an imitation of an action, composed as a beautiful object, designed to be excellent in its kind. Though an effect on audiences was implied by its form, the critic pursued the internal nature of the poem by analysing its parts in relation to the whole work.

This version of objectivist aesthetics has always tended to slide over into rhetorical study, as Bernard Weinberg has shown about Renaissance "Aristotelians." Within the Chicago school there has been a steady drift, as I now see it, toward the "corruption" of objective views in the rhetorical direction. What I have done, it seems to me, like Sheldon Sacks working quite independently, is to make this tendency explicit. *The Rhetoric of Fiction* asks, as Kenneth Burke had been doing in a different way, that we think of the poem not primarily as *meaning* or *being* but as *doing*. In place of analyses of poetic form, descriptions and interpretations of types of action or plot (with their power to produce an effect indicated, but not exclusively dominant), I look at effects, at techniques for producing them, and at readers and their inferences. In place of a classification of literary kinds, I give an analysis of *interests* and (as in the *Emma* chapter) manipulations of interests. In place of an analysis into the poetic elements of the internal structure (plot, character, thought, diction) my elements become identical with the three that one finds in all rhetorics, author, work, audience: authors and their various surrogates and spokesmen; works, and their various arrangements for effect; audiences, and their preconceptions and processes of inference.

I did try to avoid ruling my conclusions, unlike some earlier rhetoricians claiming to work from the *Poetics,* according to the peculiar demands of particular audiences. But I did not (and would not now) surrender the insights that come when the work is viewed not as a formed object, eternally what it is, beautifully whole in its form, but as something designed, or at least suited, to impose itself upon us (not, be it noted, to communicate *themes* or *norms*, as Mr. Donald Pizer and many other readers have taken it, but *itself*). Study of what the work *is,* what it has been made to *be*, will yield a "poetics," and I hope someday to produce a poetics of some kinds of fiction.[1] What the work is made to *do*—how it is designed to communicate itself—will yield a rhetoric. The two differing aspects will not be incompatible if they are done well, since a work *does* what it does because of what it *is*, and vice versa. But they will start and end at different points, and they will certainly deal with different elements in different proportions along the way.[2]

1. The editors have called my attention to the confusion that this use of the word "poetics" is likely to produce, since many other critics are using it differently these days. "Your use of the term 'poetics' jars with the way we've been using it, in our brochure and our first-issue editorial, to mean a theoretical account of the nature and function of literary genres. Malcolm Bradbury is also using it that way in his essay, 'Towards a Poetics of Fiction: An Approach Through Structure,' in our first issue. The notion of a poetics which pulls together many different approaches seems to be common— seems to correspond in fact with your plea for pluralism, and with the Chicago view of Aristotle's *Poetics* as a many-sided approach. So we are troubled by your confinement of poetics to matters of craft, to the inner nature of the art object, its isness versus its doesness."
    Though the present draft may not be quite so confusing as the one that elicited this comment, I can see that the term is so ambiguous as almost to be useless. For me a genuine poetics would *include* a "theoretical account of the nature and function of (some) literary genres," and it would "pull together many different approaches"—at least in the sense of trying to comprehend linguistic, technical, structural, and "affective" questions in a unified view. But it would by no means be "confined to craft," it would not be a compendium of all possible approaches, and its theory would be subordinated to the effort to give a practical account of how good works are in fact made and how we can talk about their special (autonomous) qualities without analogizing them to other human arts (like rhetoric, psychology, politics, etc.). Clearly someone should do a taxonomy of current definitions of *poetics*, before we all end up quarreling pointlessly about this term as we do about so many others.
2. To dwell as I am doing on distinctions among dimensions or aspects or modes is of course once again to choose one way of doing things rather than other possible ways. A critic might well prefer to deal synthetically with questions of similarities among things, and he would have good reason then to ignore the distinction between rhetoric and poetics. A good example is the procedure of Frank Kermode, in his fine recent book, *The Sense of an Ending;* he dwells on the similarities among all "fictions," including myths and sociological and philosophical accounts, and our perceptions of the shape of life itself. Nothing could be less relevant to his profound pursuit of how the shapes of literature and life resemble each other than for me to complain that it gives no help to a critic pursuing rhetorical questions.

In theory, once I had grasped my subject as the rhetorical aspect of fiction, I should have then written "the whole rhetoric of fiction." Such a work would have been different in many ways. It would have had the chapter on the "rhetoric of symbols" that John Crowe Ransom rightly demanded. It would have had much more on style, in the manner of David Lodge's excellent *Language of Fiction* (though avoiding his assumption that language is all). It might well have had a comparison of the rhetoric of literature, in this conception, with more directly rhetorical forms. Rereading it now, I am especially distressed by how little I wrote about the "rhetoric of event"—the way in which the synthesis of incidents determines how we respond. But it is clear why this was so. I still had my original polemic on my hands: of all the weapons in the writer's arsenal, it was mainly overt commentary, "telling," that had been attacked. And so the book has a great overload of defense of the author's voice. Indeed, I sometimes feel that though I set out in part to undermine those who would make manipulation of point-of-view the whole art of fiction, my own polemical stress on narrators and voices has strengthened this one-sided view of the art of fiction. I occasionally receive manuscripts by critics claiming my influence, and they are always point-of-view studies, never studies of plot construction viewed as rhetoric.

If I had wrestled harder with the rhetoric of character and event, I would, I hope, have been led to the kind of thing done brilliantly by Sheldon Sacks in *Fiction and the Shape of Belief.* I am thinking not only of his central chapters on how Fielding's minor characters serve to shape our beliefs even as they amuse us, but even more of his carefully argued distinctions among three modes of narration: satire, apologue, and "action." Against the advice of R. S. Crane, I deliberately avoided systematic distinctions between works of explicit rhetorical intent, like *Gulliver's Travels,* and "mimetic" works like *A Passage to India,* and I would still hold to this indiscriminate grouping, on the twin grounds that my general case applies to all fiction, regardless of form or effect, and that any judgment of elements within a given work must be specific to that particular work and its needs. At the same time, it is quite clear that the rhetoric of fiction must finally deal, as Sacks does, with differences of *kind* among formal intentions. Such differences are implied throughout my book, but they are never discussed for more than a few sentences. Sooner or later the rhetorical critic must face them full-on. As he does so, he will of course move into the territory of what I am calling poetics, but he will do so as a stranger in a foreign land, discovering that the *kinds of actions authors perform on readers* differ markedly, though subtly, from *the kinds of imitations of objects they are seen as making,* in the poetic mode.

IV

The position I have just described can be discovered in my book, but since it is largely implicit, I can hardly blame readers who missed it. But even as I write such self-criticism I must confess that I cringe in anticipation of what some readers will do with it. "Booth has himself admitted that the book is confused to the core. . . ." Mr. Killham, who has no room on his chart either for a poetics in my sense *or* a rhetoric will simply be further confused. Mr. Donald Pizer, who claims that in my "ethical conservatism" I am less interested in "how fiction communicates than in what it should communicate" *(College English,* March 1967), will perhaps conclude that the book as I revised it would be even more of a didactics of fiction than the one he discerns. The further I go in the direction of consistency in the rhetorical mode, the more I shall invite the charge of didacticism, and that final chapter, which has upset many readers, will when revised upset even more.

It may be true—to touch briefly on that chapter—that my interest in rhetoric springs from my being more morally conservative, and more given to imposing general standards, than I like to think. But just as there is an ethics of rhetoric, as everyone from Plato to Kenneth Burke has recognized, so there is a moral dimension to fiction as rhetoric. It does not dictate in any simple way a set of doctrines that fiction should communicate, and even in that "tendentious" final chapter my interest was not in *what* should be communicated; I asked only that the work communicate itself, that the author "be as clear about his moral position as he possibly can be" and that he "do all that is possible in any given instance to realize his world as he intends it." It is not hard for me to see how readers could take this, out of context, as an effort to ban ambiguities; after all, I did not underline "all that is possible in any given instance." To discover that I admire many great works that are both ambiguous and ironic and—to some degree—unclear, the reader would have to go back through earlier chapters with perhaps more care than one has a right to expect from one's readers. My attack was simply on the assumption that all the arguments favor a rhetoric of ambiguity.

But to deal with that final chapter would require another essay. Rather than trying here to answer or accept every possible objection to my book, I am trying simply to ask whether Mr. Killham and I belong as critics to a profession in which there is any chance whatever of cumulative discourse. Must we forever shout slogans at each other from distant armed camps? Presumably we must if, as Mr. Killham implies, there is one true aesthetic view which all must come to or perish. If on the other hand, there are many legitimate questions based on differing assumptions and definitions and amenable to differing methods, progress of a limited kind should be possible for those willing to share a mode, an interest, a language.

"Until you understand a writer's ignorance," Coleridge wrote, "presume yourself ignorant of his understanding." Most of my critics cannot "explain my ignorance," since they cannot really explain, in terms relevant either to their own interests or my own, why I do the strange things I do. They are reduced to assuming that temperamental or moral bias or sheer stupidity has led me astray, or that happy chance has led me to their own conclusions. Inevitably such critics prove useless to me (as I to them) because even when they praise me we simply do not connect. What is disappointing is that with all the thousands of words written about the book, no one has tried, so far, to wrestle with the whole conception of the rhetoric of fiction and improve it, clarify it, make it more useful to more people. Nothing surprising in that, I suppose; it is our way of dealing with each other.

I must regularly disappoint other authors in the same way. New books on the novel come out almost every week. I buy them, and I "read" them—that is, I go through them quickly, first peeking to see what, if anything, they say about my own work, then, only slightly less shamefully, skimming for agreements and disagreements. It is only by an effort of will that I can resist using the results as if they had some value to myself and others as reflections of the real books. They do not. I am told by Mr. W. J. Harvey that *character* should be given primacy in dealing with the novel (*Character and the Novel*), and by Messrs. Robert Scholes and Robert Kellogg, in *The Nature of Narrative*, that *narrative shape* is central. Are they then in conflict with Mr. Lodge, who says it is all language, and with each other? They may be, but it is more likely that when I finally get inside their books I will find not only such obvious differences but more basic differences of method and principle that will allow me to accept the legitimacy of their attempts and Mr. Lodge's too—once they have been purged of their claims to exclusive truth. As claimants to the whole truth they may even turn out to be bad books; as complementary inquiries, they could nourish each other.

In any case, it is absurd to tell them—on this superficial acquaintance—that one of them must be wrong because they "disagree," or because Michael Raimond has shown that the novel is to be seen as a *way of dealing with reality (La Crise du Roman)*, or because Ihab Hassan has taught us *(Radical Innocence)* that the basic question in dealing with the novel is metaphysical or because R.-M. Albérè *(Métamorphoses du Roman)* says that the basic question is moral. Of all these works I have just "placed" so glibly, which have I really read, which have I made my own? None, and I thus stand now exposed, not for the first time, as sinning against my own sermon. Well, I've been busy, of course, like you, and this promised article has to be completed by day before yesterday, and besides, I'm really quite sure that none of these authors will have a lot to say to— No, no, that's not it exactly, but there are so many books, so many articles—

Must we forever rush through all these books, demolishing each man's shelter to provide materials for our own? Is each new position merely a fashion to be outgrown as soon as possible? Why not change our figure to something like a series of climbing expeditions, attempting different peaks or different faces of the same peak? If we could do so, most of us would discover that most of what we have said about other critics is flatly irrelevant. Take, for example, that stuff in *The Rhetoric of Fiction* on Ortega y Gasset, based on one reading of two of his short books, and in translation too! I know from that little raid that Ortega is not just worthless but aggressively misleading about the rhetoric of fiction. But what about *his* problem? What could a man of such obvious intelligence and sensitivity have been *doing,* that could lead him so far astray? The least I can do is take an oath of silence on Ortega until I have him cold, until I can explain his "ignorance" so well that it is no longer ignorance about my problem, but a form of knowledge about his.

Part

THE
LAST TRUE
CHURCH

The glory of God is intelligence.
  —Joseph Smith

Every pupil was made to feel that there was work for him to do—that his happiness as well as his duty lay in doing that work well. Hence an indescribable zest was communicated to a young man's feeling about life. . . .
  —Price on Thomas Arnold's Rugby

So we arrived at Wellesley and found that there was a gap between expectation and realities. . . . Our love for this place—this particular place—Wellesley College . . . allowed us to question basic assumptions underlying education. . . . We are searching for a more immediate, ecstatic and penetrating mode of living.
  —Hillary Rodham, senior honor student,
   at Wellesley commencement, 1969

Fuck the life of the mind!
  —Message scrawled on a desk during
   a sit-in, 1969

THE LAST TRUE CHURCH

For a believer in Reason, there need not be any church except secular life and the effort to infuse it with some degree of reason. But if he has been raised in a church as vigorous as Mormonism and has learned the pleasures and duties of working to embody reason in an institution, he will probably make a church out of the home of reason—the college, the university. Certainly this has happened to me. Brought up to believe that "the Glory of God is Intelligence," and that "Man cannot be saved in ignorance," I turned—after a period of what I called atheism—to a God who is the totality of Reason in Action in the world, the Power and the Law. For me, He—or It—has His shrines in places like the simple Quaker chapel at Earlham College and the gothic Bond Chapel at the University of Chicago, or the libraries which, on both campuses, are a hundred paces away.

The shrines are under attack. Yesterday the library at the University of Chicago received an anonymous call stating that all of the cards in the catalogue dealing with the works of Professor X had been stolen. Since Professor X has written some things reputed by the New Left to be objectionable, the effort is apparently being made to send him down the memory chute.

The College as Church, in short, has entered the age of heresy trials.

Whether anything worthy of allegiance will survive the rising warfare of fanatical sects and schisms is not clear. But as a rhetorician disguised as educator I would not deliver my academic sermons if I did not believe that this church may have a future after all.

THE COLLEGE AS CHURCH
OR,
SCREWTAPE REVIVED

I was visited a month or so after our recent sit-in (1966) by one
of the faculty members who had been most sympathetic to the
protest group. As we talked about the grounds for the sit-in, he
began to warm up about his own motives, and soon he was saying something like the following:

What you don't seem to realize is that the students' passion comes from
a sense of betrayal by an object of love. Most of these students have
no church, no institution whatever into which they could invest their
faith or to which they could in full self-respect give their lives. They
have, many of them, fallen into the arms of the university as the only
institution on earth with any integrity left, the only institution in
which truly human qualities and values have a chance for preservation. They *expect* the university to care about intellectual integrity
and about human dignity. When they think she has failed them, they
fight back in anger.

Since I knew this man to be himself churchless, I was at first
inclined to think he might be whitewashing himself and the

Abridged from an address given to a conference of the Danforth Associates
at Estes Park, Colorado, August 1966, and printed in *The Earlham Review,*
summer 1967. Reprinted with permission.

movement he cared for. But the more I've thought about it, the more similarities I've seen between the devout members of a traditional church, especially those who through their intensity of devotion became schismatics, and the devout schismatics within the modern university. Reading in Seymour Lipset's anthology, *The Berkeley Student Revolt,* I have been struck by how many of the free speech movement members talk in terms that would traditionally have been reserved for religious controversy: they protest their moral purity, they speak of their superior devotion to the true values of learning, they even sometimes make the religious parallel explicit. Listen to Mario Savio, for example: "One conception of the university, suggested by a classical Christian formulation, is that it be in the world but not of the world. The conception of Clark Kerr by contrast is that the university is part and parcel of this particular stage in the history of American society: it stands to serve the need of American industry, it is a factory that turns out a certain product needed by industry or government." One pamphlet says, "For a moment on December 8th, eight hundred and twenty-four professors gave us all a glimpse—a *brief, glorious vision*—of the university *as a loving community*. It is ours to demand meaning: we must insist on meaning." As these young folks stand in what they call "the searing light of truth," they sound to me very much like primitive Christians.

I think we must say, then, that if a church is an institution that embodies the ultimate commitment of its members, the colleges and universities are being elevated into churches by a great many faculty members and students today. This does not mean, however, that they are all members of the same church, or that they all demand the same services or feel betrayed by the same failures. Many faculty members in our major universities have entered the communion of holy truth: they worship knowledge as an end in itself, sometimes blindly, sometimes with a passion and intelligence that does indeed have a touch of the holy about it. In radical contrast, many students seem to want the college to provide all of the services of the old church, with the Y.M.C.A. and women's auxiliary and Sunday night suppers thrown in. Caught between these extremes is the college teacher, who may have a vocation for teaching but who finds so many different competing concepts of what that means that his life is divided and fragmented and harried beyond endurance.

If the college is a church for him, it is one that arouses the same ambivalent feelings that other more conventional churches have aroused. We all know of the dangers of institutionalization. Yet we all find ourselves desperately seeking for institutional support for our commitments. An old dilemma—an old dilemma indeed.

Meditating on this dilemma last week late at night, trying to decide what to say to you, I began to thumb idly through my files—hoping to find some light. Riffling through a long catalogue of trivia, past Arbitrary Administrators, Base Bumblings and Betrayals, Dastardly Deans, and so on, I finally got down to the S's and noticed a file I'd never seen before, labelled Screwtape. I knew immediately that something was wrong here. In C. S. Lewis's book, old Screwtape, Lord of the Underworld, writes letters of advice to his earthly emissary, advice on how to combat what he calls The Enemy by leading men to their eternal damnation. I simply could not imagine why my secretary, a hard-headed, down-to-earth woman, should have started a file of imaginary letters from Screwtape himself. I took out the folder—and found to my horror that my worst fears were realized: *somebody* in the university—I have yet to discover who or where—had concluded a pact with the old boy, and in return had been receiving Screwtape's advice. Rather than explain further, let me quote—since my speech is over and we have time on our hands—from some of the letters I found.

Dr. Harley P. Sellout, Vice-President
Surrogate University

My dear Sellout,

I was delighted to learn that you have been promoted to Vice-President. The mere fact of your appointment to a newly created office is of course a triumph for our side: as you know, the enemy has always tried to maintain simplicity in university organizations, on the theory that responsibility for the pursuit of truth, wisdom, or aesthetic experience should be clear and unequivocal. Now that with your appointment the university has eight vice-presidents and fourteen deans, your opportunities to create confusion are practically unlimited. I do not mean to suggest that you can afford to relax—the university is not yet entirely ours. But victory is in sight.

Very sincerely,
Screwtape

My very dear Sellout,

Once again you have got it wrong. Sowing the slogans of cynicism and despair gets you nowhere. *Optimism, optimism* is our proper tone, and what we are optimistic about is *the future.* Our main task—I hope this does not weary you as much as it does me—is to keep the whole academic church—if you'll pardon the expression—geared to the future; the future, as you know, has always been ours, and if you can keep everyone in a "forward looking frame of mind," totally abstracted from any present contact with existential reality, it will continue to be ours. Prevent at all costs any contact with what the enemy used to call The Eternal, under whatever guise. Every faculty member and every student should be forced to see that EVERYTHING IS DONE FOR THE SAKE OF SOMETHING ELSE AND NOTHING FOR ITS OWN SAKE. We are in the service of the useful, and to be useful means *to be useful for something else.* If you think about what *this* means, you may need very little in the way of further detailed instruction from me.

Bless you,
Screwtape

Dear Sellout,

I'm surprised at your having allowed the curriculum committee to substitute a course in poetry for the course in the history of literary criticism, on the grounds that much modern poetry is either antireligious or antiacademic, and therefore on our side. It is clear that you have not understood our first principle. Let me repeat. Your duty is not to worry about the *content* of courses; rather it is quite simply to prevent all contact with what is real. Your stock in trade is the phony, which you will always call the practical or the relevant, and you can accomplish your work better with a bad critic who opposes you than with a good poet who seems to support you.

What I meant by suggesting that everything must be done for the sake of something else should have been quite clear: whenever any student or faculty member has a moment, however fleeting, of direct contact with anything noninstrumental, anything self-justifying—any genuine thought or experience, any moment of love or fellowship that calculateth not—he is likely, at least for that moment, to think that life at the university is worth living for its own sake. This will have one of two effects, depending on what kind of person he is. If he is on the make, already embarked on a career that may lead him finally to move into our organization, such moments will cause feelings of joy and gratitude that can only distract and confuse him on his path to success. On the other hand, if he has decided that he is a rebel against the new church, such moments discovered within the institution can only weaken his resolve to destroy it and hence delay the day of our triumph. Remember: We triumph, now as in the past, either by dissolving the church entirely or by metamorphosing it into the busy service of an indefinitely postponeable and meaningless future.

As ever,
Screwtape

My dear Sellout,

I was somewhat encouraged by your reply to my last. I must confess that your device of creating an office of examinations covering all outside reading was a brilliant implementation of our first principle. If as you say some students were already

reading books without thought for the morrow, it is clear that
you acted none too soon. Be sure to look into whether the same
danger does not threaten in art and music. You may have heard
of the terrible setback we experienced last month at Frangible
University, when they stopped giving the annual humanities
qualifying exam, and spent the money saved on listening booths
and a rental record collection. Have you thought of the possibility of granting some sort of prize to the student who makes
best *use* of his reading, listening, or looking in his daily life?
Or better, in his daily conversation? You might give an award
to any student (or faculty member, for that matter) who could
show that he never *wasted* any reading—always finding some
lecture or exam or bit of conversational one-upmanship with
which to garner credit. But of course you will not rest content,
I trust, as long as faculty and students are really *reading* books
for whatever purpose.

By the way, did I tell you that old Radamanthus has succeeded in organizing a national commission on the full realization of our artistic resources? Representatives from every major
college and university will work initially on the ways in which
art can be made really meaningful in filling the leisure time of
our citizens. Many of the professors who were causing us most
trouble by bringing students to an unconditioned encounter
with works of art have been induced to serve; they will spend—
need I explain?—a great deal of time in Washington for some
years to come.

As ever,
Screwtape

Dear Sellout,

Once again you have bumbled, this time almost unforgivably.
How could you have been so stupid as to persuade the curriculum committee to introduce the actual works of Nietzsche
and Sartre into the curriculum? I distinctly remember giving
you the relevant principle here: Better slogans *supporting* the
Enemy than genuine encounters with arguments *against* Him.

Your whole behavior in this regard shows that I must once again go over our rules about how to deal with ideas:

There are four slogans to repeat on all occasions:

a. Each man is entitled to his own opinion, so why bother to discuss it or read about it?

b. All ideas can be explained in practical terms as filling psychological needs in their originators, so why bother about them as *ideas?*

c. Every thinker has been refuted by some other thinker, so why bother about him *as thinker?*

d. What the world needs is men of passionate commitment to causes. The effort to think a problem through, or to think at all, is a way of putting off action.

I hope you have seen that whenever you convince a student or faculty member to repeat these slogans, you have ensured both that the actions he takes will be hasty, compulsive, and ultimately disillusioning and that his contact with ideas will always be second-hand and reassuring.

I trust that I shall not find myself having to go over this same ground again.

As ever,
Screwtape

Dear Sellout,

Your news that the president has made you his special adviser on the *proper use of students* gave me great pleasure. The whole secret now lies of course in keeping him on the path of *use.* Remind him constantly that his main goal is to build a great university in the next five years. The students now at the university are always to be treated as a step toward the next generation. Never let him think of them as ends in themselves, let alone act on the thought. It may be difficult to keep him from an occasional consideration of their intellectual welfare, but you should have no difficulty keeping such thoughts *oriented,* as we say, toward what he will be glad to call their *later* life in the *real* world. Make sure that when he talks to them he stresses the values of a college education in preparing for the life ahead. Never let him mention that real life is now. If he allows you to prepare his speeches, always insert statistics about the dropout rate and what dropping out will mean to the future income of those who drop.

As for the rest, I think you need not worry. Just encourage all the deans to continue their usual practices; they're doing all right on their own. Their praiseworthy persistence in making soul-grinding duty the sole principle of their lives sets an example to faculty and students that could not be bettered. If they will just emulate the administration, as some of them will, their lives will soon be so harried with thoughts of tomorrow that everything they do will be in my name.

Oh, by the way, and in conclusion, may I suggest that *you* suggest to the dean of the college that he gather his speeches together into a book? You can have no idea how many converts we have gained from the collected speeches of President Quagmire of Obfuscate U.

Best wishes,
Screwtape

My dear Sellout,

You ask what your line should be with students? Once again I am surprised at your inability to draw out from our basic commitment to futurism and repudiation of *now* the day-by-day practices you should advocate. But let me go over the details, albeit somewhat wearily.

In everything you say to students, suggest the following:

1. They are the pure in heart and everybody else is corrupt.
2. They have nothing to learn: in fact, as one of our best men at Chicago said during our recent sit-in, "In these matters you (students) must be the teachers of the faculty."
3. Encourage them in the notion that when they lie or cheat it is youthful highjinks, or justified white lying in the noble cause of building the future.
4. Praise them for wisdom, maturity, and a promising spirit

whenever they follow their impulses blindly. Remind them that members of the true church naturally, impulsively, do the right thing, so long as it is in the name of some abstraction about the future.

5. Do everything you can to encourage them in the belief that the only reality is political, and that every value *now* should be subordinated to the nobler world to come.

A few slogans that will be of use to you here are the following:

Scholarship is the Opium of the Uncommitted; Student Power Versus Ivory Tower; Those We Cherish Don't Publish But Perish; Only Dropouts Can Be Trusted (I might just remind you that one of our best emissaries at California, a young man named Bradford Cleaveland, said in a pamphlet, "The only large group of students I personally respect, other than the freedom fighters, are the dropouts. . . . Many have had the guts to cut their social umbilical cord, become genuinely *free,* and to begin coughing up their own mistakes.") Whenever you can find such students, your problems are solved: anyone who can get his guts and umbilical cord and coughings-up nicely mixed together like that in defense of dropping out rather than staying on and learning how to write English is a natural ally. Cultivate such with all your might.

Finally and most important, teach them to think of you and other administrators as abstractions—the best way to do this, of course, is to *act* like an abstraction. Never let any student catch you or any of your colleagues in the act of caring about books, ideas, art works, or human beings. Let them see you only as instruments to the institution's ends, and they will be sure to *treat* you as means to their own.

As ever,
Screwtape

My dear Sellout,

I know that I do not need to tell you of my pleasure in your recent triumphs. Our dorm-to-dorm survey shows that since you took office the number of hypocritical contact-hours with art works or pseudo art works has doubled, the number of genuine discussions has gone down, and the number of ego-ridden talk displays has gone up. The number of activists who are moved by genuine love of their fellows rather than delight in the simplicities of love-hate abstractions has been cut almost to zero. I especially like the way you have managed to get the *faculty* to talk past each other, in mounting hatred, over the issue of whether they are *for* or *against* the students or the administration. There was a time, a week or so ago, when I was quite worried; some faculty were asking each other what precisely it means to be *for* the students. Your device of speaking out with a clear voice against the mealy-mouthed equivocations of those who would appease students who are little more than left-wing revolutionaries was one of the most effective strokes you have taken. I note with genuine satisfaction that the little Genuine-Thought-Index-Meter that we keep in the office for each of the new churches where we have an emissary today registers lower for Surrogate than for any other university.

I cannot, however, pretend that I think you have done all that might be done with the faculty. Take for example the issue of depersonalization. You have made a serious mistake in trying to fight the proponents of depersonalization. It is true, of course —and this is what has led you astray—that any genuinely personal contact works against us. But you have failed to see that in the new church, as in the old, the best way to fight the personal is with the right kind of campaign for personalization. Just as you have discovered that the mass cocktail hour among faculty can effectively prevent any two faculty members from getting well enough acquainted to matter, so you should now work for social occasions which will encourage a great many faculty to be chummy with a great many students. The new extremist movements, right and left, can provide you with many occasions for the blind groupiness I'm thinking of. We can't hope at this stage for the kind of intensification of group relations that has marked some of our nationalistic movements in this century. But experience has shown that many a student and faculty member has been effectively saved from an afternoon of reading or thought or love making or listening to music or genuine conversation by a well-organized, brainless faculty-student tea.

In all faculty-student contacts, by the way, you should teach the students to think of themselves as academically at least the equals of the faculty, since the faculty are, as they like to say, only human. If the faculty are kept busy enough with routine classes, committee meetings, and socials, they will, of course, steadily deteriorate intellectually, and the students will find plenty of evidence that they are equal, or lower.

As ever,
Screwtape

And so I read on, far into the morning. When I finally finished, I was a confused man, believe me. Until I found those letters, I had intended to come to this conference to say that the college has become our new church, and that though this process might have its dangers, the metamorphosis is on the whole a good thing. But now I am not so sure. How do *you* feel about the following statement by representatives of campus ministries?

Summary of the Philosophies of the Campus Ministries and of the Major Denominations and Ecumenical Bodies. The university is rapidly becoming the institution around which life in the world will be centered. . . . It will be what the church was a century ago and commerce during more recent times: the source of the values by which men live. . . . This new church [these are not *my* words], as the most determinative institution in our world today, [is] under the lordship of Jesus Christ and is called upon to join God's action of liberating and humanizing man.

After reading old Screwtape I felt uneasy about this ready compliance of the men of God on campus. It was clear to me that the university is a church, that of all institutions I belong to it comes closest to being for me what the old church was to my fathers, and that it may well become the last true church on earth. But as I meditated on into the morning hours, I found myself not entirely sure whether its dominion is that of the Lord of Light and Love, experienced in the Eternal moment, or of old Screwtape, Master of the Phony, Prince of Time, Lord of the Great Postponement.

MR. GRADGRIND, 1965

I

I've been reading application folders for the College recently, and I've been struck, as I think you would be, by the poverty of vocabulary and idea shown in the students' statements of why they want to go to college. "I want to be a doctor and I have heard that the University of Chicago has a good pre-medical program." "I want to be a social worker and I have been told that these days a college degree is almost a must for such work." Honest statements perhaps, but otherwise no less depressing than the many attempts to butter us up with clichés about "wanting a liberal education in order to live a fuller life" or wanting to "round out my education before entering on my professional career." One young man talked about the age of leisure that is upon us, and he wanted a liberal education in order to have, in later life, something to do in his spare time.

What disturbs me about these statements is not that any of them are flatly illiterate or wrong-headed but that they are all

Speech at commencement convocation, the University of Chicago, winter 1965, and printed in the *University of Chicago Magazine,* May 1965. Reprinted with permission.

so mean-spirited. Each of the applications I read showed quite clearly that its author was thinking strictly in terms of the future *uses* of a liberal education. Or at least he thought *we* would be stuck in such grooves. "I want to get a liberal education so that I will be able to do this, that, or the other *with* it." Nobody said anything like "I want to get a liberal education because that seems to me the best possible way to spend my time during the next four years, no matter what happens to me after that." Nobody said, "What a strange question. Is there anything else that a human being my age *ought* to want?" Nobody said, "I want to go to Chicago because I've heard that people have more fun with ideas there than anywhere else in the world." No, it was all "I want to go to Chicago because I've heard that you have a good pre-med program."

Pre-med, pre-law, pre-physics, pre-English, pre-life. I sometimes think, as I look at what has been called the post-Sputnik era in American education, that there is no one left who learns anything because he wants to know it; it is all *pre*-learning. "Education is Our First Line of Defense—Make it Strong"—so reads the title of a chapter in Admiral Rickover's book pleading with us to educate for Freedom. Any day now I expect to see some educational measure advocated because it is good training for survival in a nuclear attack: get your liberal education packet here, good for filling your leisure hours in the bomb shelter.

Where do the applicants get such stuff? Quite obviously they get it from their mentors, from college catalogues, from articles in national magazines, from books about education. When educators publish statistics proving that college graduates earn more than non–college graduates, it is not difficult for students to infer the reasons for going to college. High school counselors, who have been counseled by college counselors, who have been counseled by graduate school counselors, counsel high school students to get such-and-such courses "out of the way" *so that* when they get to college they can be placed in certain other preparatory courses *in order* to get as quickly as possible into graduate courses *which will prepare them for* a degree *which will be necessary for* good placement in a job *which will lead quickly on up* the ladder toward an indefinite but no doubt finally glorious future. Of course, those who are counseled assume that we will read their applications with that glorious future in mind. Even our general education requirements, those courses designed to educate men as men and not merely as preprofessionals, those courses the experience of which should be the high points of a young man's life, are subjected to the same treatment. Students tell me that their advisers here frequently use the expression "get it out of the way" when talking of such courses. "The way to *what?*" I want to ask.

People often call the process I am describing a rat-race or a treadmill; the metaphors suggest activity without a goal, running for the sake of running. I think that a more appropriate metaphor for the current American educational scene would be something like the chimera chase, or winning the will-o'-the-wisp. Our activities are not goalless: the trouble is that they are entirely goal-ridden, and the goal is often almost as crude as the cash-values satirized by Dickens in *Hard Times,* the novel from which I take my reference to Mr. Gradgrind. Mr. Gradgrind runs a school in Coketown. The school and the town are both run in the service of facts, and the facts are chosen in the service of what pays off.

You saw nothing in Coketown but what was severely workful. If the members of a religious persuasion built a chapel there . . . they made it a pious warehouse of red brick. . . . The jail might have been the infirmary, the infirmary might have been the jail, the town-hall might have been either, or both, or anything else, for anything that appeared to the contrary in the graces of their construction. Fact, fact, fact, everywhere in the material aspect of the town; fact, fact, fact, everywhere in the immaterial. The M'Choakumchild school was all fact, and the school of design was all fact, and the relations between master and man were all fact, and everything was fact between the lying-in hospital and the cemetery, and what you couldn't state in figures, or show to be purchaseable in the cheapest market and saleable in the dearest, was not, and never should be, world without end, Amen.

We all recognize this as so obviously opposed to what we hope will come from our education that we may even think the portrait irrelevant to our present abuses. But three weeks ago a good student said to me, "Why must this university force us to work for grades. I don't *want* to work for grades. I have proved to myself in the past that I can work without being whipped, but from the first moment of my arrival here I have been made to understand that the ultimate goal of education is to have a good transcript to show to graduate schools."[1] A teacher told me that when he introduced into his discussion a newly published work, strictly relevant to the problems of the course but not on the reading list, he was asked by his students to stick to what was sure to appear on the comprehensive. And when I ask students in the dormitories whether they are doing any reading on their own, they often answer "No, my required work keeps me too busy."

Work required for what? Ultimately, for something good in the future. The student usually thinks that the future good he works for will be a good for *him,* but many of his mentors make it quite clear that they are thinking of something else entirely —the need for educated industrial management, the need for a citizenry indoctrinated in the principles of Americanism, the need for educated bodies to fill the factories and offices of tomorrow. Paul Goodman has reduced the whole problem to the charge that our college students are a new exploited class: they are being used, against their own welfare, for the practical needs of the economic system. Goodman's charges are always exaggerated for effect, but I must say that it is not hard to find talk about education that could be used to support his case. Admiral Rickover says that we must "upgrade the schools" in order to "guarantee the future prosperity and freedom of the Republic." The student sitting over his books at 2 A.M., experiencing the effects of upgrading in the form of tough assignments, cannot help wondering what's in it for him, and I must say that I am on his side. Though I would hope that any really good education would guarantee the future freedom of the Republic, and that it might even have some favorable effect on the Republic's prosperity, I am convinced that if we plan our education with such economic and social goals at the center, we are doomed. The practical effects we want, if practical is the word, are changes in the quality of human beings, changes not

1. Note that this all preceded the organized student attacks on grading.

only in what they can and will do in the world but also in what they are. The educated man, in this view, is himself the final justification of education, and if this is so the process of education, the quality of life led as the education goes on, is a kind of end in itself as well. You cannot, in the manner of Mr. Gradgrind, pour the facts, the proper machine-tooled responses, into the little pitchers in the hope that when the proper time comes they can be tilted to pour them back again. Every educational step we take in the name of a future payoff has immediate practical consequences in the quality of life led by those we educate; yet what they in fact become depends more on the quality of the present moments we give them than on our explicit plans. (I've noticed lately that nursery school programs, here and elsewhere, are being organized specifically as academic preparation for first grade. Whether any nursery school is issuing diplomas yet I do not know, but we can be quite sure that the day will come. Do you share with me the fear that a four-year-old child, asked to prepare for the future, may learn more about the true values of his mentors than they intended?)

Perhaps it is the very virulence of the taint we feel in many of our academic endeavours that leads us to search so zealously for that other kind of learning, free, purely motivated, untrammeled by external, practical ends. Surely it is the road traveled and not any particular destination that justifies liberal education. Surely what we mean by the free play of the mind is a play of the mind without some secret payoff in the future. Surely the ultimate justification of a university education is not something that could be destroyed if the student's life ended on the day of graduation. Ask yourself, now, whether you would consider yourself cheated if some sort of flaming disaster struck Rockefeller Chapel and took us all to the kind of unexpected death that will, in fact, meet some of us during the next year— cheated because you had spent your last years struggling for an education? I suspect that some of you *would* feel cheated, but if you would, if you do not feel any sense that these recent years have been in some degree self-justifying, I feel sorry for you, and if I had the authority I would suggest that you request a refund. Not only should these years have been filled with activities worth pursuing even if all external demands were removed;

they should also have provided you with a philosophy of life that would prevent your looking to the future for some sort of payoff for the present. Except for a handful of fundamentalist Christians, the world has learned not to look to future heavenly rewards as the ultimate sanction of virtue; but we have so far been unable to rid ourselves of the kind of futurism that sees all of the present as a means to some future fulfillment.

II

Some such thinking as I have so far engaged in, based on disillusion with phony futurism, has led to a good deal of expressed discontent with current academic practices. Some prophets of revolt—I have already mentioned Paul Goodman—seem to ask that we tear down the whole edifice of education and start over. Since the best learning, their argument runs, is learning for its own sake and not for the external rewards, then we should remove grades and other external rewards. Since administrators tend to run colleges as degree factories, grinding out grads at the fastest possible rate, the way to improve education is to get rid of administrators and allow men's natural love of learning to take over. Our colleges should teach students what students want to learn. Some students, perhaps, will not want to learn anything, and they do not matter. But the pure in heart, the true, natural learners should be liberated.

Well, such dreams are attractive. The Goodman doctrine is a flattering one—he even flatters faculty by telling them that they too could be pure if only administrators would leave them alone. It is not the first time that prophets have told us that we are naturally perfect beings who have nothing to lose but our chains. Men are good; institutions are bad; or rather, all administrators and some faculty members are bad, and all students and some faculty members are naturally good. Just set the pure learners free and then see how they will learn!

But I wonder. I wonder because of what I see in myself and what I see in other men. As for myself, the opposing parts of my double nature are quite clear. On the one hand, I have no doubt whatever, at this late date, of my genuine love of learning for its own sake. I love inquiry as I love few things in this world; I love books and working with books; I love to solve problems.

But on the other hand, if you ask me whether I would ever have learned as much as I have about literature—and precious little it is—without a strong infusion of tainted motives, I must answer "Of course not." First of all, the Ph.D. requirements: with rare exceptions, I learned most at times of external crises—comprehensive examinations, papers, and finally the Ph.D. dissertation itself. Would I have written a full-scale study, at the age of thirty, if the desire for a degree had not overcome my natural laziness? Never in this world. I would never have got started. While it is true that there were many days, weeks, even months, when my problem might have sufficed to keep me going, there were other days, weeks, even months, when nothing could have kept me going but the many external whips that the departmental patterns and my base personal ambitions provided. Similarly, I would like to think that my subsequent publication has all been done for the love of learning: I was never told that I would perish if I did not publish. But I would lie to you if I pretended that I never found need for low motives like ambition, desire to show up my enemies and impress my friends, and shame about publishers' deadlines.

There may be pure creatures somewhere who never work except when it is fun, who never write except when inspired, who are never aided by external prods. But the men I know best, including myself, are not quite that pure. To put it in extreme form, if we follow the nostrums of Paul Goodman and other Utopians and allow students to learn what and when their pure love of learning dictates, it is not hard to foresee seventeen different forms of disaster. Many of them have, in fact, already happened. I think that a list of failures in Utopian experimentation in this country would make a very interesting study: all of the efforts to do away with grading, all of the efforts to have the pupil do only what he wants to do, all the efforts to do away with administration and to rely, simply, on tired old Mark Hopkins on that worn out log.

III

You will notice that I have been playing that old game of on-the-other-hand-ism—pairing off two dialectical extremes against each other. Whenever a speaker attacks first one extreme

and then another, you can be almost sure that he'll mix his
metaphors, abandon both hands, and conclude on some in-
nocuous, wishy-washy middle ground, not to say bog or swamp,
like the pre-med conference secretary who reported: "Too much
overspecialization is a bad thing." But I have not gone through
all this simply to conclude with a comfortable exhortation to
avoid extremes. It is not enough—though it might be something
—to say that we want to repudiate both the prophets of payoff
like Admiral Rickover and the prophets of purity like Paul
Goodman. Our problem is really not simply to get as much pure
learning into the curriculum as possible, while rendering unto
Caesar, with our left hands, that which is Caesar's. The problem
is to find those kinds of external goad and reward, those forms
of practical incentive that will ultimately lead to pure learning
rather than building habits of mere reward-seeking. And as soon
as we think hard about this problem, we discover a curious
ambiguity underlying many of the most abhorred, seemingly
mechanical kinds of reward.

Consider for a moment the standard protest against "working
for grades." Everybody knows that to work mechanically for
grades is a sad business. But nobody looking at two M.A. candidates, slaving away through the night this past week on their
M.A. papers, could possibly tell by external signs which of them
was working for grades in this sense and which of them was
trying his best in order to convince himself that his best was
good enough to please his teacher. To work to please a teacher
is still not the same as working for the love of truth, but it is a
step toward it. Surely our problem is not to attempt to remove
all external motivation and organization of education, as if all
students when they come to us are forever divided into two
camps, the pure and the impure, but rather to make the motivation and organization we provide as human, as personal as
possible. When a student works for signs of a teacher's approval,
as expressed in a grade, he may be very close to working for
his own approval, and that is only a shade removed from working for the truth alone. Something human has crept in. Even
the strongest student may need, at times, some sense of support
from the practical world, but the effects will be very different,

depending on whether the whip is wielded by an admired human being or by an impersonal machine, metaphorical or literal.

Perhaps a better example can be found in the phrase "working for a degree." To work for a degree in order to get the badge necessary for working toward another degree in order to get the badge necessary to get the job, and so on, is dehumanizing and ultimately embittering. And yet to work for a degree which will be a symbol of human respect paid you by fellow human beings who really know your work and who know you as a person is another thing entirely. It may still be nothing very noble, as compared with the great free moments when the subject takes over and inquiry becomes pure. But it is no mean thing.

Perhaps there are some among you today who have been led through the whole process, as I have been, from mechanical grade-grinding to free inquiry, and back to grubbing again. How many of you mastered your second language out of pure love of learning? How many of you prepared for every examination with the light of free inquiry shining internally, behind your bleary eyes? And yet somewhere along the line you have again reversed yourselves: something human has subverted the institutional machine, or something in your subject has come alive. You wouldn't have come to such moments without external support; if the external support had been entirely dehumanized, you would not have come to such moments at all. But having come to them you do not need, temporarily, any further external support.

When I was an undergraduate I became convinced that academic ceremony was phony, and I swore that I would never walk in an academic procession. Contemptuous of external trappings, I was pleased to stay away from my own bachelor's ceremony—though as it happened my triumph was somewhat dampened by the fact that I could not have gone if I'd tried: World War II had already dragged the young idealist into the mire of basic training camp. But as I later went through the M.A. and Ph.D. programs here, I noticed a subtle shift in my attitude. Maybe I just got older and more corrupt; perhaps I was just lucky in finding teachers and subjects that made the degrees seem something more than phony trappings. Tainted by all kinds of low human motives, goaded by external prods, I walked to receive my diploma with a strong conviction that I would do the whole thing again if I had the choice. The thought didn't occur to me then, but as I look on it now, I would say that if that flaming disaster which everyone fears these days had struck in 1950, I would not have cursed my bad luck in having spent four years preparing for the nonexistent future. The quality of those four years was somehow self-justifying. The goal seemed important just because the path leading to it was something more than a mere utilitarian preparation for that goal.

What I am trying to say today is that I hope there are at least a few of you here who feel the same way.

THE LUXURY
OF LIBERAL LEARNING

*A computer, MANIAC 2000, is printing out an essay by one
Professor Zukunft, entitled, "Who Killed Liberal Education?"
The professor programmed it into the machine in the year 2000
just before he died, the last educated man. Professor Zukunft
spent an interminable time on the visible enemies of education;
he now turns to the struggle with his friends.*

In spite of many such attacks, liberal education might have
survived if its defenders had themselves behaved like educated
men. But instead of thinking about how to keep education alive,
they fell into the same kind of empty-headed sloganeering that
was used (more skillfully) by their opponents. The result was
the most popular game of the twentieth century, Polarities, one
version of which was sold under the name of Wholemansman-
ship. It went like this:

Excerpted from "Who Killed Liberal Education?" an address delivered to
the undergraduate Liberal Arts Conference at the University of Chicago,
April 1968. An earlier version was given to a conference on the liberal arts
at Wayne State University. Abridged form reprinted with permission from
Graduate Comment, vol. 11, no. 4 (1968).

Dean of a College: You graduate scholars are destroying undergraduate teaching, because you teach dry subject matter and fail to educate the whole man.

Graduate Professor: You undergraduate buffs are so concerned with students' personalities and psyches that you are failing to educate them at all, whole *or* part.

Dean: Nonsense! What you forget is that a subject is meaningful only insofar as it becomes real to the student, meets his concerns and needs, and takes on existential relevance.

Professor: Double nonsense! No man can claim to be whole these days who has not mastered a special field. Your *whole* man is maimed by incompetence.

Dean: You ignore the flesh-and-blood creatures you would teach. They have passions; they must make vital choices; and you, in your ivory tower, would teach them dry facts and irrelevent theories . . .

And so on. The counters in this game were clearly marked, the moves all laid out in advance; nobody had to think to play it.

There were, of course, sound reasons for the popularity of Polarities in the sixties: war always polarizes, and an undeclared and rightly unpopular war polarizes with especial viciousness. A young man who must choose whether to accept the draft cannot resist being polarized: there are only two boxes to be checked, yes or no. He cannot, by taking thought, invent a third box, "None of the above." So it was not surprising that everything else got reduced to two boxes too.

For liberal education, the most destructive of these reductions was that between research and teaching. Publish or perish? For or against? Research or teaching? For or against? Many highly intelligent defenders of liberal education, shocked by its enemies, fell into the trap of talking as if it were possible to choose up sides. One of them, William Arrowsmith,[1] even recommended that the country should set up research institutes in large numbers, divorcing research entirely from the places where liberal learning could take place. That a man with so

1. A guest lecturer for the conference.

much true learning could have recommended such a divorce
of teaching from discovery shows just how hard it was, in 1968,
to think clearly about the causes and possible cures of the decline of teaching.

For David Riesman the poles were *professional* versus *intellectual,* making it impossible for anyone to aspire *both* to the
fullest professional competence *and* to the intellectual's passion
for ideals. For many graduate professors they were *professional*
versus *incompetent,* which had the same effect but with a
rhetorical push in the opposite direction. For Martin Duber-
man they were *student-initiated learning* versus *teacher-
initiated learning,* and the resulting polarity was so compelling
that even when a great many of his students complained that
they hadn't learned enough because he refused to teach them
anything, he dismissed their complaint with the charge that
they had been corrupted by their early training!

Here I should like to quote from an unpublished speech by
an anonymous dean, dated "University of Chicago Liberal Arts
Conference, April 1968." It is clear that at that time it was still
customary to hold Easter festivals of learning, and that somehow
there was in the popular academic mind an obscure connection
between Christ and Athena, or perhaps even Apollo, with their
resurrections of the spirit of learning. Be that as it may, at one
of these festivals this harried dean said the following:

The absurdity of blaming research for bad education can be shown
quite simply:

First, ask yourself who have been the really valuable teachers in your
own life. Then check those who have been actively engaged in some
kind of research and publication which they themselves cared about.
For me the figure comes out to better than 95 percent of the good
teachers I have known, *including* my high school teachers. Mr. Arrowsmith, Mr. Friedenberg, Mr. Kamen, and Mr. Hildebrand[2] all do research, and the results of their research become part of their teaching,
both in print and in the classroom. I have studied under only two
really good teachers who did not publish, and both of those were doing
what *I* would call research—they were actively engaged in inquiring
into questions other men had not yet answered.

Secondly, make a list of the teachers whose classes were for you

2. All speakers at the conference.

absolutely worthless. Note that I am not asking you to make a list of
people you consider bad teachers. That might come later. When I
make such a list, I find that all but two were *not* doing any kind of
research, let alone publication. Three were, I admit, publishing the
crummy results of crummy research. But the point here is that eight
out of ten of my poor teachers were poor partly because they didn't
know enough; they had nothing to teach me, though they thought of
themselves as genuine teachers devoted to their work.

Third, add to list number two those teachers who you think were
bad simply because their techniques were bad or because they neglected their teaching in favor of research. Then ask, How many of
these would have been better teachers if they had spent less time on
research and more on their teaching? I find only one man I feel clear
about here. The rest would have been just as bad if they'd spent weeks
of preparation on each class, and worse if they had done no research.

I conclude from these three simple mental experiments, [the worthy
but obscure dean goes on in a learned allusion to David Hume] that
to talk of research and teaching as antithetical gets us nowhere. It
cannot be research in itself that leads to the obvious neglect of teaching, and it cannot be a simple decline in what we call teaching that
produces the decline in liberal education. As for the tendency to
blame graduate schools for the decline, we must never forget that
every graduate professor, every institute researcher, and every graduate student, was once an undergraduate somewhere. What he is must
in part be a result of what happened to him in the four years of
college. If he is not liberally educated, who is to blame?

But of course many graduate professors *are* liberally educated, and
they are, pace Arrowsmith, conducting liberal education with their
graduate students. If we searched America today to find where genuine
cultivation of the mind occurs, with professional consequences and
personal ambitions left to fall where they may, we would surely find
as much of it going on *after* the BA as *before*—in a few law schools,
some business programs, an isolated English or philosophy or classics
department. I know one graduate professor of physics who gives his
Ph.D. candidates, belatedly, a liberal education. Graduates of famous
liberal arts colleges, they still are barbarians when they come to him,
but they leave him changed men.

But I must leave the dean's rather shrill rhetoric and continue
with my own dispassionate analysis.

Besides the polarizers, the chief culprits responsible for the
worst crime of the century were the many inventors of plausible
substitutes for the real thing. Defenders of liberal education
were fairly well armed, after all, against their open enemies.
When businessmen asked for more "practical" courses, colleges

knew the answers in advance, and gave them. When government tried to force indoctrination programs onto the colleges,
the good colleges knew the right answers in advance, and gave
them. When graduate research programs stole money and
equipment and time from undergraduate classrooms, they may
have in part succeeded in the theft, but nobody was fooled into
thinking that what they did was done in the name of liberal
education, or that nothing had been lost. But when the defenders of liberal education themselves grew more and more confused about what it was, then there were no true defenders
left.

All of the proposed substitutes for liberal education, offered
in the name of liberal education, were of course good things.
They could not have been dangerous, and finally effective, if
they had not been obviously good things. Perhaps it was inevitable that in a time when most intelligent men had lost their
faith in all other institutions, they should have called upon the
universities and colleges to take care of all of the values remaining in society.

Perhaps the most important of these was love. With the
church dead, at least in the opinion of most faculty and students, it was natural to demand that the colleges should provide
a loving community of the saved, an institutional embodiment
of everyone's hope, even in these non-Christian times, that love
may save the world after all.

I quote from a statement by a graduate student in 1967:
"With the exception of Hannah Arendt," he said, "I doubt that
any of my teachers cares whether I'm around or not—so long as
I learn what they have to teach." When asked if he didn't think
that *teaching him* was from his own point of view the most
important form of caring, he denied it: "When teachers care
too much for the truth, they become inhuman. I'd even prefer
Professor X, who, unlike Hannah Arendt, has a mediocre mind
but who really cares about his students and makes them care for
him, to Professor Y, who will trample everyone in his way as
he struggles to get at the truth. The university is really cheating
me out of my tuition if it makes a God out of truth. Truth
simply is not an end in itself—it is a means to the development
of people." And then he went on to say that he thought it his

own duty as teaching assistant to shock his freshmen into changing their lives, not to teach them simply how to be effective in the world of ideas.

And so he and others called for a loving community of the saved, living together in spiritual equality, like primitive Christians. In such a community, what could be more inappropriate than grades—can we grade a man's soul? And how can we make invidious distinctions between faculty members and students? In the kingdom of love, it is one man one vote. And in contrast, what is wrong with the kingdom of intellect is that it presupposes, or seems to, distinctions of rank, power, and ultimate value among men. It leads to distinctions between wisdom and foolishness, between knowledge and ignorance, and finally between teachers and learners.

But if such distinctions violated love, they even more obviously violated the principles of egalitarian democracy. And since most faculty and students had lost their faith in government and political parties as embodiments of their highest political aspirations, it was natural to demand that the university and college become the last best manifestation of democratic political ideas. Of course in practice this meant that the university was viewed as a kind of state or city, to be manipulated or used for particular political ends, and the community of equal participants was often defined rather narrowly. Even professors were found leading demonstrations demanding that universities ban certain persons from the campus. One advanced graduate student in one of the traditionally liberal arts, mathematics, when reproached for violating the right of free entry to the campus, said, "Let's not have any of that civil rights bullshit!" Of course he felt very moral as he said it, because he was speaking on behalf of participatory democracy, and participatory democracy was obviously such a good thing that all other values could be sacrificed to it.

It's true that the motives for seeking egalitarian universities were not always exactly pure. One spokesman for what in those days was called the new left was quoted as saying that if you're travelling on the Titanic, there's no point in going steerage. But liberal education was not killed by men with such grubby motives; had there been anyone around to defend it, such attacks would have meant little. But too many of those who might have been defenders had decided that as between two goods, democracy and truth, or political effectiveness and truth, they would choose democracy and political effectiveness. Truth is just too obviously one of the worst of tyrants, one of the worst discriminators.

Third, it was natural, when civil society found itself no longer able to support a genuine cultural life (except in sporadic outbursts like the good popular music of the time)—it was natural, I say, to ask the universities to become patrons of the arts, sponsoring every good thing because every good thing would die if it was not sponsored by the university. Theater, modern dance, contemporary music, architecture, cinema—older societies provided private or governmental support for these arts. But the universities found themselves with orphan after orphan dumped on their doorsteps, and who could be so cruel as to let the orphans die?

And speaking of orphans, social services were increasingly left to the universities. With the local, national, and state governments no longer able to solve social problems, what more natural than to ask the universities and colleges to cure all social ills. When universities found themselves spending more money annually on their brand new departments of urban studies than they spent on the whole of undergraduate education, the end was in sight. A few shrewd educators, seeing where the future lay, transferred from college positions to departments of urban studies and worked subversively in them, teaching students how to think freely, using urban problems as subject matter. This worked for a while, until the free thought got in the way of the doctrines of the urban planners; then of course the practical demands won out.

So the process was clear and inevitable: asked to become church, political savior, patron of the arts, and social agency, college after college simply forgot what it might once have been to be thinker and teacher of thinkers. The university should relate to society in one or more of these ways, everyone came to say, without even having to think twice about it; the truth was so obvious that soon no one remembered that before two things can really relate, they must really be two things, different from each other. If a university is just an extension of society, without a unique and essential role of its own, it cannot relate to society; it *is* society.

By 1984 no one was left to state such counter truths, and nobody felt compelled, consequently, to attack the ivory tower. But a decade or so earlier there were still a few traditionalists saying that universities were or ought to be somehow distinct and unique, and consequently young men could still feel quite self-righteous and courageous in attacking what one of them called the "complacencies of the Academy, 1967." I shall quote from his article, which was printed in the first issue of what pretended to be a new and radical journal, the *New American Review*. Pleading for the obvious virtue of courageous outspokenness on public issues, the author, one Professor Roszak, made four comparisons:

> Let us suppose, then, that an instructor in American history takes an active part in organizing a thoughtful, well-conceived campaign against capital punishment in his state. He musters the students to the cause and succeeds in engaging public officials and people generally in a searching debate of crime and punishment. Has he not made a more genuine intellectual contribution than if he had written a definitive study on the decline of cotton factorage in the American South for the period of 1865–94?
>
> Or, again, suppose that a psychology instructor, feeling that the politics of his community has gone slack, undertakes to run for Congress, with an eye to stimulating serious public discussion of pressing local problems. His campaign is responsible from start to finish, and he forces his opposing candidates to take clear-cut stands they would otherwise have avoided like the plague. How shall we assess the man's intellectual behavior? Is it more or less valuable than an exhaustive study of olfaction in the unrestrained rat?
>
> Suppose an English instructor devotes a large amount of his time to organizing "freedom schools" in the slums and conducting a creative writing workshop there. Should we [not], for purposes of promotion and tenure, count his intellectual efforts as highly as if he had produced a critical study of Golding's translation of Ovid's *Metamorphoses?*
>
> Suppose an anthropology instructor busies himself organizing a teach-in on the Vietnam war. Perhaps he even travels to Vietnam for

the Inter-Universities Committee and then writes a solid analysis of the effects of the war on the rural population for the *Atlantic Monthly* or *The New Republic*. Is his work worth more or less—intellectually speaking—than a study of unity and diversity in the celebration of cattle-curing rites in a north Indian village?

Now we can leave aside the obvious point that Mr. Roszak deliberately describes academic studies more trivial or contemptible than most *actual* studies he could have named. We can also forgive him for not knowing that each of the studies he pooh-poohs turned out during the next three decades to have unpredictable practical consequences (we all remember how important Blitz's study of the olfaction of unrestrained rats turned out to be in making possible the survival of the human race during the Great Smog of '88). Leaving all this aside, what kind of mind do we see revealed here, and what conception of the operations of mind? Are these supposed to be arguments? How is one supposed to judge the worth of "a solid analysis of the effects of the war on the rural population for the *Atlantic Monthly* or *The New Republic*"—except that we are told that it is "solid," which must make us all very happy? The organizing of "freedom schools" in the slums and the conducting of a creative writing workshop are obviously achievements of the highest order, if anyone ever succeeds in doing them well, and they are achievements that would obviously require a good mind. But to place them in competition with writing a critical study, even of the most important kind, is entirely misleading. The world did not need to choose one or the other kinds of activity: it needed both, but it did not get both because it pretended that they are achievements of the same kind.

Mr. Roszak went on to make quite explicit his notion that thinking and acting are not separate, since analysis and discussion are political *acts*, and "to think, to speak, to teach, to write: all these are forms of doing" and are thus "indispensable parts of the political process." And since this is so, the value of a man's political actions, especially if they are in the "dramatic form of civil disobedience"—should be taken into account when promotion time comes. In 1967 Mr. Roszak deplored that "the barest handful of schools in America took 'citizenly conduct'

into account when making professional decisions." But we are
now in a position to see how quickly that situation was reversed.
Having been taught by Mr. Roszak and others that "citizenly
conduct" was equivalent to intellectual achievement in the
academy, universities and colleges were soon hiring and firing
according to the instructor's social value. At progressive institutions, faculty committees found themselves trying to decide
between Smith's creative organization of protest demonstrations, Jones' good teaching, and Brown's good book. At conservative institutions, committees of course fired Smith for
leading demonstrations (uncitizenly conduct), but they had a
hard time comparing Doe's citizenly work for the John Birch
Society with Roe's splendid testimony before the House Committee to Investigate Student Protesters!

We can see now that the graduate schools were, in fact, the
last and strongest bastions against the Roszaks of the world,
and thus against the loss of one of man's great values: the cultivation of intellectual power as a good thing in itself. Though
all of the colleges had, by 1984, ceased to teach any subject
except as it could be proved immediately useful, a few graduate
schools went on believing in knowledge and the pursuit of
knowledge and mental excellence as self-justifying goods until
—well, until the end. By 1984, in other words, every college
student in every minute of his day was engaging either in public
service, in political activity, in industrial work projects, or in
that minimal amount of study necessary to get into graduate
school. But it was not until 2000, this very year, that the last
graduate department officially gave up the ghost; that school
was not, as men in mid-century would have predicted, the art
department, or the music department, or the English department, or the philosophy department: these had long before
declared disinterested curiosity out of bounds. No, the last bit
of free curiosity pursuing its own ends was in the business
school, where a group of professors got together once a week to
discuss a variety of theories about why no student had been
heard laughing for at least two years. They all got very excited
by their theories and they neglected "their own research"
terribly as they conducted their studies of what had happened.

Finally one man hypothecated that the students were joyless because they were no longer curious, and then somebody suddenly noticed that nobody teaches curiosity any more, and yet curiosity is surely one of the things that modern businesses most want—and why don't we have any courses in curiosity? So they voted a proposal to the business school faculty for a program of six courses in Curiosity, Curiosity 101, 102, 103, 111, 112, 113. Everybody thought it was a very good idea, because certainly all graduates of business schools should be curious, and so Curiosity was finally entombed, perhaps forever, in six very dull courses at Gradgrind University.

But I have no heart to continue. Why should I continue? With everyone now leading "useful, happy lives," what possibility is there that my account of the death of a value could be of interest? After all, it is a value the usefulness of which can never be demonstrated to anyone unless he is already convinced of that value—unless, that is, he thinks it is a good thing to be curious and to have curiosity satisfied and to learn how to do a good job of satisfying curiosity, and especially of satisfying that supreme curiosity about what curiosities are most worth satisfying.

It used to be said that it was natural for man to want to learn. We have now proved that civilization can overpower such a seemingly natural urge, that the most luxurious of all societies can get along without the luxury of liberal learning. Everyone, as I said at the beginning, is very happy about it. There are no educational problems when every high school knows that its task is to prepare for college entry, when every college knows that its task is to prepare for graduate school, and every graduate school knows that its task is to prepare the nation's human resources for industry and government and consumerism, when every researcher is pushing for results and for publication whether there are any real results or not, when every teacher is willing to doctor what he knows in order to give the students what they "want to learn," when every student has learned to parrot what his charismatic teacher says, either for grades or for love and approval. I am told that last week at my own university, from which I retired in 1992, the students *voted in* a new

Ph.D. program in Feelie Science. Some of the older professors of subjects like Video Science, Entertainment Journalism, Cinematographic Chaos, Creative Collage, Controlled Hallucinogenetrics, and Hermeneutics of Happenings, opposed the program on the ground that the Feelies as an art form did not yet have enough popular support to justify a whole Ph.D. program in Feelie Science; they thought that the M.A. went far enough. Besides, there was only one slot left open in the computerized time table of Ph.D. programs—the program in Free Logic and Loose Analogies—and the professors in those subjects were strong in defending these traditional disciplines. But the day was lost when it came out that nobody, not even the professors themselves, could explain what logic was or how analogies work. The Committee on Liberal Education recommended that there could be no education truly worthy of the name liberal if it could not *freely* accommodate the new disciplines as they came along, and the vote was assured.

As for myself . . .

Professor Zukunft's manuscript and MANIAC's print-out end here, leaving me terribly puzzled, not to say curious. Why, if Zukunft is so hot on totally disinterested, nonpractical curiosity, why should he want to communicate with anyone else about it? Shouldn't his idle curiosity have been enough, in itself?

REASON AND
EMOTION IN EDUCATION

One often hears it said that we should not be interested in education of the "mere reason," that we should instead want to educate the "whole man," with special emphasis on the emotions and on moral commitment. "Mere reason," it is said, has long since been shown to be inadequate for the solution of man's problems, and we should work at "educating the emotions." In a recent seminar on education for women, for example, many participants implied that if we "merely" trained the minds of our women students, we would not be doing our jobs, and one speaker explicitly contrasted reason and emotion, suggesting that those of us who work at the intellectual disciplines, those of us who talk of training our students' minds, are somehow overlooking the main point. After all, "Nobody ever gave his life for a logical proposition."

Now there is obviously some truth in all this—reason by

Reprinted with permission from *Earlham Review*, summer 1967. I include the essay here, though it now seems to me a relatively primitive treatment, because the attacks on the intellect that I found in a Quaker setting about twelve years ago have now swelled to a great national hymn extolling the truths of the heart.

itself is *not* enough—but it is only a half-truth, and in some respects a dangerous one. It is especially dangerous in a college founded by a religious society—it is so easy to enlist on one side or the other in the old war between science and religion. It *is* an old war, but I see no reason why, if we consider reason and emotion carefully, the war should break out again here and now.

I have been troubled in our debates by the implication that because a particular mental power or faculty can't do everything, it is therefore somehow suspect or inferior. Even if we accept the implicit equation of "reason" with "mere logic," and admit that "mere logic" can't make me a good or wise man, it still remains true that logical thought is one of the noblest achievements of man. If "mere logic" can't make me wise or good, neither can "mere" emotional commitment—as the history of the various *isms* of this century makes clear. Similarly, if "mere" logic or cold scientific method cannot make a scientist, it is equally true that there was never an effective scientist or scholar, in any discipline, who had not mastered the logic of that discipline. Even if logic deserves the adjective *mere,* it is still an obviously essential element in all effective human action, whether painting a picture, testing a hypothesis, or raising a child; although it can't do everything, nothing at all can be done without it.

But why should we accent the equation of reason and logic? Do we have only two faculties, reason or thinking or logic on the one hand and emotion on the other? Few philosophers or psychologists have been content with such an oversimplification. The term *reason* has almost always been used to cover an area far larger than is covered by logic. Plato and Aristotle used *reason*—both *logos* and *nous,* I'm told—to refer to the capacity to discover sound first principles, to make *assumptions,* or to formulate alternative hypotheses, as well as to the capacity to test those principles or hypotheses dialectically and to construct chains of argument from them logically. My knowledge, for example, that a given thing, say Carpenter Hall, cannot both *exist* and *not exist* at the same time, though it cannot be proved, is still a rational first principle from which all my other thinking and acting springs. How I discover this knowledge, and why I say that I "know" it even though it cannot be proved, may be matters for debate, but the process of its discovery can hardly be called either emotional *or* strictly logical. It is part of my thinking activity, part of what most earlier philosophers would have called my reason. What is more, I can, as Aristotle pointed out, test it rationally, because I can discover that the alternative —"Carpenter Hall *can* both exist and not exist at the same time, even if we maintain the same definition of the term *exist*" —leads me to consequences which I cannot accept. Further, I discover that if anyone tries to disprove it in argument with me, his arguments depend for their validity on the very principle he is trying to disprove.

It is true, of course, that once I have recognized this principle rationally, I am almost certain to feel an emotional commitment to it, and I may even become angry if anyone denies it. But no amount of emotional training or experience could have taught it to me. Even if we adopt the modern usage and say that I know it "intuitively," we should recognize that for most men throughout the history of thought, the word *reason* has included this kind of sound intuition, and when they have talked of education as the schooling of the reason, they have meant to include the process of learning how to test and compare our various intuitive beliefs, many of which are unsound even when *felt* as strongly as this one.

For example, I once "knew," with absolute conviction, that I was number one in the universe; like Saint Augustine, and like everyone else, I discovered early in life, long before I was aware of conscious reason, that everyone else should bow to my will. My emotional commitment to my own absolute primacy was great indeed. But it was in conflict with certain other beliefs about which I have gradually become aware: "Other men feel the same way about themselves," and "I have a strong sense of guilt whenever I violate, in the name of my own quite obvious primacy, the equal but less obvious primacy of any other man." These beliefs about "the brotherhood of man" did not, and do not, automatically subdue the forceful belief about my own centrality; one spends a lifetime of what I would call rational schooling—consciously and unconsciously comparing the impulses that spring from the one misleading "first principle" with those that come from others. Put in simpler terms, I *feel* a sense of duty to myself, but I also feel or come to feel a sense of duty to others. I think that most men have these two *feelings* in a strongly developed form. But only by reasoning about them, only by examining the impulses which each one produces and by comparing the consequences of each can one discover, first of all, that one's self-centeredness must often be subordinated to one's sense of brotherhood, and secondly, that there is after all no ultimate conflict, since to learn to lose one's life—one's absolute self-centeredness—is the only way to find one's true life.

Further reasoning can lead me to reassess even this belief of the unique importance of men as brothers by comparing it with further principles discovered intuitively: for example, the sense we all share, at first in an extremely vague form, that there is "something bigger than any of us." The whole of the existentialist movement, it seems to me, is an unavoidable attempt to reason through the contradictions revealed by comparing our sense of man's importance with our discovery that God or the universe often seem to treat man as of no importance whatever. Against such a contradiction, it is perhaps not surprising that many existentialists have decided to surrender reason rather than surrender either man's importance or the existence of God. Men are always discovering that particular contradictions between seeming first principles force them to give up belief in reason and a rational universe. But they are also always rediscovering that the contradictions can be resolved either by rejecting one belief or by discovering that both beliefs are really reconciled in a higher one.

In any case, whether we choose to accept all this talk about reason or not—and I know that to some of you the term, though not the process, is distasteful—I think it *is* important in our discussions to recognize that when we talk of educating men to reason we mean something more than "mere logic." Right or wrong, we think we are talking about something so inclusive that it covers a good deal of what we ordinarily mean by intuition and "emotion."

While we may disagree about the dangers of "mere reason," I suppose none of us are in disagreement about the dangers of "mere emotion." We are all too aware of what some emotions, unchecked, can lead to. Indeed, to talk at all of "educating the emotions" always implies that some emotions are *better than* others, regardless of which axis of values we are operating on; the very notion of education presupposes the notion of improvement according to *some* scale. Gandhi was emotionally committed; so was Hitler. The campus heroes who defended us against that most awful of fates, loss of "school spirit," were emotionally committed; so were those who brought them to task.[1] Obviously what we are all after is the good kind rather than the bad, whichever side we are on.

There is nothing that distresses me so much in our faculty discussions as the frequent suggestion that the defenders of liberal education in the more "academic" sense are not interested in schooling the emotions, and do not care whether men are good or bad, whether they become hoodlums or productive members of society. We all desire, I believe, graduates who are committed emotionally to whatever way of life they think is best. We are all thus interested, in one sense or another, in educating the emotions, just as we are all interested in an education that is practical—according to our own definition of what is practical. What we seem to disagree about is the *method* most appropriate to a college, or, in other terms, the degree to which a college can profitably deal with the emotions in emotional terms without too great a cost.

There are clearly many methods, more or less effective depending on the practitioners, for schooling the emotions. One method, highly effective in the hands of a Christ or Gandhi, a Billy Graham or a Joseph Smith, is that of direct personal conversion. Psychic revolutions are obviously of great importance to mankind—when they are in the cause of truth and right. Whenever they are *not,* according to our standards, we start using names like "holy roller" or "propagandist" or "rabble-rouser" or "fascist" or "Communist." The direct emotional

1. Ah, how remote that little episode of student protest in the late '50's now seems (1970 note).

appeal of a personality and his deeply felt message seems, unfortunately, to work as well in the hands of a Hitler inciting his
followers to viciousness as it does in the hands of a Gandhi
leading his followers to a great nonviolent revolution. I don't
suppose that any of us thinks that the two kinds of personal
conversion are of equal value; we would all agree that Gandhi
is, in a sense, "educating the emotions" of his followers, while
Hitler is rabble-rousing. But how do we decide that this is so?
If we answer that we decide on the basis of our *feeling* that it is
so, then our educational task becomes, I suppose, that of con-
verting as many people as we can, by emotional appeals, to feel
the way we do. There seems to be no reason against our doing
so, and we can easily discover "reasons" for employing Madison
Avenue to fight Madison Avenue, as it were; the more TV
preachers and the more roadside signs proclaiming our cause,
the better chance we will have.

The question would seem to be, however, whether it is the
main job of a college to enter into this particular kind of battle
for souls. I doubt that many of us would stay in business for very
long if we thought that it was. A college by its very nature presupposes that there is something more to men's commitments
than a battle of personalities and of propaganda devices. We
might, of course, by reorganizing ourselves and hiring a new
staff obtain a higher percentage of commanding personalities
who could effect conversions. But conversions to *what?* However we answer that question, we all believe that the answer has
a somewhat more firm basis than a mere personal opinion that
our position "feels" better than the alternative position. We all
believe, in short, that there is a meaningful choice possible
between a passionate commitment to a Hitler and a passionate
commitment to any of the world's genuine prophets. We believe,
that there are *reasons* why some things are better than some
other things, why true propositions are truer than false ones,
beautiful objects more beautiful than ugly ones, good actions
better than bad ones. The "dialogue" of a college differs from
the dialogue of the church or market place, important as they
are, in that we are committed to exploring and clarifying the
genuine reasons which make human choice meaningful rather

than meaningless. All choice has emotional concomitants. All choice can be rationalized. But only *some* choices—whether of action, thought, or feeling—are reasonable. Unless we want to reduce ourselves simply to the level of being one propagandistic organization among others—the victory to go to the best propagandist or the strongest personality—we must sooner or later be willing to test our reasons. A college is first of all a testing ground of rational choice. Whatever else it is or does should be judged according to whether it assists or hinders this unique function.

All of this certainly does not mean that we should refuse to deal directly with students' emotional problems. We should have trained counsellors—I think more of them—to work with the student's emotional life directly; we will always have some students whose emotions are so tangled that only direct manipulation, through individual or group therapy, can free them to the point of being able to listen to the "dialogue"—to a reason when they encounter one. Nor does it mean that we should actively avoid making personal "conversions," whether to our favorite form of marriage or our favorite philosopher, so long as we are sure that the kind of conversion we are likely to make can withstand the light of reason in the broad sense in which I am trying to use the term. But we cannot set up a psycho-analytic institute any more than we can set up a college of saints and prophets. Within the limits of our finances and abilities, we are qualified to deal with the emotions primarily in one way: we are, or pretend to be, qualified to teach people how to use their minds, how to solve problems, how to compare motives and preferences and insights and emotional commitments and to choose those which can stand the light of day. In Plato's terms, we are, or ought to be, qualified to give help to the charioteer, reason, as he attempts to guide those two wayward steeds, the emotions and the desires.

We do, I suppose, have a duty to help provide a wider range of emotional experiences than our students know when they come to us. Bach and Elvis Presley can't be compared effectively by a student who knows only Elvis; the rewards and consequences of a Quaker religious experience and an old-fashioned revival can hardly be compared by the student who knows only the revival; the comparative value of Arthur Miller's tragedies and Li'l Orphan Annie will never be recognized by a student who knows only the comic strip. But it will be noticed that in each of these instances, one is not simply providing one emotional experience in place of another, but rather one is providing an experience in which emotion and reason are so deeply interfused that the experience can withstand the most rigorous of rational criticism. I would seriously doubt that a college could ever afford to spend very much of its energies dealing with the emotions except in such rationally defensible forms.

For the most part our students seem to me pretty well set in their basic natures when they come to us. They are the products of their homes and churches and peer groups. If a time ever comes when we receive each year a freshman class made up of a job-lot of Hitlers, nothing we can ever do will change them much in four years. But so long as society sends us, as is fortunately the case, a group of thoroughly confused but well-meaning young people who want to find a good life, who have a vague longing for education but very little notion of how to work for it, we *can* hope to help them in clearing up their confusions and finding *their own way*. In short, we can cultivate their reasoning powers in such a way as to aid them in finding direction through the circumstances and problems of a future we cannot predict. If we don't do this, nobody else will. And if we fail to do this because we are too busy meddling with matters about which we really know very little and over which we have very little control anyway, we are committing a kind of irrational crime of our own—though with the best of intentions and the firmest of emotional commitments.

THE UNIVERSITY
AND PUBLIC ISSUES

You would expect an administrator to come before you and say that the issues are more complex than you have realized. Well, what I want to say is that the issues are more complex than you have realized. The issue I have been asked to discuss is whether, as some have argued, the university should, as an institution, be urged to declare itself opposed to our present policies in Vietnam. But instead of dealing immediately with Vietnam, I think it is necessary to back up a bit and ask about the general question of institutional stands on public issues.

Let me begin with what I take to be some facts—some of them unpleasant—then move to some principles on which I think we are probably all agreed, and finally go to some controversial points on which I am reasonably sure we will *not* all be united.

Fact 1. Nobody knows for sure, but I think it's a fact that most universities, if they did speak out *as institutions* on the Vietnam issue, would speak out in opposition to the point of view that

Delivered at an open meeting sponsored by students at the University of Chicago, fall 1965. Though my estimate about campus votes would now place them much closer to "my side," I think the principles remain unchanged.

217

you and I favor. I can't speak for any board of trustees, of course, but I suspect that at many colleges and universities the trustees would support the extreme right, if they spoke at all. And one needn't confine it to boards: the faculty and student body of perhaps 1800 of the 2000 American colleges and universities would not oppose our involvement in Vietnam— or so I guess. The interesting thing is that we are not even sure that we can get a majority vote among the students of this campus, reputed to be, rightly or wrongly, one of the most liberal in the country.

Fact 2. As things stand, even though the presidents, the boards, the faculty, and the student bodies of most colleges do not oppose the Vietnam policy, at most institutions those who *do* oppose Vietnam policies are free to speak their piece without reprisal.

Fact 3. Such freedom can be lost. It is not at all clear that universities can long maintain their freedom if they adopt the policy of taking an official stand on all important public issues, especially if those stands are determined by popular pressures, whether from students or the community. In Minnesota, for example, there is now an active movement by the Junior Chamber of Commerce to get business interests to organize to put pressure on the university to stamp out left-wing elements, as they are called. The pressure will be resisted, we can be sure; but suppose we ask ourselves why we can be sure? Only because the university has managed to preserve a tradition of freedom of inquiry and statement—and managed to educate the public, however dimly, to that tradition.

I read this week in a journal from South Africa of a student demonstration at the University of Pretoria. These students were deeply concerned about social issues, and they were annoyed because the university officials were not taking a strong stand. The young men and women, deeply committed to social action, marched around the university and through the town, demanding official action—and for what cause? *For* a stronger support of apartheid, *for* a stronger pro-government line, *against* the student groups protesting apartheid, *for* an absolute banning of integrated meetings. But I don't have to go to South Africa: many formerly free universities have been mutilated with the help of student protest groups, supporting fascist or communist governments, protesting what this or that professor has said in the classroom or in public.

The fact is—if fact is the right word here—that there are not many countries in the world where one can find *any* free universities left, universities where a student can be sure that what the teacher says in the classroom is what the teacher believes, whether it is true or false, objective or biased.

PRINCIPLES AND JUDGMENTS

1. A university should be a place where all men, students, faculty, and administrators, can speak their minds on any issue without punishment or reprisal. At Chicago we tend to take this principle for granted, but I need not remind you that there are many colleges and universities in the United States and throughout the world where the principle is regularly violated. I asked an administrator of a college in Texas two years ago whether there had been any student support for civil rights. "Well, we've fortunately not had much of that element down here," he said, "but I think we'd pretty well know how to handle 'em if they came." I know a college at which a teacher was told that he was not promoted because he believed in evolution and another one where teachers did not dare to put Kennedy stickers on their cars in 1960. The administrations of these three institutions had decided, you might say, to *take a stand* on three issues, and to make that stand effective in the world. I assume that none of us would want to be at any of those three places, and that we would not want to be at an institution that was essentially like them—even if the official position was one we approved of. At least I would not want to be at a university which put pressure on my colleagues to believe a given line—even if the pressure was in favor of my own beliefs. And I assume that when students these days ask universities to take a stand on social issues, they do not mean to ask for so firm a stand that minorities within the university suffer for their minority position.

2. I would assume agreement among us also that if either a free university or a free society is to work, men must not only have the right to speak their opinions, they must speak their

opinions, even when their opinions are unpopular. This hardly needs discussion this morning, except to say that even in our society it is honored more in the breach than the observance. If men do not honestly speak out, no society depending on free exchange of opinion can thrive; yet we all know that scarcely anyone speaks all of his opinions freely, and that to do so would require saintly self-sacrifice on the one hand, or perhaps satanic willingness to be cruel on the other. Still, men ought to be honest, whether they are or not, and the closer we can come to a public honesty and debate of free opinions, the better chance we have of making democratic society work.

3. I'm not so sure about general agreement on my next principle, but it seems to me an inescapable one for anybody who thinks about what he means when he asks for honesty. It is this: Nobody has a right to ask for behavior from other men that he is not willing to ask from himself. If I ask other men to speak out honestly at great personal risk, I must be willing to expect honesty of myself. If I ask other men to make sacrifices for the sake of truth, I must myself be willing to make sacrifices for truth. Doublethink is found in great quantity in all institutions, and I think we should deplore it. But we lose our right to deplore as soon as we engage in doublethink ourselves.

4. Principle four I'm reasonably sure you'll agree with: there are *some* issues on which universities have a moral obligation to speak out. One can prove this one most easily by pointing to cases on which most men would be in agreement: Nazi universities; the University of Chicago against the Broyles Commission; loyalty oaths; the defense affidavit. Why am I so sure of these? Because the university as a free institution is itself threatened in each of them, and every university has, or should have, an absolute determination to preserve the conditions for its own continuation as a place of free inquiry.

We have now reached, though with some rather big gaps, the following statement: a university has a moral obligation to speak out on any issue when its very existence as a true university is threatened.

5. Now let me move further in the controversial direction. My fifth principle is this: It is both foolish and unfair to expect institutions to be judged by as high a moral standard as we

expect of individuals. I sometimes hear people accusing this or that institution of duplicity, when all that could possibly be meant is that the institution is divided, made up of men with different points of view. I don't deny that individuals in institutions often show duplicity, sometimes for selfish reasons and sometimes because they have come to believe, like the Communists and some Jesuits and some of the leaders of the Free Speech Movement in California, that a good end justifies extreme means. But let me give you an example of institutional duplicity and then ask you whether you think I should condemn the persons involved as dishonest. Last week I was asked to speak to this group this morning, on the topic of institutional responsibility in such issues as Vietnam. I agreed. Early this week I learned that a campaign was being carried out to boycott classes this morning. Nothing had been said to me about it, yet surely it was a rather crucial element that I should have been told about before deciding whether to join you. O, lackaday, *the organization had betrayed me.* Perhaps even Mr. Ross had betrayed me. When I phoned him, he said, just like a dean, that the organization was rather loose and he had not known, when he talked to me, that these other plans were afoot. Being a dean, I believed him, and instead of cursing the organization and saying that it has now become a corrupt manipulator of deans, I simply said, "It is an institution; it is behaving the way institutions—especially free institutions—behave." Ladies and gentlemen, free spirits all, you are an institution, and you have behaved immorally!

But it would be naive of me indeed to say that your institution of this morning is corrupt. And it would be even more naive of me to expect you to respond, efficiently, clearly, and morally—as a group—to every issue that comes along. You are united, at least most of you, for a purpose, to protest American policies in Vietnam, just as the university is a group of men who have united, for another purpose, which is not to protest American policies in anything, but to maintain a forum for free inquiry and for free teaching of the results of free inquiry.

As an administrator of the second institution, asked to join the first, I have no great difficulty, so long as I am asked to join only as an individual, and not to speak for my institution (let me ignore the problem of keeping this distinction clear—many people, including the public press, will not want to keep it clear, and thus administrators have great pressures on them, pressures both moral and sleazy, to temporize, pressures of which none of you can even dream). But as soon as you ask me to work for a statement *from the institution as a whole,* I face a deep conflict: I am convinced that to do so would soon destroy the university as a place where such meetings as this could be held, on any side of any question. I am also convinced that our policies in Vietnam are sadly, terrifyingly wrong, and that every citizen should do all that he can to protest.

As a student, you also have the same conflict, whether you feel it strongly or weakly or not at all. On the one hand, you are probably not as convinced as I am that to ask the university to speak out, as an institution, in response to pressure from an organized group, would destroy its true character very quickly. What is more, you probably do not feel as much loyalty to the institution as an institution as does someone who is spending, as all university administrators do, most of their waking hours trying to make the thing go with as few creaks and compromises as possible. But even so, your true interests, both as students here, as citizens, and simply as human beings, lie with the preservation of our forum of inquiry, with all its loose-jointed, exasperating need to temporize. You have, on the other hand, an interest in preserving your country and the world from annihilating war. What other interests you may have, noble or ignoble, constructive or destructive, only you can know. But if we rule out the sheer destructive impulses that many of my generation claim to find as the chief motive of your generation —and I think this is nonsense, because all generations are both constructive and destructive—if you leave out such matters and think really of what your responsibility is in the present moment, as a scholar-citizen, I think the issue appears as I have described it: a conflict of two judgments, based on two important values and two important fears of destruction.

My own judgment is that if you can find a way to describe the present situation that really fits the extreme conditions of, say, Nazi Germany or Stalin's Soviet Union, then, since universities will all be destroyed soon anyway, you might as well try to sacrifice the university to the end of peace in Vietnam. Before you do so, I would point out, just in passing, that President Johnson, with all his power, hasn't a chance in the world of silencing you and me this morning, nor has he ever shown that he would even try. I think you would be drastically wrong if you came to any such conclusion, but I think you could make a moral case for yourself.

But speaking practically, I think you would be *foolishly* moral, even if your assessment of the world situation is much more pessimistic than mine. For the various factual reasons I gave at the beginning, I am quite convinced that any effort we might make to enlist universities as institutions on our side would backfire: President Johnson got, the morning paper tells me, a thirty-two foot pat on the back from 2057 University of Michigan students and faculty members yesterday. Make no mistake—if any group at Michigan tries to get the university as university to speak out on Vietnam, that thirty-two foot petition, and not any position you and I would espouse, would be given the name of the university. As it is now, student and faculty groups and deans on both sides can speak out from the university, and in a sense, but only in a limited sense, use the university name. I personally am horrified at the prospect of a university that would spend its time trying to arrive at political decisions, in order to speak to the community with a unified voice.

By the same token, I am proud to be at a university where I can speak at meetings like this, say exactly what I think, and know that when I walk from the building there will be no reprisals.[1] To preserve a forum of that kind is to me the basic task of the university.

---

1. I did not suspect that within three years, fear of reprisal would be fairly common even at my university—reprisal from the so-called left, not the right. By 1970 professors were subject to some harassment *for their opinions* —and the students were thus slightly less justified in assuming that what anyone said was what he really believed. That the students in general were thus the true targets of the crusading spirit of *some* students seems to me self-evident. Even where this repression from the left does not lead, as it generally will, to larger-scale repression from the right, it has already done immense harm.

THE COMPLEAT EQUIVOCATOR
OR,
HOW THE DEAN
ENTERED WITH UNQUALIFIED
SYMPATHY INTO MANY
DIFFERENT AND UTTERLY
CONTRADICTORY INTELLECTUAL
POSITIONS AND EMERGED
SMELLING LIKE A ROSE

I must confess at once that I'm troubled by the way that *enfant terrible,* Peter Ratner, has set this thing up. Think for a moment about that mixed metaphor he committed—"mired in a philosophical vein." Was he subtly imitating the similar mixture in the title he wormed out of me in a harried moment, some time ago—"Strange Bedfellows: Some Notes on the Ancient Warfare of Scholarship and the Arts"? I suspect that Ratner's program is designed to free us all from what that other *enfant terrible* McLuhan calls "the linear bonds of the pre-electric age." Once we've done that we can call a truce, silence the guns, take a fresh look at how the ball crumbles, clean out the stale air in the spaceship, and lay down a fresh reconnaisance into the future which, by golly, lies ahead.

But there's a more serious problem about that original title: it belies the number of terms in my profound dialectic. Any true Chicagoan ought to know that a two-term dialectic, like the one between scholarship and the arts, produces pretty feeble and predictable stuff. As soon as I had given my phony

The opening address for the Festival of the Arts at the University of Chicago, May 1969.

title to Ratner, I began to drag myself through the obvious
stages of the argument that it dictates: on the one hand, there is
scholarship, and it has such-and-such to be said for it; but, on
the other hand, there are the arts, as indeed we all know, and
there is much to be said for *them*. Conclusion: *on balance,*
scholarship has much to learn from art, and art much to gain
from scholarship, and all of this learning and gaining takes
place ideally in a university community, etc., etc. I was just
sinking into this soggy little piece when my secretary came in,
her arms laden, as usual, with correspondence. "There's something funny this time," she said, and handed me from the top
of a pile a manuscript entitled "Strange Co-pilots, Some Notes
on the Ancient and Glorious Warfare Between Scholarship, the
Arts, and Politics—By a Friend." Well now, since a three-term
dialectic is obviously fifty percent better than a two-term dialectic, I read through that twenty-page piece with great anticipation; but it was terribly disappointing. The author was an
activist who first showed why scholarship or the search for truth
in itself is deficient, because it leads men to ignore the pressing
problems of the world, and the arts by themselves are deficient
because they provide an escape from one's duty to solve those
problems; but a *proper* scholarship, in the service of political
reform, of course, and a *proper* art, in the service of political
reform, of course, should be encouraged. And of course the
proper home for such encouragement would be within a radical-
ized university. Well, for an old retiring dean, this one clearly
would not do either.

What I wanted was either a strictly neutral analysis, present-
ing each of three or more cases so cogently that you would be
forced to make up your own minds, or a *seemingly* neutral
presentation, that would subtly but surely guarantee your
coming out with my point of view about how the arts relate to
everything else in a university. So I wrote, God protect us all,
an educational quartet—four-term dialectics are, I think thirty-
three percent better than three-term. All voices in this quartet
are strictly equal, but I leave it to you to see whether perhaps
some are more equal than others.

The scene is Authentica University. Only in Authentica in

1969 could four people of such clashing views talk for as long as I'll have these people talking without coming to blows. The four participants are Bookmaker, a devoted professor; Artsman, a gifted representational painter; Goodman, a selfless political activist; and Feeler, an antiformalist, anti-esthetician. I have scrupulously awarded each participant just exactly 1543 words to make his case, though some of the words are, by the nature of the case, less consecutive than others. There are other speakers who would like to get into this conversation, but these four talk so much that nobody else can be heard.

Bookmaker: I just don't understand what all the fuss is these days about the irrelevant university. Anybody who compares the universities of today with those of five or fifty or a hundred years ago must see that they are much more involved in the contemporary, much more involved with the arts, much more involved with social problems. I just saw the opening of a huge Festival of the Arts, one that makes me wonder whether anybody's going to have any time to do anything at this university for the next month. Obviously everybody here is allowed to do whatever he wants to do in the arts. We have three orchestras, three choruses, two art studios, a modern dance instructor, and the best facilities for showing movies within a radius of four blocks. If Robert Maynard Hutchins ever compares us now with the purified academic university he was proud of, it must curdle his blood. What's all the fuss about?

Artsman: That's not even the way the question should be put. Of course you can point to a lot of peripheral artistic activity, and of course there are many of us who manage to battle against the general trend and get some art into our lives. But "battle" is the word. If professors and students had to work as hard to have courses as Ratner had to work to get a Festival of the Arts, this place would fold in a week. The question ought to be put the other way around. It seems obvious to me that art is more important than anything else men do.

(Goodman at this point tries to interrupt, but Artsman doesn't let him.)

Artsman: The question therefore ought to be: What possible justification can you give, Bookmaker, for setting up a university which places the creative act of *making art* lower than the act of *talking about* art and then further defines both of these acts as a whole lot less important expenditure-wise than performing laboratory experiments or running data through a computer? It's the dry-as-dust scholar who ought to be required to defend himself.

Bookmaker: I'm sick and tired of that "dry-as-dust" bit, and I think anyone who'd use the word "expenditure-wise" is in need of some good scholarly training in how to use English. But the point is: obviously there is bad scholarship and good scholarship—learning that dries up and learning that irrigates, to accept your tired metaphor. And it seems equally obvious to me that a university must place its main emphasis on intellectual inquiry and training, subordinating everything it does for the arts to the primary task of teaching men to think.

Artsman: Well, it's not obvious to me at all. Do you have any reasons other than your own inability to create a work of art?

Bookmaker: In some ages and climes a crack like that would have called for a duel. What I mean when I say something is obvious is not what you artist-types might mean—that I "feel it but I can't express it." No, I mean that there are so many good arguments on one side, and so few on the other, that I can't see how an honest man who considers the question can come out on any but one side. May I run over the reasons?

Feeler (paying something resembling attention for the first time): Like, I mean, man, like reasons. If you feel, uh—

Artsman: Of course, go ahead.

Bookmaker: The structure of my argument is simple, though it has ramifications. I see you smile; I hear you laugh; and I get your point: everything I say has ramifications—right. Things are more complex than they look, all things. But remember, it was God who built this incomprehensibly complex universe, and it was the Devil who tried to reduce it all to simple *pro* and *con* choices.

Artsman: All right, yes, go on.

Bookman: Well, it goes like this: (1) Learning how to think well is terribly important both to individuals and to the society in which they live. (2) If the university doesn't take care of thinking, nobody else will. (3) If the university spends its energies trying to teach people to paint or act or write poems or do creative dancing, it'll not have the resources in energy, money, or time to educate minds that are critical, clear, and free. Do you follow that?

Artsman: Oh, I follow it all right, but it seems to me that all three steps are questionable when put in your form. Of course it's important for men to learn to think, but to say that begs the question of what learning to think means. If what we need is only men who can think as clearly as a machine can think, that's one thing; but if the only human thought worthy of the name is the thought that's informed by creative personality, as many people would say—if, as Polanyi says, all true knowledge is personal knowledge, then—

Bookmaker (interrupting): But you're parodying me. Of course I'm not thinking of mere linear programming, though I confess that I'd be happier if more of our students and faculty were capable of it as a kind of bare minimum; to know whether one should accept a piece of argument *is* after all terribly important to every individual and to society. But intellectual inquiry for me stands for the whole activity of the mind addressed to the problems of human life—including the apprehension and testing of first principles and purposes as well as "reasoning" clearly from or toward them. The university is, in fact, uniquely charged with preserving standards of inquiry and argument, and if, as seems to be the case with this one, it lets other matters, whether artistic or political, get in the way of hard thought, thought suffers and may in fact be doomed.

Artsman: But how is a university to stimulate something more than mere logical clarity? How can it make for creative thought if it relegates creative matters to weekends and festival periods?

Bookmaker: No, you haven't understood. I'm saying it's the university's task to preserve and extend the intellectual life of man. That intellectual life of course includes the highest creative acts of which the intellect is capable. In any historical perspective, this university is comparatively saturated with the arts, as I said earlier. It's true that a decade or so ago at this university performing arts were really in disrepute. Hutchins was pleased to boast that unlike almost every other American college and university, we gave no credit for nonintellectual pursuits. Last year I was told by a lively, cultivated alumna in her sixties that the decline of the universities began when departments of music and art were added. "It's these subjects," she said, "entirely inappropriate in the true university, that have replaced the old solidly intellectual subjects like the classics and turned our universities into places that don't really know what their purpose for existence is."

Well, I never heard Hutchins go quite that far, but he was fond of explaining why courses in musical performance or in painting or creative writing did not belong in a university. Courses should concern themselves, he would say, with teaching men to think and to deal with bodies of knowledge. Why should there be *academic* credit for work that has no stateable theoretical content and no structure of teachable knowledge? There are, after all, other more appropriate forms of "credit" for success in writing a novel.

Now we all know that most universities, including this one, have stretched themselves in dozens of ways in recent years to accommodate various creative arts. We give degrees in the fine arts; we give credit for creative writing; we give credit for musical composition. Unlike most American universities we do not as yet give credit for playing in a band or orchestra or for movie-making. But that time, God help us, will come. What is more, our best departments are themselves centers of creativity very much like that found in the arts, as our mathematical friends are very fond of telling us.

(Now I should like to point out that while Bookmaker has been going on with this discussion of which he is obviously very proud, Goodman has been angrily smoking one cigarette after another, snorting, writhing, and generally looking disgusted—when he's not been trying to break in. Feeler, on the other hand, looks happy. For the last five minutes he's been staring at the water pitcher as if entranced. From time to time

he scratches himself without shame. A while ago he walked to
the window and smiled benignly on the universe, then returned
to stare at the pitcher.)

Bookmaker (unaware of any of this): No, it seems to me that
no matter how broadly you define thinking, you can't define it
in such a way as to reduce it to what men do when they create
or enjoy works of art. Last week I heard a young philosopher
named Ted Cohen say that there was no point in a philosopher's
teaching Thoreau because there are no *ideas* in Thoreau worth
teaching, not as a philosopher would teach them. And there's
an element of truth in that. If a philosopher spends his time
teaching the half-formed "ideas" of a Thoreau, he will not have
time to teach the efforts at fully-formed thought of genuine
philosophers. It's the creative *intellectual* achievements of man
past and future that will die unless the universities manage to
make them live.

Artsman: But you don't seem to realize or to care about the
fact that we seem to have reached the *same* point with the
arts. The arts will die too, unless the universities preserve them.
Ours is the first culture in which the universities preempt most
or all of the cultural life of the community. If they don't become
patrons of the arts, the arts are doomed. So our argument finally
boils down to a different view of the importance to man of the
arts and of scholarship. I suspect you may be right that the
university can't maintain what it now calls scholarship and do
what it should do for the arts as well. To me the conclusion is
obvious: give up most, though perhaps not all, of what is *called*
scholarship because it's not, under any definition, preserving or
encouraging anything that's half so important to man as is a
lively artistic culture.

Bookmaker: You depress me. You keep insisting on a choice
that may be forced onto us but that a man should never have
to make. It's the nature of life that it cannot be lived in the
exclusive service of one value. I'd never say that an individual
man can or should live by learning alone. I listen to classical
music and rock music passionately; I happen to play both the
classical guitar and bongo drums, and I care for this side of my
life as passionately as I do for my teaching and research. In fact,

I care for my family even more than for either of them, and I suppose if I had to make a personal and final choice of Goods, as you seem to want me to do, I'd give up first the drums, then the guitar, then Aretha Franklin, then the Beatles, and last of all scholarship, if necessary to preserve the family I love. But it's "the university" that must subordinate everything to the intellect, not the men or women in it.

(At this point, Feeler seems for the first time to be really listening. Goodman appears especially disgusted and breaks in.)

Goodman: You guys really make me sick. You both sit here making lists of this and that bit of precious life you care about, and while you talk, the world is burning down around your ears. This university is so far from where the real troubles are that it's sailed right around back into them again from a different angle. But if you think the quarrel is between artsy-fartsy-craftsy-crapsy Bach and Michelangelo on the one hand and pure clean Plato and Aristotle and Einstein on the other, you'd better reexamine your curriculum vitae!

(There is a long pause. Finally Bookmaker speaks in a low voice.)

Bookmaker: What do you think the university should be doing?

Goodman: How can you even ask a question like that? It's so plain that anybody not blinded by tradition can see it without having to be told. While we sit here eliting away, just a few little things are happening in the world, just a few little catastrophes which just might be more important than whether an argument is logically unassailable, or whether enough people got Beethoven in their lives—like the most depraved and vicious and corrupting war this country has ever been in, a war which this university connives in by remaining silent and by doing its scholarly and artistic and investment business as usual. Like millions of people starving in the world, from Biafra to Evanston. I just can't see how you can be so deaf to this shrieking, bloody message. People are dying of physical and mental and emotional starvation within a few blocks of this university, and you can sit here worrying about whether Thoreau, who at least had the guts to take a stand on the problems of his own time, was a true philosopher or just an artist; and then you, Bookmaker, make a list of things that are important in your life, and I didn't even notice on it anything to do with improving the bloody lot of your bloody fellow man.

Bookmaker: But we were trying to talk about something else. Give us a chance. You're trying to reduce everything again to two categories only—social improvement and all the worthless remainder of life. Most of us do what we can—admittedly not much—about the direct alleviation of suffering you seem to be talking about—ah, er, *(Bookmaker is visibly embarrassed, as you see)* a check here, ah, a telegram there, squeezed into my *central* life, which is and must remain working in and for the university so that as many men as possible can share the values that it conserves and extends.

Goodman: Crud, absolute crud! You just admitted that you spend what you didn't call your "leisure time" playing the guitar and bongo drums, while people, godammit, die of starvation a few blocks from your art-filled home.

Artsman: Now wait just a damn minute here! You're the one who's talking nonsense. If we start playing the game of who's inconsistent, we're all lost, because you'll turn out just as guilty as the rest of us. Where did you spend your vacation? Somebody told me it was in Mexico, right? Why didn't you give the money that trip cost to the poor instead and spend that time working for free in the slums? That's one inconsistency. Nobody *I* know has really "sold all that he hath," to quote a great creative artist, and given it to the poor. But even if he did, he wouldn't have solved the problems you raise. The whole question we're slowly beginning to wrestle with here is how should a man live, because the answer to that question will determine how a university should be run. And you're just angry, threshing about in favor of one very real value, without at all playing fair.

Goodman: Playing fair! Fair's exactly what I'm trying to play, and my whole point is that this society, like every other one I know, has never played fair. It's set up to allow leeches like you to sit around sniffing at scholarship and the arts, using them as perfume to cover the smell of the corpses all around you.

Artsman: But wait, wait! I'm trying to say something that ought to be important to you as well as me. Can't we all calm down a minute and ask what it is that makes the lives we all wish we could save worth living at all.

Goodman: Calm down all you want to, but what makes anybody's life worthwhile is working together with other people to improve the world.

Bookmaker: Yes, but isn't the question exactly what does the word "improve" mean? If you get everybody clothed and fed and housed well, and they're all intellectually subhuman—

Artsman (jumping in quickly): Please keep out of this for a minute, Bookmaker. Phrases like "intellectually subhuman" will only make him mad. I've got something more important from *his* point of view, and that is the question: Would you be satisfied if everybody had equal income and nobody had any art in his life?

Goodman: I thought I'd made clear that Bach and Shakespeare and Da Vinci are irrelevant.

Artsman: No, I mean art, art of *any* kind. You know I've been asking for a course here at the university in jazz. Jazz is a dying art, like most of the other arts except the various forms of pop music. Would you think that a world without jazz, Goodman, would be a poorer world?

Goodman: Well, yeah, a little bit poorer, maybe, but even jazz is mainly irrelevant to—

Artsman (interrupting): But let me go on a bit. Would a world without soul music be a poorer world?

(Feeler looks up; he's heard that word "soul.")

Artsman (plowing on): You don't seem to list the arts of the people you are interested in when you lash about you, but that's art too. I'll give up on Beethoven for a while, but do you want to live in a world in which the Aretha Franklins are thought to be irrelevant? Just because the time people spend listening to her should be spent on economic improvement in the slums?

Goodman: I don't get you.

Artsman: My point is that for me the total purpose of everything we do, in and out of the university, can be summarized under the notion of "improving the quality of life." A world without music or painting or dancing, defined any way you want to define them, a world without all of what you would call the "useless arts," would be a terrible world—even if everybody had a full stomach. Wouldn't you agree, at least if I allow *you* to define quality and allow *you* to say which arts are permitted?

Goodman: I'm not sure. I say first things first, and first we gotta get people alive and secure from violations of their dignity, and then maybe we can turn to the nicer things.

Artsman: And meanwhile, I suppose you're willing to sell your stereo and all stereos and close all jazz and rock and soul nightclubs, along with the symphony halls and the opera halls and the art museums, and devote all of our money and energy to social ills?

Goodman: Now wait a minute. You're reducing my position to absurdity. It's the university I'm concerned about; I don't want to tear down everything but to improve it. I wouldn't tear the museums down; I'd turn them into places of living art, for the people. I wouldn't tear down the concert halls; I just want to equalize the opportunities for everybody to get into them. I'd open the universities to the people. I'd—

Artsman (interrupting again): But supposing there were still some people starving, while the "museum of the people" was filling the spirits of those people, and the "universities of the people" were teaching the arts and politics of participatory democracy. Would you think that these universities and museums should be closed also until the last social injustice was removed? Because if you would, then you'll be forced to say that there's really only one supreme value, however you define it, and the *quality* of life lived by those you claim to have saved just doesn't matter to you. Besides—

Goodman (interrupting this time): But you don't seem to realize that I'm talking about a *temporary* closing down of education and luxury so that we could then build a society that could create an education of true equality. The art we now have is itself so tainted by our crazy elitist values that it's often worse for a person to take part in it than not. The art that we might have, on the other hand, if men were free—

Artsman: But do you think that any society can just whomp
up an artistic culture by political fiat, once the social and economic inequalities are removed? All the evidence of the past is
to the contrary. The artistic traditions that grace our lives,
including the most recent ones like jazz and rock, depend on
long histories of what you call luxury. One of the painful and
inescapable facts of man's history is that, without economic
inequality, providing for what you would call "useless leisure
time," most of man's cultural achievements would never have
occurred. Without spare cash to be wasted on activities like
going to nightclubs, for example, jazz would never have got
started in the first place. In fact, the man who hoarded his
pennies and bought a clarinet or trombone instead of feeding
the poor was violating the standards you seem to have set up.

Goodman: Oh, you go on taking everything to absurdities.
It's not the cheap clarinets of the people that are shameful; it's
the expensive art departments, wasting money and time on
meaningless research into the Gothic cathedral and Renaissance
frescoes and—

Feeler (at last coming to life): Absurdities! Abfuckingsurd-
ities! You guys are all so far off the point, I can't even see you.
You sit here *unwrapping,* and nothing happens. I mean everyone of you is asleep, dead, ya know? So abstract you don't see
anything or feel anything that's really going on. Like, wake up
and look around you—that pitcher, I'm the only one here who's
even *looked* at it, and I *made it into something.* You start talking like you talk about scholarship and art and politics, your
phone's disconnected. If you would just listen to what's inside
you, you'd know that there is stuff called art and it'll freeze
your guts, and there's other stuff, mostly not called art,
that'll melt you down and pour you into a new mold. And then
there's scholarship, which is used for self-protection. And there
are—I'm afraid I have to admit I've seen them—a few men
around here who do things with their minds you wish you could
do yourself. *(There's a pause. He's embarrassed by his last point.
He flares up again.)* I mean culture with a capital K is the killer
and you don't know it. I mean, well, I've already said more—
But you take the intellectualistic analysis of art— I mean you

ask the university to load everything with so much mental freight that everybody gets run down by it. It's only a question of waking up here and now, that's all. The real things all around us: see that mike, look at that beard, and dig those poles in the yard outside. *(Everybody laughs politely at the reference to the delightful colored poles planted in the college lawn.)* If the university would close all its classes and not "give all it hath to the poor" but instead spend its money on events, like you could have a Committee on Novelty instead of a Committee of the Council, and that committee would have to turn up an original event every day or it'd be kicked out. The Living Theatre as a repertory company, concerts by John Cage or whoever is newer, exhibits by Henry Wallenstein, séances and happenings by continuous ad hoc curriculum committees. You could—

(But he pauses, and finally subsides into dreamy, inarticulate gurgles. The other three are deeply offended and start up in chorus: "But that's—" And then there's more silence.)

Goodman (finally): That's sheer self-indulgence and irrelevancy (except maybe for the Living Theatre). More fun and games but of a different kind, while the war and the starving go on. Why is your kind of fun through formlessness and novelty any more important or any less self-indulgent than Artsman's artistic fun through beautiful forms? The world burns, and all three of you titillate your precious souls.

Feeler: Yeah, well, you can all talk better than I can. Like I— I get distracted from your linearities to other things. You know, seeing that groovy, wobbly shimmer of that fluorescent light there and somebody cooking something good next door, smell it? But I'm right, I know I'm right. Nobody has to argue about that. I got more soul in my left nostril than you got in your whole body, in bed or upright. I mean like, sex, but I've said too much. But just one thing: you're not really fooling anybody with all that bullshit. If you two *(looking at Artsman and Bookmaker),* if you two were in the right orbit, you could just shut up and float down loose. And if you *(turning on Goodman)* think the world will cure itself without the people being cured first, you're having your own kind of seizures. I'm leaving. Just don't use up all the flowers for firewood, that's all I ask.

(He goes out, a rough beast slouching toward Bethlehem to be born. And there is silence.)

Goodman (rousing himself): I'm going to have to hurry on out after him; he'll have the whole chapter high, confused, and incompetent within ten minutes. But before I go, I want to make my position clear. I'm not saying that universities in all ages have to give up pure art and pure scholarship in the service of politicial and social reform, but there are times when things get so bad that everybody oughta stop and make them better before he has any right to do anything else. In a just world, I guess it would not be wicked to hold a festival of the arts. In *this* one, to play with artistic amenities is like playing in a ballroom orchestra on the Titanic, to soothe the passengers while it sinks beneath them. Except this is worse because on the Titanic the musicians couldn't do anything to prevent the sinking. But here everybody *could* put down his instruments and move to where the action is. I'm leaving you to your toys for now, but if you go on playing long enough, you'll find either that the university will change itself and drive you out into the streets where you belong, or that it will be destroyed as utterly irrelevant.

(He strides out, anger exuding from every pore. There is a long silence.)

Bookmaker: I've never felt so depressed about the future of genuine learning as I feel today. I'm not thinking mainly of Feeler's and Goodman's attack or even of the recent direct assaults on learning that some of his associates have carried out, like the suggestion last year by a member of SDS that the Rare Book Room be burned or the recent removal of some cards from the card catalogue to push unpopular books down the memory chute. What depresses me most is you, Artsman, and your casual assault on learning in the name of creativity. If you, who honor much of what the university honors, cannot see either the essential creativity of good scholarship or the way in which the arts are dependent on the kinds of feeding they can only receive from the intellect, then who will defend us?

Artsman: Well, you deserve to feel threatened; you've sat far too long on your traditions—to put it politely—there in your ivory tower, surrounded by your books and laboratories, and in fact feeding off the creative minds of the world. Shakespeare writes his plays, and generations of you guys make your livelihood by turning him into fodder for books and lectures. An Einstein, a Marx, a Freud, a Stravinsky does his creative work and you turn him into grist for your mills. All I'm saying is that it's past time that the universities transform themselves into the places of grace and beauty they could so easily become.

Bookmaker: But why must everything be laid at the door of the university? Why should universities, already failing to train people to think, be required to take on the task traditionally assigned to government and social agencies, as Goodman would require, or to patrons and city councils, as *you* would?

Artsman: Why not? If no one else is willing or able, and the universities *are* able, they should certainly be willing. Why must we be satisfied with the traditional narrow view of a university based on a Cartesian image of man's disembodied intellect, operating in a depersonalized, value-freed, pseudo-objective vacuum?

Bookmaker: Now wait! You're cheating, you're ranting, you're—

Artsman: I'm not cheating. Anyone who thinks about the question at all must recognize that the thoughts of emotionally and artistically deprived men are dry and fruitless thoughts. A university of deprived faculty and students will produce a scholarship that's lifeless when it's not positively destructive. Just look at our daily lives here in Chicago: breathing bad air, meeting in gray and dirty buildings, in rooms with unadorned walls. Why, any tenth-rate college in this country'd be ashamed to ask its faculty and students to work in quarters as ugly and unadorned as Wieboldt and Classics. And look at how the arts are housed. Have you ever visited the Midway Studio that you talk about? Have you ever *looked* at Lexington Hall where the music department is? How can any university expect its citizens to treat each other with grace and sweet reasonableness when it treats the arts like this?

Bookmaker: I'm glad you mentioned those tenth-rate colleges. Whenever anybody wants to beat up on Chicago, he does so by saying that Purdue has a better Student Union, and Indiana has a school of grand opera. The line goes, "Why even at Surrogate University they have . . ." and then fill in the blank. It never seems to occur to anybody that one reason we're not tenth-rate intellectually is that we're willing to be tenth-rate in most other matters, ranging from football to festivals of the arts. *(Pause.)* But I must leave, to go to the faculty meeting and try to follow the non sequiturs committed by my colleagues. Even they can't think straight anymore, you know. *(Pause.)* My *main* point is this: your conception, both of the nature and value of scholarship and the seriousness of the threat to its survival, is entirely inadequate. A university that devotes itself to scholarship, in the highest sense, and obviously I'm not defending scholarship in anything less than the highest sense, is the last refuge of the probing mind in this uncritical world. Man is everywhere threatened by intellectual chaos, by absurd abysses, and by nameless voids. The true scholar grapples with the void, discerns shapes in it, wrestles with them, tames them, and gives them names. The simple and profound act of critical understanding is one of man's greatest achievements. Some would say it is his greatest. We don't need to agree with them; we could admit that the peaks of art and literature are as important as the peaks of philosophy and criticism and science, and still recognize that the essential shaping action of the mind as it works on recalcitrant experience is in itself a great creative thing, comparable in its mysteries and in its beauties to the mysteries and beauties of the purest art. And this kind of creation, perhaps more accurately called discovery, has only one home—the university. If you destroy that home in the name of organizing departments of music and art, already with us, or departments of cinematography or video-grammar, no doubt just around the corner, you'll find that the arts you think you have built a home for will be finally homeless too. Look at the kind of degradation of art that Feeler would put in art's place, with all of his honest passion and foolish theories. He'll replace you, too, mark my words, once you've removed mind from the center of the university. The arts can't thrive without criticism, and the critical, the judging mind has left to it in our society only one home, and that home is threatened from all sides. Think on it; think on it well.

(He stands, assumes a meditative pose, and walks slowly and a bit portentously out of the room. Long, long silence.)

Artsman: Now I am alone. What shall I say? They all had it wrong, even Bookmaker—*especially* Bookmaker. What really saves us from the void is the capacity to make forms, to make order where all was chaos and dark night. The only scholars worth defending are, in fact, artists in this sense. Regardless of their subject matters, they're the men who have experienced or created beauty and who can then write about that experience in forms that are themselves beautiful creations. The mathematician, the physicist, what do they write except poems—that is, forms expressing their vision of order wrung from seeming chaos? The true mathematician, the true physicist, that is. What the university can't live without is those who love what they do and say, and there can be no love except in the presence of beauty. I wish I could've made him see that I really agree with him about the value of scholarship, *when it becomes art,* when it's done as it must be done for the love of the thing, and not either for the sake of abstractions of the kind he utters or for the practical improvements Goodman requires, or for the thrills that Feeler places first. Things do look dark outside. To preserve a clean, well-lighted place seems to Feeler too easy, to Goodman a selfish travesty, to Bookmaker a matter for abstract intellect, with art used as, at best, a pleasant handmaiden. Maybe if I can talk with Bookmaker again I can get him to see that a festival of the arts is indeed properly at home even in the house of intellect.

THE POWER TO BE
A UNIVERSITY

There's an old game which some of you may have played called conjugation of adjectives. It goes something like this: I am firm; you are obstinate; he's pigheaded. I'm neat; you, my friend, are fussy; he, my enemy, is compulsive about germs. I'm scholarly; you're pedantic, he's dry-as-dust. I'm flexible; you're flabby; he's wishy-washy. I'm bold; you're a bit pushy; he's got his nerve; and so on. I've noticed that it is a game frequently played in talk about power and politics on campus. *My* side shows shrewd tactics; *your* side sometimes cuts corners a bit; my *enemies* are unscrupulous. My side adapts its rhetoric to the needs of the audience; you cannot quite be relied on to tell the same story twice; my enemy is a damned liar. As dean, I have sometimes had to exercise with discretion my legitimate authority; some of my fellow deans, I regret to say, enjoyed throwing their weight around too much; and some people I know are just plain bullies.

But even if we stop kidding and take a serious look at the word power, we find that it means many different things, and

A lecture originally delivered at a conference of Danforth Associates and students at the University of Chicago, August 1969.

before we ask how a power structure works or should work, we ought first to have some idea of what we are talking about. I don't need to tell you that many people these days are using the word loosely—the powers that be, the power elite, the sources of power. "The power of the university is finally the power to use the state's violence against students," I read in a recent journal. "What is your position on student power?" a student reporter asked me. And when I say that I am both for it and against it, depending on what it is, the reporter gives me that sneer that student reporters reserve for deans when they think we're protecting ourselves by equivocation.

But it's no equivocation to say what everybody ought to know: if power is the capacity to effect changes in the world outside ourselves, power within a university is many different things, as many as there are different ways of effecting changes in other men's minds or deeds. Hannah Arendt wrote a splendid essay last year, delivered first to one of our freshman courses, in which she distinguished true power from violence, violence being the kind of ersatz power one turns to when the true power of legitimate authority has broken down.[1] I think we need many more such distinctions if we are going to talk together meaningfully about such a word as power, and I hope it won't seem too pedantic of me, merely "scholarly," if I spend a few moments on them before turning to the college scene. Of course I'll really be dwelling on that scene surreptitiously all the while.

Although one could easily make a long list of ways we can

1. The complexities of our situation, both in terms of our rhetoric and our use of power, are shown nicely by the conflicting interpretations that have been given to Miss Arendt's speech. I heard it as *primarily* an effort to educate young extremists about the dangers of resorting to violence against the "powers" in the university; secondarily a warning to the powers about looking to their legitimacy. A student activist tells me now that he heard it as unequivocally directed as a warning to those in power about the ways in which they are squandering their legitimacy—and he claims to have Miss Arendt's agreement with his interpretation! Fortunately my use of her distinction between power and violence is not invalidated on either reading, but it is disconcerting to know that the same speech could be taken in opposing senses by two members of the same university, each of whom prides himself on being rather careful in his interpretations!

change the world or get other men to work for change, I find
that most of them fall clearly under a three-fold division: force,
influence, and persuasion. There is first the way of force, the
essence of which is either harm to others or a threat to harm
them, and the effect of which is always that the man who changes
his words or deeds does so against his own true convictions. We
all know the old saying, "The man convinced against his will
is of the same opinion still," and of course such a man will
revert to his original beliefs and behavior just as soon as the
threat of harm is removed. The most obvious forms of force on
our campuses these days are the sit-ins and the guns and the
billy clubs. But the students quite rightly remind us that other
forms have not been totally absent in the past. Although I
wouldn't, as some students would, deny the difference between
physical force and mental or spiritual force—there is an important line there—I think the students are quite justified in
reminding us of how threats of harm of various kinds can be
used and too often have been used in the running of classes and
the settling of academic disputes. The professor who uses the
threat of a bad grade as his chief pedagogical device, the professor who threatens to leave the university if his chairman
doesn't do what he asks, the dean or president or board that
adjusts salaries according to political loyalties, the student who
threatens to take his case to the provost or to the SDS chapter,
all these and many others are playing the same game as the
political activists who said this year to our president, "Either
you rehire Marlene Dixon to the sociology department, or we'll
stage a sit-in." I cannot take time here to discuss the problem
of ends and means that their threat of force raised. The president *didn't have the power* to hire Marlene Dixon to the sociology department, and I am quite sure that some of the people
who issued that ultimatum, though by no means all, *knew* that
the president didn't have that power; one had to wonder
whether they were really working for the announced end or
whether they specifically wanted to be able to put us in a spot
where we couldn't move and there would thus have to be some
kind of demonstration. (That's my first nonobjective, personal
remark; there will no doubt be others later.)

There are clearly degrees of community acceptance of various levels of threat and harm. I'll try to show later that there is also a great difference between a threat administered by someone with "legitimate authority"—the very phrase that is questioned by so many people these days—and a threat by someone who is usurping authority. These differences, denied by many, are terribly important, but they don't obscure the fact that "formally" the mode of enforcement, if it can be called that, is exactly the same whether it's "Do what I say or I'll give you an F in my course" or "Do what I say or I'll kill you" or "Do what I say or I'll withdraw your tax money or my annual gift" or "Do what we say or we'll expel you." In form, I think, they are all alike, though there are great differences otherwise. All of them work directly to change a man's action without changing his mind, without changing his belief about how he ought to act, and all of them are thus, whether legitimate or not, properly felt by what we usually call the victim as a violation of rights. He may or may not be right, but it feels that way to him.

A second kind of power available to those who govern might be called influence. I'm a little uncomfortable about some of the connotations of that word. I don't have a good word for it, but I am thinking of the kind of influence that some men carry quite independently of what they may say in arguing for or against a particular decision, and quite independently of whether there is power available of the first kind. The weight of respect or love that they have earned over the months or years carries into the present situation *for* them and *on* those around them and thus influences the outcome, sometimes even if their present arguments are weak. I think of one member of our faculty, a man who has never had any position of so-called power; he would never accept an administrative position or be offered one—it would be foolish to offer him a job as dean for reasons I won't go into. He is simply a professor and scholar. Nobody ever *has* to consult him about anything. He is not in the line of channels anywhere and, what's more, he is so deeply wedded to Chicago that there is never any threat about his leaving if he doesn't get his way; he never would think of saying, "Do it my way or I'll go somewhere else." And we wouldn't believe him if he did. Yet, again and again, I've noted that presidents, provosts, and deans call him to ask his opinion before they act. To be able to say in an argument that "X thinks I am right" carries great weight—not *decisive* weight; not enough, usually, to settle the matter, but enough to make a difference. Everybody knows that he is a "power" on the scene, an influence to be reckoned with, and he is that because people love and respect him.

Just as there are degrees of badness and goodness in the first kind, ranging all the way from armed assault to the threat of arrest if you go through a traffic light, so there are degrees here. The corrupted version of influence is revealed in the old phrase, "It doesn't matter what you know; it only matters who you know," or in the phrase "influence peddling." I'm sometimes amused—if you will allow some more biased commentary by the way—to see how easily members of the new left can have their minds changed if they are told that such-and-such a campus hero has said this or that; the hero shifts, of course, from month to month. I am equally amused—and here I am balancing my bias, you see—to note how some faculty members can do backflops if they hear that this or that leader has spoken; it is quite clear that they haven't the slightest fear of harm to themselves if they disagree; it is simply that they are ready to be influenced, not to say seduced, by the first words that come from the right man's mouth.

Though I think my amusement is sometimes justified, it remains true that no one can avoid depending to some degree on the influence of those he respects. Lord David Cecil once said that if Tolstoy disapproved of something he did, he wouldn't lose a single night's sleep over it, but if Jane Austen disapproved of him, he wouldn't sleep for weeks and weeks. We all have—or ought to have—moral heroes whose mere judgment, without the reasons given, will cause us this kind of uneasiness. And we all know other people who seem to be equally intelligent, equally good men, who somehow don't carry that kind of influence. Every really successful campus leader, from student body president through dean of students to university president, somehow manages to build for himself sufficient respect concerning his past behavior to earn the right to influence any present or future crisis. He must do so, because he is not going to have time to give all the arguments. Any leader must have enough credit to allow him to act in a crisis without having to go back over all of the reasons with every person for whom he acts. Needless to say, in America these days we suffer, as several of our speakers have already said, from a great dearth of leaders in this sense—like the man in the *New Yorker* cartoon who said, "Of course, I don't trust anybody under 30; I don't trust anybody *over* 30 either." But in spite of growing mistrust, influence does still work. We see it operating every day.

The third kind of power is the power of persuasion. If I have no power to harm you or if I refuse to threaten to harm you, and if your respect or love for me will not influence you to do as I say, then I must persuade you with reasons or with emotional appeals. Here again there are important distinctions to be made—between honest and dishonest forms of persuasion, and between the man who persuades me to do something good for me and the man who persuades me to do something bad for me and good for him. But in spite of these differences, persuasion is the mode that we all most often praise or at least give lip service to. I have heard or read hundreds of statements in the last year saying that reason is the proper arbiter in university affairs; I've even written some of them myself. Students read these statements by faculty members, and since they know of many instances in which issues have been settled by the exercise of the other two kinds of power, they accuse the faculty of hypocrisy. Faculty hear the same kind of statement by administrators; they too laugh up their sleeves. Yet in spite of the fact that we often fail to practice our beliefs, most of us do believe that the proper governance of the university, old or new, ought somehow to be based on reasoning together, on talking together, on working things out. We may or may not embrace the democratic model of "one man, one vote" as the proper way to record and implement the results of our reasoning together, but most faculty, students, and administrators (the exceptions are, I think, mostly very recent and very few) would still claim that reasoning together is the way we *ought* to run our institutional lives.

This near unanimity is really sort of surprising, especially in an age when many claim that there is no consensus about values and that we have nothing but incongruence and conflict in our lives. But if we all believe in it, why is it that most of us, most of the time, seem to be disappointed by failure to live up to it? What is the source of the fantastic wave of mistrust and disillusionment that has swept not only our students but our faculties as well?

Without pretending to answer fully such a complicated question—obviously there are many causes that go into a thing of this kind—I think we can see part of the answer by turning to a term I have so far avoided, namely *authority*. For some people these days, authority is a swear word; for others it is an appeal against the hordes of barbarians at the gates. In actual practice, I would say that most exercises of power of all three kinds, no matter who does the exercising, make some sort of explicit claim to authority, either legitimate because established, traditional—"this is the way we've always done it" or "this is the way our constitution reads" or "this is the way the faculty council works"—or legitimate because morally superior to the old ways, *legitimated* by a superior conscience or a superior sense of justice or whatever. The professor threatening to fail a student or requiring him to do a doctoral dissertation that serves the professor's ends and not the student's own (and I know of some specific cases of that; I am sure there are a lot of exaggerations about it, but it is not just a myth) wields his threat of harm in the name of an authority conferred upon him by the university. The committee or dean who tells the young man either to shape up or ship out speaks again in the name of the authority of the university. The students who occupy a building claim the authority of a superior morality or sense of justice, and they usually try for a further legitimacy through a democratic vote. The faculty committee that expels students does so in the name of legitimacy established in their eyes by tradition, law, and a reasonable moral code.

Once we begin to think about that word "authority" we can see that one mark of our present difficulties is the near collapse of the whole notion of *any* kind of authority that can be conferred on *anybody*. Nobody, it seems, can legitimately speak or act for anybody else. More and more faculty and students are making the claim that every man must be in on every decision about anything that concerns his life. The students write into their codes that no student shall be held for any rule or regulation that students have not made. In some codes it is even written that a student cannot be held to any code that he has not himself participated in making. I had an experience this winter with a negotiating committee for a sit-in who came to us with a set of formal demands which they announced were nonnegotiable. As we began to talk about some aspects of them, I could tell they didn't believe in their own nonnegotiable demands and that we were really surprisingly close to agreement. After we had talked for awhile, they caucused briefly and came back to say, "We can't talk like this; we have got to go back to our constituency and get further orders" (they didn't use the word orders, but that is what they meant). They were not *authorities* even though they had been elected.

Similarly faculty members automatically deny to their administrators any right to make decisions and implement them. "Nobody asked *me* about it" is the refrain on every campus. "*You* made the decision, now *you* carry it out." I found recently that the same mistrust extends to elected or appointed faculty or faculty-student committees. Once elected, they are immediately mistrusted. It was taken as simply antidemocratic to say, as I tried to say about a committee that had worked months on a problem, that they should now be granted the authority of experts because by studying the problem longer than anybody else they now knew more about it than any of us. "I was not consulted, and therefore the decision doesn't bind me." Our own elected faculty council has suffered the same fate: "It's true that we elected them, but that gives them no right to make decisions for us." I have also found, I think increasingly over recent years (and I am now getting old enough so that I can say that with some dignity) that the loyalty of committee members to their own committee has diminished. When I first began teaching, a committee would work on a problem, come to a decision, and then go before the faculty with confidence that all committee members would defend their decision. Now, generally speaking, at least half of the committee members will pretend they had nothing to do with it and also claim they never got most of the memos anyway. I don't have to tell you that student organizations, both local student governments and national bodies, are having exactly the same trouble; they simply cannot find representative persons for themselves. For ten years now, every student government at Chicago, indeed every student government *official* at Chicago, has been rendered ineffectual by student mistrust. The mere fact of being chosen seems to taint them very quickly; within a month or two in office, they are rendered suspect and are off by themselves; some of them have become very lonely people.

This crisis of authority may not be the deepest crisis we face in our society, but it is surely one of the most troublesome to deal with, especially in light of our democratic traditions and the new developments given them by the rise of "participatory democracy." If men who believe in democracy cease to believe in the process of representation, they are, I believe, doomed ultimately to fall into either anarchy or tyranny. (Plato has some good stuff on that.) And we seem to be more and more victimized by especially vicious forms of so-called democratic beliefs, particularly the notion that authority is required only where men are *evil* and must be controlled for their own good: the honest of heart and the clear of mind don't need to delegate authority to anybody. If we were all as pure as we ought to be, we would need no authorities. After all, if we only stripped the corruptions produced in us by modern civilization, wouldn't we find in all of us a natural capacity for love and generosity that would require no institutional control and hence no institutional hierarchies or authority?

Well, leaving aside the theological difficulties in such a picture of man's pre-Adamic glory, I think it can be shown that even if we *were* all good, we would still need to delegate authority in order to work out our corporate good together. In a recent article on authority, Father Buckley, one of the few people who has spent some time thinking about it, reminds us that the Utopian rejection of authority is not new. "In the Middle Ages

a classical conflict was waged, framed in one of the questions to
which Simon adverts [in *Philosophy of Democratic Government*]: 'Whether man in the state of innocence would be under
human authority' "—an old fashioned formulation of exactly
our problem. "The Augustinian answer to this," Buckley goes
on, "was No, that human authority only arose because man was
evil or deficient, and that the function of authority was either to
correct the evil through coercion or to remedy the deficiency
through instruction and care. Aquinas differed with Augustine
here. . . . There is indeed this remedial function of authority,
. . . [but] authority has essential as well as accidental uses. Even
among the mature, the developed, and the virtuous—even
among Angels—authority is needed to achieve united action.
Any society is faced with a number of variant possibilities to
accomplish its end. . . . Granted that some of these possibilities
may equally accomplish the desired good, a decision must be
made among them if the society is to move. Granted that there
are several ways to get to a fire, the fire department must decide
upon one in order to get there at all. . . . The most essential task
of authority is [thus] to understand the common good and, as a
consequence, to coordinate the activities of the society so that
this good [can] be obtained which is, indeed, the realization of
the freedom of the members" of that group to act as a group.
The group simply is not free to act as a group unless it is organized in such a way as to be able to act. "Authority then, is, the
instrument—the indispensable instrument—of freedom, and if
authority is destroyed or its practice made impossible, the
society is no longer free, [because it is] unable to determine
itself. [An individual] man is enslaved who cannot choose because he is too torn apart by internal disorder, unresolved conflicts, pathologically dominant passions, and clashing intentions. So a society is simply not free when anarchy, injustice,
illiberality, or party passions have destroyed its ability to choose
operational patterns and to obtain its determined purpose,
whether that society be a university, a family, or a body politic."

Father Buckley goes on to quote Walter Lippmann to the
effect that failures of authority are especially likely in democratic societies. "With exceptions so rare that they are regarded

as miracles and freaks of nature, successful democratic politicians" (and I suppose that there is no question in anybody's mind that deans and presidents have to be politicians to some degree) "are insecure and intimidated men. They advance politically only as they placate, appease, bribe, seduce, bamboozle, or otherwise manage to manipulate the demanding and threatening elements in their constituencies. . . . Politicians rationalize this servitude by saying that in a democracy public men are the servants of the people. This devitalization of the governing power is the malady of democratic states. As the malady grows, the executive become highly susceptible to encroachment and usurpation by elected assemblies; they are pressed and harassed by the haggling of parties, by the agents of organized interests, and by the spokesmen of sectarians and idealogues. The malady can be fatal. It can be deadly to the very survival of the state as a free society if, when the great and hard issues of war and peace, of security and solvency, of revolution and order are up for decision, the executive and judicial departments, with their civil servants and technicians, have lost their power to decide." He wasn't writing about universities—in fact he wrote this before anyone suspected that this would be a problem in universities to the degree it is—but I think we can translate university issues immediately into his terms. A similar list of "great and hard issues" could be constructed for almost any one of our universities or colleges, and I think that these days it would be a rare president or dean who could honestly claim that he has not, at least to some degree, lost the power to decide. Whatever the process of selection that chose him, he has not been granted by his constituents the authority to govern.

Where does authority come from? Where *could* it come from? How does one earn it? How does society recover the processes of delegated responsibility once they have been lost? All three of the modes of governing, force, influence, and rational discussion, require legitimate authority if they are to work properly, and this means that the authority must be accepted as legitimate by those over whom it is exercised. But what *is* the legitimate authority of a college administration or faculty in a time when men are widely questioning the validity of *any* authority?

Tonight is hardly the occasion to run through the possible sources of governing authority, searching desperately for one that might work for us in this century. Even if this were the time or place, I don't feel myself qualified to do the kind of professional job that is needed—and I think it might very well call for a professional job, the job of somebody who had thought longer about it than I have done in preparing this talk. Such a discussion would have to begin with tracing the way in which each successive idea of authority has broken down over the last three centuries. First, the doctrine of divine right or delegation (which by the way I don't even find mentioned in the most recent edition of the *Encyclopaedia Britannica* as one of the possible modes of authority, so outmoded is the notion of divine delegation of authority); then the doctrine of the organic society in which each part receives its greatest good from the organic health of the whole; then Rousseau's notion of the general will granting to the leader the right to know better than the follower what is good for him (sounds bad, but if you think about it, that is really what good universities claim for themselves: that the leaders of the university, namely the faculty, know better than the followers, the students, what is good for them educationally); then the rise from this of various democratic and liberal doctrines in which the voice of the populace replaces the voice of God or the general will, or in which was developed the notion of the rule of law rather than the rule of men.

What's important at this moment, perhaps more than ever before in the history of the West, is that many young people are denying the legitimacy of all authority except that of the *individual* will, the individual impulse. Some go one step further and refuse to let the individual of *today* legislate for the same person's individual will tomorrow for fear the will may change by then. At such a time we're forced as never before to look at our own first principles in the hope that if we push ourselves hard enough about them, they may turn out to be acceptable to other men, *if* we really get to the first ones and not the second and the third. Here I must take a moment to say how misguided is the reaction of some well-meaning persons who are trying to entrench themselves against the barbarian hordes when they decide that communication with those hordes as they see them is flatly impossible. Listen just a moment to the "Report on Academic Alienation: An Outline of the Problem and Relevant Action" by three members of the National Council of Scholars, a group of new conservatives dedicated to thinking through and combating the errors lying back of our present academic mess. "An attempt to enter into a dialogue with the ideologically alienated should be avoided. There is no basis for a rational discussion with them since they have opted for a world of their own making and removed themselves from ours, so that meanings are not the same to them as to us, and their words conform to the laws of struggle rather than to those of discourse. The mere appearance of dialogue will only provide the activists with a disguise that is useful to them in obtaining the support of non-alienated or nonideological followers." Now I have to admit that as an ex-dean I understand the source and ground for this attitude. I've been bit many a time by someone asking for a "dialogue" only to discover that what he wanted was only evidence that I wouldn't listen to him, since *after* the dialogue I wouldn't come to full agreement with him. But I think it is dreadful to respond to such experiences, no matter how often they happen, in what amounts to the same spirit. "There is no use talking to you because you are unreachable." Even if we are bitten seven times seven we must bounce back and try again to probe beyond what Paul Saltman calls the "license plate slogan level" and get to possible bases for honest and clear discourse. Because, you see, the only other alternatives are the use of influence (of which we ain't got none) and force, the use of which corrupts the university, changing it into something else. I won't say that we'll never need to use force in the years immediately ahead, against students, against each other, or against raiders from outside the campus. The latter has already happened at Chicago: we had a little raid from—well, we never did find out if they were telling the truth when they said they were John Birchers or Minutemen, last year; obviously when they came in force, they had to be met with force, but I will say that the use of force against those who don't recognize the legitimacy of the authority of those who use it is not the mark of a university, but the mark of something else—a civil society perhaps, but certainly not a university.

Is it possible to find, by thought, by discussion, by meditation, by prayer, a set of principles and practices that might legitimate what a university does with each of its three kinds of power? At commencement time, our president says to the students, "By the authority vested in me by the Board of Trustees and the State of Illinois, I confer upon you. . . ." Well, if I read the situation right, fewer and fewer of the students and faculty see any meaning in that formula whatever; the fact was dramatized for us this year when the faculty, by the authority vested in them by the Board of Trustees and the State of Illinois, expelled some three-score students. I have talked with many students about that action and I can remember only two out of several dozen who would even agree that the faculty has the authority of expulsion, let alone that the authority was exercised properly in this case. To them it was a case of raw illegitimate force. To me, it was a case of legitimate force, nonviolent but still force, into the use of which the university had itself been forced, thereby becoming temporarily less of a university but necessarily so once the thing got started. When I pressed my conversations with the distressed students, themselves not expelled but bitter because the university had, as they saw it, betrayed their peers, I found a surprising agreement with them at one point. What would make a university justified in such an exercise of authority, they said, would be if it were *really* serving truth and justice as it *pretends* to be but is not, and if the expelled students had been *really* threatening the service of truth and justice. An institution and its officers earn their authority, we all agreed, by serving genuine values. But again and again I heard the refrain, "That doesn't go for this university; it's hypocritical; it professes to serve truth; it really serves the self-advancement of the faculty and the Pentagon." Or, "You pretend to believe in reason but you use force whenever you think it's required. As Paul Goodman says, 'Students are the most exploited slave class in the modern world.'" "What would you say about the expulsions," I asked in one of these conversations, "if the university were in your view really living up to its ideals? If the sit-in had disrupted what *you* consider an ideal university, would you think

the disrupters should be punished and that there was any authority who would have the right to do so?" The answer, I think,
was significant. "Yes, but that wouldn't happen, because if the
university *were* doing that, there wouldn't be a sit-in."

Well, I couldn't be quite so hopeful about that last point.
I've seen some young people lately who think that what they
want to do is disrupt at all costs, and I don't think that they
would be stopped, some of them, even by an ideal university.
But it was clear that at least for the students I was talking with
—and I am sure they are far more representative than the few
who are out to destroy—we had found a common basis for exploration of the problem of authority; authority for them and
for me comes to any institution in its service of the common
good, the good proper to the particular ends of that institution.

I was so encouraged by this agreement that I tried to move
further to show them why I felt that this particular university,
on balance and with all of its faults counted up, was really
serving education in a surprisingly effective way. Improvements
were needed; but surely, I said, you would agree that education
of inestimable value does take place here and that we ought to
preserve what is good while trying for the better. As you might
predict, the dialogue broke down at this point, or at least the
agreement did, though I would say that with some of the students it will continue; it broke down on the problem of *who
decides on the values.* Who decides what is education? In other
words, it broke down again on the question of authority, now
put in a different form. "*We* think that what this place *calls*
education is too often irrelevant, stultifying, Mickey Mouse
stuff." When I asked them where they obtained the authority
to decide on a version of education superior to that of this established institution with its traditions, how they had earned
the authority to make such a statement, they at first quoted some
authorities to me, books and articles they had read by prophets
like Paul Goodman; then they fell back on the relativism of
generations: "Our generation defines it one way; your generation defines it another. And since we're the ones who need the
education now, what right have you, what authority have you
to impose your notion of education on our generation?"

At such moments I sometimes envy the old Catholic professors who could fall back on the authority of the Church and ultimately of the good and learned Lord who surely knows, if anybody does, what true education is. But as it was, we bogged down this time, as I have bogged down so many times before, on their version of the easy relativism that is to me the chief plague of our academic lives today. I could have asserted to them, but clearly didn't have time to prove, that educational values are not all *that* shifty, that they in fact remain surprisingly constant from generation to generation. It is simply not given to each man to decide how he will be educated or whether he *is* educated. Though there must surely be many valid ways of being educated, there are many more ways of remaining hopelessly and arrogantly miseducated or uneducated, just as there are no doubt several roads to heaven but an unlimited number of roads to hell. And the individual person cannot with any kind of security judge which kind of road he is on. I remember a wonderful exchange in the *Times Literary Supplement* once between F. R. Leavis and a reviewer who had said that he had a boorish style. Leavis wrote the *Times Literary Supplement* saying, in effect: "I do not have a boorish style." And he tried to give his reasons for thinking his own style not all that bad. The reviewer replied that unfortunately for Mr. Leavis, the person who decides whether your style is boorish is the person reading you and not you yourself.

In short, whether a man is educated or not cannot be left to his own biased judgment, and whether an institution is serving true education or not is in one sense an objective matter not to be settled by the freshman who happens to come along preferring something different. Nor is it settled, of course, by a dean's declaring himself the judge. The point is that subjective preference is not the test: either education is taking place or it isn't. And in passing judgment, each man trusts, in this modern and intensified egalitarianism of ours, his own brand of miseducation. Every student thinks that he can whomp up between breakfast and his ten o'clock class a better curriculum than the prescribed one. He naturally assumes that in prescribing programs of education, nobody is an expert. We cater to his assumption, we professors, by the way we talk to him about our

mutual ignorance. It has become a national way of life to protest that no one knows any more about anything than anybody
else, except for some scientific matters in which a few know
everything and the rest of us know nothing. The mucker's pose:
"Gee, ain't we all ignorant though! Why don't you just tell me
now what you would *like* to learn because *you're* the one who
knows most about that." This pose is killing us and it will go
on killing us until we find roads to an authority that can
organize our lives, govern our universities, and teach our classes,
roads that can lead the ignorant, including ourselves, to recognize the difference between knowledge and opinion. We must
discover once again a passion for *learning*—a word which
always implies that there is a difference between knowing and
not knowing. You cannot *learn* unless there is a *truer something*
ahead of you somewhere, and the surest way not to learn is to
assume that there is nobody who can help you do it. I am not
denying that we are all ignorant mortals, but we professors
sell ourselves short when we talk of ourselves as having nothing
to teach and start taking democratic votes on what should be
learned. If we really have nothing to teach, we should take up
some other line of work. Socrates knew how to talk of his own
ignorance in such a way as to demonstrate the greater ignorance
of those around him. We might all begin in our search for lost
authority in education by rereading the Socratic *Dialogues*.

Such talk as I have been indulging in here leads inescapably
to questions about the ultimate commitment to ultimate authority. What is it that we really serve? What or who is our
supreme authority? I would submit that what has corrupted
American education and its governance in the last decades is
that in the place of God whose supreme truths men like Harper
and other founders of our universities worshipped, we have
substituted a set of lesser gods, most noticeably the shabby gods
of futurism. We worship a future that can be discovered by voting on what it should be. Universities that worship the future,
undefined, nondescript, attained through a "progress" that cannot provide the criteria for distinguishing itself from regress—
such universities cannot answer, even if given unlimited time
for discussion, the charges of those serious students who accuse

them of "serving the military-industrial complex," to use one of the slogans. They *are* serving a military-industrial complex if they allow themselves to climb onto the same spiralling escalator on which the national economy, with the GNP, climbs. Futurism has a natural appeal, since obviously we move toward the future whether we want to or not, but the gods of futurism are the gods of futility. If I seem to be speaking with undue feeling about this, it is because I have been having to think about the future a great deal lately. My son was just killed by a car a month ago, at the age of 18. I find, of course, that "the future" for him does not exist in any immediate or obvious sense, and yet in a very real sense that fact does not matter. My *grief* matters, to me, but somehow his life is fulfilled at the moment of his death, and the payoff is not to be found somewhere else. What I'm trying to say about education is similar: the payoff ought to be *now,* so that if at the moment of graduation, as I sometimes used to put it long before I had experienced this kind of personal grief, the atomic bomb were to fall and everyone were wiped out—graduated in a different sense— everybody in that convocation hall would say to himself, "That's the way I would want to have been spending my last four years; *that* was the fulfillment—the way I lived those last four years." The gods of futurism on the other hand are the gods of futility because they proclaim at such moments: the past was prelude, now the payoff will not come.

The student critique that is best is the attack on that university governance which forgets the service of human values in the present, forgets the human needs of this generation right now, this year, this month, this day, and aims the bureaucracy at both preserving itself and at building a national reputation of some kind in the future, at raising the average SAT scores of the entering students *for the future;* at increasing its Nobel prize winners *in the future.* This is a governance that cannot command the love and loyalty of either faculty or students, because when it is challenged about its gods, it can find no authoritative reasons for what it is doing, now.

On the other hand, where the students go astray is in their own brand of futurism. Children of America, they naively look to a glorious day when all of our sins will be washed away and the true university shall walk forth onto the fields of light. Like their elders they are too often willing to corrupt and sour the present in the name of an abstract dream of an impossible future, which is to say that they lack that education in history and philosophy, in religion and the arts, that could teach them about their own frailties and make them less confident about the reliability of their pure immediate impulses and ideas. If we deny them that education simply because they ask us to, that is our crime, not theirs. We keep telling ourselves that we are in a time of great crisis. Some argue that in dealing with the crisis we need only listen to the young, and they'll lead us out of it. Others retreat into unlistening and self-righteous battle for our traditions. What I am trying to say is that if we take our talk of crisis seriously, we will undertake a steady, unhurried, but radical critique of where we are, a critique that will be far more radical than anything most of the so-called radical faculty or students will be able to manage. If it is radical enough, it will take us, in our quest for a genuine authority to guide and justify our actions, to the only Author of all true authority, the Author of that single standard which should guide and which always judges our gropings in the world.

Part

IRONIES AND THE NEW SCIENCE OF IRONOLOGY

A little credulity helps one through life very smoothly.
   —Cranford

IRONIES AND THE
NEW SCIENCE OF
IRONOLOGY

As anybody once said, in a credulous age the wise man will avoid irony. It is always embarrassing and sometimes dangerous when readers take as straight what one has intended as obviously absurd. What do you do when you get a letter from the Institute for Language Research asking whether your imaginary edition of poetry using only Basic English was ever published, because they'd like to include it in their bibliography? What do you do when a colleague questions your sincerity in claiming that *Tristram Shandy* influenced Homer retroactively?

What I have done is try to "write a book" on the hermeneutics of ironic literature. It still does not get itself written; it resists. Interpretations of irony always come out so much less lively than the thing itself. And so I often find it easier to create *eirons* than to think about them. Most of these fools and knaves I leave undeveloped and unpublished (the inventor of a lead codpiece, Permotect, for the age of fallout; the PR man in the Goldwater headquarters who in his heart knew Goldwater was wrong; the autocratic dean—"A Small College But My Own"; the tyrannical president of a church-related, tidy

265

little college who faces his first rebellion in the form of a white-washed message on *his* mountain overlooking the college— "Fuck You"; the founder of Schismism—these and many others lie fallow). But about once a year I tear loose with something that really ought to be signed with a pseudonym.

This is only a roundabout way of saying that any resemblance of the first-person narrators in the following pieces to myself is purely.

FARKISM AND HYPERYORKISM

I have never tried to conceal from anyone that I come from American Fork, Utah. But I have never flaunted my origins either, and I wouldn't bother about them now if American Fork had not recently become more and more important in determining my own future, and, for all I know, the whole future of the English language.

My problem isn't a new one. I first became aware of it twenty years ago when a maiden aunt of mine, who had been spending ten years' savings on a summer in New York, came to visit us in American Fork before returning to her teaching job in Lehi, three miles closer to Salt Lake City. The first thing I noticed was that she said she had enjoyed her visit to New York very much. I had thought her visit was to New Yark, and asked her why she said it funny. She said she wasn't saying it funny, that that was the way it was supposed to be said, and that American Fark, which should be pronounced Fork, was certainly the home of more vulgar mispronunciations than any other place in the country. I was pretty sure that she was wrong. Everybody I

Reprinted with permission from *Furioso,* summer 1951.

knew said New Yark and American Fark, just as they said carn and harse. What's more, my aunt had taken several other queer stands on pronunciation even before her vacation, and I knew that if she could be as wrong-headed as she was on envelope she could be wrong on bigger matters.

There was only one thing that made me doubt. I remembered that my father had always insisted on our saying Lord instead of Lard. In fact, so many fathers in that religious town insisted on the distinction that the children actually picked it up and made it their own. When someone in Sunday School or Primary or Mutual Improvement Association would accidentally say Lard, someone else was sure to laugh and say that the *Lord* didn't like to have people talking as if they cooked with Him. Of course, this popular correction didn't change anybody's mind; we all knew that the real pronunciation was Lard and that the distinction was introduced merely as an artificial expedient for clarity and homage. Still, if the true pronunciation of such a fundamental word could be changed by popular agreement, analogy argued that Fark and Yark could be changed, too. So that I was none too sure of my position until I noticed the difficulties my aunt got into in following her new ways.

I didn't know it at the time, but her troubles all came from the fact that *all* the ahs in Farkist speech are not ohs in Yorkist. It wasn't long until she began to stumble over this basic illogicality, and once she had begun, she kept it up until she just about had to start all over again and learn the language from scratch. The first sign I had of her troubles came when she asked me to go upstairs and get her some bicorbonate. That same day she was talking to my mother about her trip, and clear in the next room I heard her say, "It looked to me like the people in New York never even thought of suppressing their cornal desires." Next thing we knew she was corving the meat and denouncing people who played cords and raving about the Bord of Avon until we all got pretty sick of it. About half the time she would catch herself and start over, getting things more or less right, but her efforts to correct her errors became more and more exhausting, to her and to everybody else. On the day before she left, she was making some pudding at the cupboard, for supper,

and she said, "Louise, where do you keep your carnstorch?"
Then she corrected it to "cornstorch" and then to "carnstarch"
and finally to "cornstarch." As I watched her fuss along helping
mother with the rest of the meal, I could see she was pretty
upset. Her lips kept moving in silent ahs and ohs, and I wasn't
surprised when she forgot what she was doing and set the pudding on the table first, completely bypassing the main part of
the meal. I snickered, and she came to.

"My goodness," she said, "there I go getting the cort before
the harse." Then she went into her little act again, trying all the
combinations and finally lighting on the Yorkist version. She
knew, of course, that all her credit with me was gone, and she
didn't try to present any last arguments for cultured speech
before she left. But if she had, I would have just felt sorry for
her. I knew that nobody anywhere else could talk the way she
had been talking, and I knew that even if anybody did, the
Farkist way was better and more consistent, and that even if it
wasn't, the attempt to change to foreign ways was silly and
dangerous.

Such a childhood conviction, arrived at through observing
the downfall of a once-respected adult, does not die easily.
When I left American Fark to seek my fortune, I took Farkism
with me wherever I went. When I was drafted into the Army,
I was as belligerent about saying Arder of the Day as the ordinary soldier was about certain more basic matters of vocabulary
and pronunciation. When I ended up at U.S. Army University
No. 1 in Shrivenham, England, I was as careful to maintain myself as the right sart as the officers and gentlemen were to maintain other kinds of status. Even when I got discharged and went
to the University of Chicago, where everyone is a little self-
conscious about not being Harvard, I clung to Farkism as if it
were my last support in a world gone Eastern. Indeed, it was
only with my employment by a Little College in The East that
my defenses began to fall. For the first time in my life, pro-
tective coloration became a necessity rather than a luxury.
"New Yark" was as dangerous socially here as "American Fork"
would have been in American Fark. In short, there was nothing
to do but to forget my aunt, whom I now for the first time began

to think of as my awnt, and retreat judiciously into conformity.

As you would expect, I was no more fortunate than she had been. Like her, I began by changing ah's that really *were* ahs into ohs. It was all very well for my good friend Jarge to become my cultivated friend George. But at the same time my friend Martin became Mortin, somewhat less willingly. Before long, everything was confused. I contributed to the Hort Foundation; I accepted a port in the faculty play; I approached words like fort and forte with increasing apprehension.

And then the metathesis began. I should perhaps have remembered my aunt and taken alarm when, in the 1950 campaign, I asked someone to tell me about a certain dork harse candidate. But I ignored what was happening until it was too late: I found myself metathesizing consistently. Whenever an oh could be felt approaching, however far in the distance, the sphincter muscles would begin to work, and any ah coming along would automatically take its place. I caught myself looking in the phone book under the Co's for the Cornegie Carporation. I invited a friend to eat at Harn and Hordart's. I advised another friend to swear off John Borleycarn and still another, a man who had worked up an excellent rhythm act with false teeth and an amplifier, to go on a bornstarming tour—

You may wonder why I did not retreat, at this point, to out-and-out Farkism and let myself be written down, or off, as a character. As a matter of fact, I tried, but Farkism had itself become unnatural to me by this time, and it came from my lips as affectedly as Yorkism. Trying to go back merely made me more incapable of remembering how an oh or an ah should be pronounced; I found myself more and more frequently ending an attempted statement completely inarticulately, trailing off into a series of ahs and ohs—more like the grunts of a beast than the noble speech of man—as I sought in my mind for a memory that was no longer there.

The crisis came last week when I was talking with the wife of a member of the board of trustees, at a faculty tea. Aware that under such stresses I was especially likely to transgress, I had what I considered a tight hold on my sphincters. But the conversation swung to music, and I began to air my theory of the modes of musical influence. I was making, I felt, quite an impression, but I got overconfident and tried a sequence that should never have been tried.

"All this becomes clear," I said, "if we look at the influence of Thomas Marley's 'Mighty Lard of all Creation' on Mozort's 'Concerto for Harn and Archestra,' or the influence of the latter on the music of Bortak. But it is even clearer when the works are heard on the horpsichard—"

Now I knew that at least part of what I had said had been garbled, but I hadn't the slightest idea of where to begin my corrections, and I knew that in correcting I would make other errors. So I merely smiled helplessly. *She,* on the other hand, burst into deep, admiring laughter.

"But you're so clever," she said. "Do it some more."

It took me a moment to see what had happened. But in that moment, I became a new man. Do it some more I did, and needless to say I have been a tremendous social success ever since. How long this can be expected to last I don't know. But unlike my aunt, who, I forgot to tell you, ended in a sanitorium, I have always made it a cardinal point not to tarment myself with worrying about things that are beyond my control.

THOMAS MANN AND EIGHTEENTH-CENTURY COMIC FICTION

All my life I have been extremely careful to avoid the pitfalls into which I have observed my associates falling. I perhaps need offer no more compelling evidence of this care than the procedure I followed when I came to write my Ph.D. dissertation. All around me I saw graduate students getting into difficulties with their dissertations. Some of them were choosing authors whom everyone knew to be insignificant, and were trying their best, against all odds, to make them seem significant. Others were choosing authors whom everyone recognized to be great—I mention only Shakespeare—and were trying to find something fresh to be said on a subject already exhausted. I of course took the middle path: I chose to write on a figure who was unquestionably the greatest in his genre, but who had never been given his full measure of praise. The choice made, I then carefully avoided other pitfalls: I did not try to treat my man exhaustively, or even originally, as some of my more reckless companions were attempting to do with their men. Rather I limited myself to what my thesis chairman liked to call a "negotiable

Reprinted with permission from *Furioso,* winter 1951.

scope." Though it was clear to me that *Tristram Shandy* was the greatest novel ever written, I did not try to establish that point —a task that could easily have taken a full year to complete. Instead, I made a simple and cogent study of Laurence Sterne's journey to Toulouse (via Auxerre, Lyons, Avignon, and Montpellier) during the winter of 1763.[1] I did not even try to establish that this period was the turning point in Sterne's career; I was content to show—and no one has as yet seen fit to attempt a refutation—that this visit is reflected quite clearly in *Tristram Shandy*, volume III, chapter 27, and again, though perhaps less clearly, in volume VIII, chapter 30. As a result of this modesty —I might even say integrity—of aims, I finished my degree before any one of my contemporaries in the English department, except my close friend who, sacrificing quality to speed, was content to do a study of the critical reputation of Beroalde de Verville in America during the nineteenth century. Since no one in America had ever mentioned this follower of Rabelais until twentieth-century scholars noticed him apropos *Tristram Shandy*, my friend's conclusions were largely negative, and the whole job took him just under three months, two of which were spent in supervising the typing and proofreading.

I mention all this to make credible what I can now only call my blind caution in my first productive scholarship after the degree was conferred. With my usual prudence, I had looked ahead to discover what errors my colleagues were inclined to commit in the years of work left to them when they were once free. It will be no surprise to my readers, if they are at all familiar with academic pursuits, to learn that the most frequent and fatal error was dissertation bleeding. The annals of *PMLA*[2] are filled with the names of scholars who have spent their lives developing the claims they staked with their dissertations. I perhaps need mention only Dr. F. M. Q——, who earned his degree with a study of Giles Fletcher, the younger (1588?– 1623). He of course discovered that Fletcher was much more important than anyone had before realized, since, contrary to

1. See Wilbur L. Cross, *The Life and Times of Laurence Sterne* (New York, 1929), p. 660.
2. *PMLA, Annals,* passim.

all previous opinion, he wrote two plays in addition to his poems: *Emunctories Cleanséd, A Masque,* and *In Praise of Fools,* a dramatization of Erasmus's *Encomium Moriae.* These plays, he found, were really the finest artistic flowering of Fletcher's whole period, being in reality the models aimed at (and sometimes indeed surpassed) by Shakespeare in his last period.[3] The dissertation finished and tucked away in the stacks, he began to read, for the first time in many years, literature written after 1623. He found that everybody who wrote plays after Giles Fletcher, the younger, was influenced by him much more than the scholarly world had ever suspected. He read Otway, and to him Otway seemed merely the Restoration Fletcher. He discovered that *George Barnwell, The Cenci,* Dickens and Collins's *No Thoroughfare, A Drama,* Wilde's *The Duchess of Padua: A Tragedy of the XVI Century,* and, among other modern plays, *A Streetcar Named Desire*—these and many others he found derived either their dramatic form or their more important representational devices, or, in a surprising number of cases, both, from Fletcher. He quite naturally began to write and publish essays about his discoveries, and before he was aware of what had happened, he had collected the essays, published over a twenty-year period, under the title *Giles Fletcher and his Followers: The Great Tradition.* Upon his retirement, his students and colleagues considered putting together a memorial volume of his critical essays over four decades, but they were so embarrassed by the monotony of the subject, and the monomania of its treatment, that they abandoned the project. He did not get his memorial volume!

To see this happen to only one man would have been sufficient warning to me. But to see the same kind of wasted life result for one after another of those who failed to see their man in the context of the whole made me determine to get away from Sterne the day after graduation, and to stay away. I was of course aware of a strong tradition of belief in Sterne as a powerful influence; I had read essays on "Sterne and Jean Paul," "Sterne und Goethe," "Sterne and C. M. Wieland," "Laurence

---

3. The plays were written when Fletcher was a very young man.

Sterne und Wilhelm Raahe," "Sterne et William Combe," and "Sterne and Lord Aboyne." But although some of the evidence offered in these articles, *qua* evidence, seemed quite sound, I was not in the least tempted to abandon my caution. In fact, painful as it now is to admit it, I refused to see Sterne's influence anywhere. As I began my first reading beyond 1767 in five years, I systematically blinded myself to any evidence that might have indicated that Sterne was anything more, to borrow a phrase from the great George Saintsbury, than just another one of the "four wheels of the novel wain," the other three being of course Richardson, Fielding, and Smollett.[4] When I heard of *The Life and Opinions of Miss Sukey Shandy of Bow Street, Gentlewoman, in a Series of Letters to her Dear Brother, Tristram Shandy, Gent.,* I of course recognized the similarity of the names, but I did not leap to the assumption that this was a Shandean imitation. Rather, I took pains: I obtained a photostatic copy from the British Museum. The book did indeed resemble *Tristram Shandy* rather strongly, but, incredible as it now seems, I was able to convince myself that the resemblances were really due to the author's borrowing rather heavily from authors whom Sterne had borrowed from: Beroalde de Verville, Bruscambille, and others. Similarly, I refused to believe, what everyone now accepts, that *A Supplement to the Life and Opinions of Tristram Shandy* (1761) was directly inspired by *Tristram Shandy* itself.

It should not be hard to understand that with such an attitude I was not converted easily to recognizing Sterne's true influence. It happened only gradually and would never have happened at all if I had not decided to leave the eighteenth century and, for the first time since entering graduate school, read a modern novel. In one graduate course Joyce's *Ulysses* had been praised, with a boldness not often encountered in graduate school, as a "pivotal" modern work. Since I was determined to read nothing but pivotal works, I began to read *Ulysses*.

Even then, even on first reading—even before I so much as suspected what I now know—I felt—I'm sure that I can re-

4. George Saintsbury, *The English Novel*, 1767, p. 320.

member feeling—an uneasy conviction that I was encountering echoes of Sterne. These were nothing like my earlier suspicions, so easily put down, about *Sukey Shandy* and *A Supplement to Tristram Shandy*. I *knew* I had something that I could not ignore. Joyce's deliberate attempt to maintain a consecutive story on several levels at once—the elaborate play between actual duration and poetic duration—the use of stream-of-consciousness (a term which at that time was unknown to me, although the phenomenon was clear even without a name)—all seemed—and I tremble even now to remember the confusion in my heart as I saw the dangerous and exciting new territory opening before me—all seemed fairly obvious imitations of Tristramshandeism.

Of course I was still cautious: I said nothing. Even when, with Molly's final yes, the total picture of Joyce's attempt became clear to me and I became absolutely convinced, I still demurred. I hid the book behind my five-volume illustrated set of the complete works of Bruscambille, including the "Prologue on Long Noses" mentioned by Sterne, and tried to forget. But one day as I was sitting in my office reading *Farrago,* by Pilgrim Plowden, Esquire (London, 17—), an academic friend—one of those who can never let another man's man alone—came to me with a copy of *James Joyce: Two Decades of Criticism*.

"This should interest you," he said, thrusting the book on my desk before me, opened to page twelve. It was a bit of reminiscence by Eugène Jolas:

It is not very difficult to follow a simple, chronological scheme which the critics will understand [Joyce was saying to him]. . . . But I, after all, am trying to tell the story of this Chapelizod family in a new way. . . . Only I am trying to build many planes of narrative with a single esthetic purpose. . . . Did you ever read Laurence Sterne . . . ?

I am afraid I lost my head. I plunged homeward, trying to remember what role a Chapelizod family had played in *Ulysses*. I flung the Bruscambille from the shelf, snatched down *Ulysses,* raced through it—and found nothing. I hurried back to my office, and read Jolas's passage again, finally studying the context. It was explicitly, as I should have noticed from the beginning, a reference to *Work in Progress,* now known as

Finnegans Wake, rather than to *Ulysses.* For the moment I did not know quite what to do with this confusing detail. That *Finnegans Wake* is an imitation of *Tristram Shandy* was perhaps a useful discovery, but my original feeling had been inspired by *Ulysses,* and it was evidence about *Ulysses* for which I thirsted. To those who thirst will drink be given,[5] and I finally found what I desired, a statement in *Le livre jaune* (August 1945) to the effect that *Finnegans Wake* was simply the logical development of tendencies to be discovered in *all* of Joyce's earlier work. It followed that anything *Finnegans Wake* was, *Ulysses* was, and my original feeling was now demonstrated to have been sound.

Well, I wrote my article. "Tristram Shandy, Ulysses, and Finnegans Wake," I called it, with what still seems to me admirable restraint. Much to my surprise, the editor of *Modern Philology,* to whom I sent the piece, scribbled "Oh, come now!" on the title page and sent it back. At first I thought he had had some difficulty following the argument, which indeed was occasionally somewhat rarified: I had had to abandon the reading of *Finnegans Wake* after several attempts, so that my *arguments* were all about *Finnegans Wake* and my *evidence* was all drawn from *Ulysses.* But I am now convinced that the editor had read only the title page. It was of course a mistake to have given away in the title the full force of my break with tradition. I have since learned better rhetorical techniques (cf. my present title), and have some reason to believe that at least one editor read more than one-third of one article I sent him (there was a "God!" pencilled in the margin on page 35) although like all the others he did not print what I had to offer. But I am getting ahead of my story.

In spite of editorial indifference, I was on fire; I knew instinctively that my discoveries had just begun. Yet I was determined to move slowly and with caution: I read another pivotal work, *A la recherche du temps perdu.* As soon as I saw that it was narrated in the first person, I knew that my choice had been justified. And when I finished reading, three months later, there

5. *Guide to Research in English Literature,* 5th ed., 1950, article on "Thirst."

was nothing to do but write another article—or I should say chapter—"Proust and Sterne," in which I argued, quite simply, that *Tristram Shandy* is the *comic* story of a narrator writing a book, and *A la recherche du temps perdu* is a *serious* story of a narrator writing a book. Proust's so-called originality consists in nothing more than adapting Sterne's suggestions to a different kind of narrator: the hypersensitive, pathetically isolated genius-type. The body of the paper demonstrated the chapter-by-chapter parallelism, in too great detail to allow for reproduction here. I need only say that it has been called by at least one Sterne scholar, to whom I showed the manuscript, a model of deductive scholarship.[6]

Now to understand my situation at this point it will be necessary to recapitulate briefly. I had read a total of two modern novels. Both of them were rated as pivotal, yet both of them had proved to be hardly more than third-rate extensions of techniques magnificently originated by Sterne. Nevertheless, maintaining my customary circumspection, I refused to generalize without further evidence. I chose another pivot: Gide. Eduard's journal in *Les faux-monnayeurs* proved of course to be nothing but a *serious* condensation of Sterne's *comic* digressions on his art. As soon as it became perfectly obvious to me that Gide was simply copying Sterne, I did not even bother to finish the novel, but began to look around for some external proof, for those readers (and editors) who might object if I duplicated my exclusively *aesthetic* treatment of Proust. I leafed through the *Journal des faux-monnayeurs*. To my surprise, Sterne was not mentioned as one of Gide's models. I

6. The reader may well wonder why I did not wait for some external evidence of the compelling kind I had previously discovered about Joyce. Needless to say, I searched for whatever could be found, but there was nothing. I knew a girl who was compiling an index of names occurring in all of Proust's works. She told me that neither *Sterne* nor *Shandy* was in her index. I asked her what about *Tristram,* under the Ts, but for simplicity she had indexed everyone under his last name: Lescaut (Manon); Dick (Moby); etc. I felt that my internal evidence was really strong enough to make further search for external evidence a work of supererogation, and consequently my failure did not disturb me. It was, incidentally, only after my work on Gide that I began to understand the true significance of Proust's silence about Sterne (see below).

decided that I must work with more subtlety. I said to myself:
"If *you* were writing an imitation of Sterne, would you mention
Sterne, in a journal describing your writing methods? Of
course not. You would mention, as Gide does, Proust, Stendhal,
Dickens, Dostoievsky, Tolstoy—anyone *but* Sterne."

That this approach was sound was shown when I read
through *all* the journals. I discovered the first explicit reference
to Sterne in Gide's entry for April 23, 1932, where he quotes
with seeming unconcern from *Tristram Shandy,* obviously
striving to indicate that he is reading the book for the first
time. Certainly this is one of the shrewdest moves ever under-
taken by a novelist desiring to cover his tracks. Gide pretends
to be reading *Tristram Shandy* for the first time, *six years after*
his own imitation was published. Now it is certainly not to my
purpose to attack Gide here; it is enough if the reader recognize
that Gide even more clearly than Joyce openly betrays that he
owes everything to Sterne. That he somewhat ungraciously dis-
guises the avowal may make us think less of him as a *man* (and
by the same token more of Joyce), but it does not affect the
quality either of his novels as imitations of Sterne, or of my
argument.

It was only now, having encountered Gide's deceptiveness,
that I was able properly to evaluate Proust's silence concerning
Sterne (see above.) One need only consider the number of pages
which Proust wrote, in his novels, his newspaper sketches and
reviews, his letters, and his journals, to realize the enormity of
the revelation he makes of his own plagiary in never mentioning, on any one of those thousands of pages, the man who was
not only the greatest novelist of all time, but the man who of all
other writers had the greatest influence on Proust. Again I do
not wish to indulge in unpleasant talk about the morality of
men whose works, since they embody principles discovered by
Sterne, I admire. Yet one can hardly refrain from comparing
Sterne's open-hearted confession of indebtedness to Rabelais,
Cervantes, Swift, Montaigne, etc., with the awful silence of
Proust.

But I digress. It was clear to me now that I must begin to

protect myself. I already had a book on my hands, *Tristram Shandy, the Father of the Modern Novel,* and if I maintained my one-hundred percent average, it would be a trilogy within a year. Yet it was equally clear that since no one had been willing to publish any part of my discoveries as yet, no one *would* publish the book unless I took pains to clear myself of any charges of bias. What was worse, my own fears of dissertation riding were as strong as ever. Had I really been working honestly? Was not my growing conviction that *all* modern fiction depended from Sterne a sign that I had fallen into the very error I had been so anxious to avoid?

Clearly the thing to do was to look for an undeniable exception, in order to be able to moderate my claims, for the sake of my own peace of mind and my reputation for objectivity. But if *everything* was to turn out to be Shandean, how was I to find an exception, without expending several years of my life in the search? I thought at first that some reference work would give me the help I needed. But a hasty survey of the titles I had copied years before in Research Methods 301 convinced me that only a personal interview with a man of wide *modern* scholarship would yield the answer I desired. The question was: Who?

That I did not think of the solution sooner I can only attribute to my graduate training. Contempt for little magazines had been carefully nurtured in us from the start, and it was only with effort that I could bring myself to realize that the very fountainhead of knowledge about modern literature must be the little magazine editor. But when, by dint of sheer ratiocination, I finally came to the truth, I acted swiftly. I inquired and discovered that the only little magazine edited in my vicinity was *Boom.* I went to the editor of *Boom* and asked him, after appropriate introductions, which of all the great modern novelists was least likely to be a mere imitator of Sterne. He answered without hesitation.

"Thomas Mann is *der Mensch.* I would risk my international reputation as *redacteur* of *Boom* on the categorical assertion that Thomas Mann has never lifted a line from *Tristram*

Shandy. Trivia would not interest Thomas Mann. Thomas Mann is an artist *sans peur et sans reproche.*"

"What has he written?"

He blanched.

"You ask what Thomas Mann has written? You have not read *Boom's* Memorial Issue? Thomas Mann has written, in chronological order, *The Beloved Returns, Buddenbrooks, Joseph and his Brothers* (consisting of *The Tales of Jacob, Young—*"

"But," I interrupted, "you do not understand about the disciplines of productive scholarship. You read everything. I want to read—when, as now, I am out of my beloved decade—1757–1767—only the *right* thing. Please forget the *corpus.* Tell me only which of all the titles you have named or could name, which *one* is least likely to have been influenced by Laurence Sterne."

He hesitated.

"If none of them is an imitation, how can there be a question of degree? However, if you merely want to know which of all Mann's works you, in your—ah—enthusiasm, could not claim for Sterne, perhaps I can help." And he began to mumble. "*Death in Venice?*—No, there is a digression which might be mistaken—*The Magic Mountain?*—No, the experience with Madame Chauchat and the pencil might be mistaken for Shandean bawdry. . . ."

I waited for perhaps fifteen minutes as he ran through them all. At last he smiled.

"*None* of them, as I said, has *anything* to do with *Tristram Shandy.* But there is only one, the newest one, that I can really trust *you* to read without making ridiculous discoveries. It is an adaptation of the Faustus legend, which, by the way, Sterne never touched. If it does not serve, nothing will. Mann is the least Shandean of modern authors; *Dr. Faustus*—for that is its name—is the least Shandean of his books. If, to save you from—ah—*vos critiques fâcheuses* and from yourself, you must find an Anti-Tristramshandy, *Dr. Faustus* is my recommendation."

I read it.

That is, I started to read it. I started to read it, and in the first paragraph found Serenus Zeitblom, Ph.D., the narrator, saying:

I intrude myself, of course, only in order that the reader—I might better say the future reader, for at this moment there exists not the smallest prospect that my manuscript will ever see the light. . . . Indeed, my mind misgives me that I shall only be awakening the reader's doubt whether he is in the right hands: whether, I mean, my whole existence does not disqualify me for a task dictated by my heart rather than by any true competence for the work.

My heart pounded, and not without reason. This was the most deliberate, undisguised borrowing from Sterne I had yet encountered. I went on, of course—I went on and found scarcely a transition, scarcely a narrative device, not taken from Sterne's pen. Not only is the narrator, like Tristram, careful to set himself up as self-conscious about his devices—and secretly master of them—but he is always copying explicit tricks of Sterne's narrative manner:

Here I break off, chagrined by a sense of my artistic shortcomings and lack of self-control.

It is all there. The reader is brought on the stage and asked to watch the writer at his desk, going through his antics, making his digressions, getting involved in the complexities of his material, masterfully coming through in spite of all obstacles.

I am entirely aware that with the above paragraph I have again regrettably overweighted this chapter which I had quite intended to keep short. I would not even suppress my suspicion, held on psychological grounds, that I actually seek digressions and circumlocutions . . . because I am afraid of what is coming. . . . I herewith resume my narrative.

But I could go on with these quotations indefinitely. Indeed, when I came to write up my discovery, I found that I was able to quote exactly *two-thirds* of the original text in support of my argument, surely ample proof in itself, aside from the high *quality* of my evidence, that Mann's work is simply another avatar of *Tristram Shandy*. I am tempted to quote almost as largely from these proofs here, because it is at this point that my case in all its fullness either stands or falls. But perhaps one splendid example will have to do: the beginning of chapter 9, where Mann avows his debt explicitly. In case this quotation looks too formidably long for the readers of *Furioso*, who, like

all readers of literature outside the eighteenth century, are ac-
customed to being, as one might say, spoon fed, I shall underline
the most significant sections (italics mine):

> And so, half jestingly, I would address those who in that last mon-
> strous chapter have been guilty of some skipping: *I would remind
> them of how Laurence Sterne once dealt with an imaginary listener*
> who betrayed that she had not always been paying attention. The
> author sent her back to an earlier chapter to fill in the gaps in her
> knowledge. After having informed herself, the lady rejoins the group
> of listeners and is given a hearty welcome.
>
> The passage came to my mind because Adrian as a top-form student,
> at a time when I had already left for the University of Giessen,
> studied English outside the school courses, and after all outside the
> humanistic curriculum, under the influence of Wendell Kretschmar.
> *He read Sterne with great pleasure.* Even more enthusiastically he
> read Shakespeare . . .

I did not read further, except to look at the first paragraph
of the Epilogue:

> It is finished. An old man, bent, well-nigh broken by the horrors of
> the times in which he wrote. . . . A task has been mastered, for which
> by nature I was not the man. . . . In actual fact I have sometimes
> pondered ways and means of sending these pages to America, in order
> that they might first be laid before the public in an English transla-
> tion.[7]

No, I did not read further. My case—the case I had not
wanted to make, the case for Sterne as the father of all modern
literature—was so firmly established that I did not need to read
further. Mann, the last resort of my doubts, the last hope of my
desire to limit myself to a negotiable scope, had been found to
be as derivative as all the others.

There is little point in reporting on my further, and, as appears now, final steps. I read a little in Henry James, not really
out of any doubt as to what I should find, but simply to make
my case complete. It is unnecessary to report on what I discovered about the narrator in such works as *Daisy Miller, The
Author of Beltraffio,* or *The Aspern Papers*—to say nothing of

---

7. As *I* look back on what I have written, I sometimes think I shall have it
translated into Latin, in order that it might first be published in a language
fit for timeless scholarship.

the longer works—because those of my readers who have read them with any perception, and *me* with any sympathy, will already have seen who James's inspiration was, and those readers who are still holding out are undoubtedly so committed to the belief that all great works are, as they are so fond of saying, *sui generis,* that nothing, not even the most rigorous scientific proof, could convince them of any further instance of Sterne's universal influence.

I, on the contrary, have now adopted without reservation the belief that all modern literature is essentially one, that not only is it *not sui generis,* but it has *one* source and fountainhead: *TRISTRAM SHANDY.* All literary works written since Sterne —novels, plays, poems—exist, for me, now, simultaneously. Indeed, it is to me as if *all* literature except *Tristram Shandy* had been written in 1768, the year following the publication of Sterne's final volume. Only dull readers will be surprised at that word "all." For why, if my discoveries are sound, should I limit their application to works written after Sterne? If Sterne is the fountainhead of all modern literature, is he not also the culminating receptacle of all previous developments? Indeed, who, having followed me through this account, can question the essential conservatism of my claim that in this sense every Western writer (for I am not, at least as yet, ready to include any other than the Western tradition) before Sterne was but preparing the way, proclaiming to benighted times fragments of the Truth which was to come? And if this is true, is it not safe to say (borrowing a phrase from the Stagyrite) that *Tristram Shandy* is the "Final Cause" of all Western Literature? It is with this aspect of my discoveries that my decology, on which I am now putting the finishing touches, is to deal. I am still looking for a title, but although it seems to suggest a less sweeping claim than I have in mind, I have tentatively settled on *Laurence Sterne, from Homer to Hemingway: A Study in Influence.* After all, there is no harm, I believe, at this stage of my inquiries, in maintaining an air of restraint.

DAWN, DELIGHT, DEW, DOVE

A couple of summers ago I taught for six weeks in an orientation program given to foreign exchange students who were to enter American graduate schools in the fall. There were many remarkable things about this program that I would like to talk about, if I had time—the care with which the students were screened before leaving their home countries, insuring that no one with false opinions or dangerous attitudes would get through; the careful and bounteous directives issued by the State Department outlining what could not be discussed with the students and listing which documentary films and which books could not be used; and so on. But important as they are, they seem insignificant when compared to the discovery I was led to make of a new use for Basic English.

You must understand that, besides the State Department directives, we received many other documents, perhaps the most useful being the weekly teaching guides prepared by the supervisor of English instruction. He would bone up on background material for drill in phonetics and grammar; then he would

Reprinted with permission from *Furioso*.

mimeograph his gleanings for the rest of us to use on our classes. It is true, of course, that some difficulties in the use of this material resulted from the mixture of nationalities. In a class of ten students, I had four nationalities, each of them with its own linguistic problems. But a hearty will and an honest internationalism can overcome almost any problem, and it is impossible to place a limit on what we might have accomplished if we had continued in this vein for the full six weeks. But it was not to be. On the morning of July 8, I found in my pile of English suggestions a copy of *Basic English Self-taught* and carbon copies—to this day I don't know precisely where *they* came from—of three supplementary lists, an Economics List, a Business List, and a Poetry List. I am a little ashamed to confess that I ignored both the book and the supplementary lists for several days. I was—let me be frank—skeptical about the value of Basic English, perhaps because of an earlier brush with Esperanto. In my first year in college I took beginning Latin, and I have no doubt that I would be a passable Latinist even today, had it not been for Esperanto. My roommate, who had announced himself on our first day together as a Socialist, a Communist, and a Pacifist, became converted during the first semester to Esperanto. He argued so cogently against wasting time studying a dead language, when one could just as easily be learning the language of the future, that I dropped the Latin in midstream and worked on the grammar of a somewhat simpler language. As a result, I have no Latin, and my consequent inability to hold my own in bouts of Languagemanship has produced an aversion to linguistic schemes of any kind.

So that it was not until the evening of July 11, as I was sorting out the directives for the week into the various piles and the wastebasket, that I happened on the Basic English materials again. I was about to send them to the fire when my eye fell on the Poetry Supplement. I began to glance through the one hundred words—and suddenly I was electrified. My life was changed in a moment. I knew that at last I had found the key to all my teaching problems, and I read the list through again and again with mounting excitement. Then I turned to the book and read the much longer list of Basic words; then I returned to the Poetry Supplement.

It was tremendous. It is true that, even then, I was dimly aware of certain problems presented by the lists, but—problems and all—it *was* tremendous. Perhaps the best initial idea of the list's power and scope, and of my subsequent difficulties, can be given by copying the entire list at this point.

POETRY LIST

angel, arrow
beast, blind, bow, breast, bride, brow, bud
calm, child, cross, crown, curse
dawn, delight, dew, dove, dream
eagle, eternal, evening, evil
fair, faith, fate, feast, flock, flow, fountain, fox
gentle, glad, glory, God, grace, grape, grief, guest
hawk, heaven, hell, hill, holy, honey, honour
image, ivory
joy
lamb, lark, life, lion, lord
meadow, melody, mercy
noble
passion, perfume, pity, pool, praise, prayer, pride,
    priest, purple
rapture, raven, robe, rock, rose, rush
search, shining, shower, sorrow, soul, spear, spirit,
    storm, stream, strength, sword
their, tower, travel
valley, veil, vine, violet, virtue, vision
wandering, wealth, weariness, weeping, wisdom,
    wolf, wonder

I hesitate now, as I would have hesitated then, to call this list a poem in itself, but I do not hesitate to point out the rhythm and the irony of

Angel, arrow, beast, blind

or the condensation of the Ophelia archetype in

Passion, perfume, pity, pool.

The devisers of this list were, it is clear, poets in their own right. Whether they realized the full implications of their development is, however, a moot question. Certainly I wished again and again that night that their instructions had been sent along with the list. As it was, I had nothing to rely on but my own powers and the inspiration of the list itself.

Since it seemed obvious that the list was intended as an aid in reading poetry, the problem as I first saw it was to find a Basic Poem. I began my search—a true measure of my growing fatigue and confusion—with children's poetry.

Twinkle, twinkle. . . .

But of course twinkle does not occur on either the Basic or the Poetry List. I looked for synonyms. The closest I could come was

Be shining, be shining, little star [*all from the Basic List*]
How I [*Basic*] wonder [*Supplement*]. . . .

I thought I was doing all right up to this point, and I would have gone on if I could have continued to do as well. But *what* does not occur on either list. I must have spent thirty minutes looking for an equivalent. "How I wonder *that* you are"? "How I wonder *about that there* you are"? "How I wonder *about the qualities you have and your structure and substance?*" This seemed all right, but it was all done with the Basic List, and I was anxious to use the Poetry List. So I looked for a more suitable poem. After rejecting a great list of them, as being impossible on the face of things ("Humpty Dumpty," "Hickory Dickory," and so on), I settled on "Mary, Mary, Quite Contrary."

Mary, Mary [*self-understood "supplement" to the Supplement*] . . .
Quite [*Basic*]. . . .

But what could I do with *contrary*? *Opposite* lacks the proper connotation, though undoubtedly *contrary* was excluded from the lists on the ground that *opposite* would serve as a synonym. I looked over the list of Qualities, both General and Opposites. "Mary, Mary, quite (in)dependent"? "Mary, Mary, quite (self-)important"? (Ir)responsible? Violent? Female? "Mary, Mary, quite opposite in a female way"? OK!

Mary, Mary, quite opposite in a female way,
How does your field of flowers increase in size? [*all Basic*]

Obviously, my great reliance on the Basic List indicated that I was not choosing materials sufficiently poetic. I needed something with "glad, glory, God, and grace," or their equivalents. Milton? Of course, Milton!

This false lead took another two hours of my precious time, and to no avail. There is no poem of Milton's which has more than one of the poetic words in the first two lines, and most of them have none at all. So I decided to try something modern and very colloquial. Maybe Yeats at his simplest:

> Others, because you did not keep.

This was very encouraging. Every word on the list, even though not on the *Poetry* List.

> That deep-

How to convey "deep-sworn vow"? *Sworn* or *swear* do not appear, though among the *s*'s, on the supplemental list, we *do* have *shower, spear, storm, stream, strength, sword,* and *shining. Vow* does not occur, although I found *valley, veil, vine,* and *violet* among the *v*'s. And no use looking for *oath*—there is nothing at all among the *o*'s. "Deep promise to be true"? But even *promise* is missing. Again I had to stop, defeated.

Something was wrong. I went back to look at the Supplementary List. Perhaps I should search for poetry with these specific words in first lines. I began with *arrow,* and ended with this couplet:

> I sent an arrow quickly in the air.
> It came down to earth, I had no knowledge where.

Finally at about 6:00 A.M., I fell to my pallet exhausted. I remember only saying to myself, as I was falling asleep, "I am a failure. I can go no further. I must either obtain help from a higher source [I was thinking of writing to Richards] or quit."

Suddenly I awoke, having dreamed a dream. A man named I. A. Coleridge had appeared to me as I slept. He was obviously under the influence of dope, but the glitter in his eyes was from a deeper source. He put his hand on my shoulder and said, "My son, hear this: 'My soul is like an angel and a beast. . . .' " And he went on, reciting a whole quatrain (ABAB) using only words to be found on the two lists.

In a fever, I began to write down what he had said. But I had written only the first line when the phone rang; it was the director of the Orientation Program, asking me where the hell I was. Classes had started ten minutes ago. I dashed to my classes, and three hours later, when I returned and tried to remember what Coleridge had given me, it was gone.

Enough of the excitement of his visitation remained, however, for me to understand the true import of The List: it should be used in the *writing* of poetry, not the reading of it. And clearly I had been chosen as the First to develop the New Way. I went to my desk and tried to reconstruct the whole stanza. Slowly it came back to me:

> My soul is like an angel and a beast.
> It's split [No, *split* doesn't occur. Shot? No. Ah, yes:]
> It's speared with bow and arrow through the breast.
> In one way it's a bride and I'm the priest;
> In one way it's a blind and faith[less] guest.

I now saw that even the interruption had not been accidental. The reconstruction of the forgotten lines had been just sufficiently difficult to get me into the swing of the thing, and I was now able to go on through the whole list of Poetic Words in the same way, concentrating on two letters per stanza, but not hesitating to borrow other words from either the Basic List or the other sections of the Poetry List when necessary. This gave me nine and one-half stanzas (there are no k's, o's, q's, u's, x's, y's, or z's), an average of one per student in the class, counting Mr. Brontini, my Italian, as one-half because he was not interested in poetry.

From the next day on, my procedure was simple and unvarying. I required each student to memorize his stanza, define each word in it (confining himself to Basic English in the definition), and use the word in a couplet of his own (here I allowed the addition of the Poetry List and, on two occasions, words from the Business List). When I was assured that each member of the class knew all the poetic words of at least two letters, I put him to writing his own poem. The results of this exercise were astounding. Although I am now in the process of editing these poems for publication, I think I will not spoil their ultimate impact too greatly if I print here the poem of Miss Susukai, of Osaka, Japan, as it reads in its final form after four weeks of polishing:

> My soul is like a crown and yet a cross:[1]
> In strength it showers sorrow in a stream;
> Yet with a sword it spears me like a curse,[2]
> And searches through my spirit like a storm . . .

Addendum: Twelve years after publishing "Dawn, Dew, Delight, Dove" I received the first sign of its having been read— as follows:

INSTITUTE
for
LANGUAGE
RESEARCH
249 Rose Street, San Francisco 2, California   MArket 6-3577

                                              27 September 1965

Dr. Wayne C. Booth
Department of English
University of Chicago
Chicago, Illinois

Dear Dr. Booth:

Among the projects under way at the Institute is a Bibliography of Basic English, which now numbers several hundred entries and which includes your "Dawn, Delight, Dew, Dove" (*College English* 15:3: 171–6, December 1953) .

In this article you mention poetry in Basic written by your students which you were "in the process of editing . . . for publication." If this ever reached published form we would appreciate bibliographic data. If not, would it be possible for you to supply us with copies of any of the verse for our library?

Any other pertinent information would, quite naturally, be most welcome.

                                             Cordially,

FB:dj

                                 Fredrick Berndt, Director

---

1. Miss Susukai, by an accident of accounting, was given letters far apart in the alphabet—the *c*'s and *s*'s. She professed to me her desire to begin with the *s*'s and end with the *c*'s; I felt that this radical reversal of alphabetical order would be against the true spirit of the whole exercise, but I did allow her to work with the two letters concurrently.
2. It should be noted that Miss Susukai was far too sophisticated to be satisfied with anything short of what, for want of a better term, I shall call "metathesized rhyme."

THE ART OF
SINKING IN PROSE
BY PROFESSOR
JOHN R. BUTHNOT, PH.D.

For six years I conducted a snide little column in The
Carleton Miscellany, *"Department of American." We offered,
and often actually paid, up to $10.00 for pieces of "bad writing
by people who ought to know better—professors, college presidents, deans, professional authors."* The Art of Sinking in
Prose, *from which I have selected only the worst portions, was
thus part of what seems to me now a rather over-extended series
that always skirted both pedantry and sadism.*

*My original principle was to mock the bad writing only of
those who were "bigger than me." As a youngish teacher at a
small college I found that this offered more than adequate
scope. I named all names and had my quiet, self-indulgent fun,
even including along the way examples of my own printed
sinkings. But as I look at the stuff now, I feel less easy about
naming those people—none of them known to me, some of them
no doubt suffering more serious mockings from life itself, all of
them surely kind to children and working vigorously to get
us out of Vietnam. Reprinting may be unfair to them, and it*

Reprinted in abridged form from *The Carleton Miscellany,* fall 1960, winter
1961, spring 1962. © by Carleton College.

is certainly unwise for me when it names those who, like Dwight Macdonald, are big enough to lick me with one hand tied behind their backs.

So I have expunged most of the names. But I have still ignored the advice of my best and severest dedicatee that I should, out of sheer self-protection, cut the whole thing. After all, even though she is right in saying that by including The Art of Sinking *I place myself in a glass house, why should I not be willing to sacrifice myself to a good cause?*

I warn only that any bad writing the reader claims to find in the next few pages—even the bad imitation of bad writing— is deliberate.

Introduction

The truly astonishing thing is that so far as the present writer can discover, which is pretty far, no one has ever attempted a Rhetoric of American before. In attempting one now, I am deeply, not to say profoundly, conscious of the risks taken by any pioneer. But I think I can say without fear of being contradicted that the primary orientation of American studies will receive a new image as a result of my spade-work.

Chapter I
GOOD AMERICAN IS DEMOCRATIC AMERICAN

[Five pages of the History of Democratic are elided here] Though it may seem radical to some, then, it is high time to recognize that it is undemocratic to do anything *too* well. We all know that the most *comfortable* pianist is the one who plays most like ourselves, *l'homme moyen clumsy*. And is not the friendliest tipist the one who tipes and spels like me? Well, then, I'm sure all you students will agree with me in extending this little principle to writing, and your teacher will too, for he or she is after all just another student, a little older perhaps, but still learning right along with you. No one knows very much in this world of ours, and it ill behooves any of us to write as if he did. In fact, it is the writing *that reads most as if the author knew how to write* that offends all of us the *most*. We've all known the gnawing envy that can be raised in us by a sentence beautifully turned. How much more skillful, how much more gracious, to please your reader, or readers, by making him or her feel that he or she could have done it better!

It was undoubtedly some such motive as this that motivated Prof. —— —— to adopt the sinking style as he exhorted the writer of children's books to employ "craftsmanship":

Mustering all the craft he possesses, he must so order, so balance, so proportion his writing that, stylistically, it is right in its form and feeling as well as in its life sources and its words.

Now, then, can you see why this is real democratic skill? You or I or any number of democratic writers might have managed that sentence up to the last clause. We *might* have thought of the pyramidal redundancy of three "so" phrases and even the splendid confusion of "stylistically right in its form and feeling as well as in its life sources." But who of us, who even of us with years of writing experience, would have thought to add that final swoop, that final steep glide, "and its words?" Our writing must not only be stylistically right in its form and its feeling, not only in its life sources, but also *in its words!* This is democratic writing, writing which makes us envy its very capacity (oh, subtlety!) to forestall envy. And it is writing that leads us to our first, or is it our second, principle.

Principle I: Slovenliness Is Skill

Whenever possible, avoid building your sentences into meaningful wholes. Honest, realistic thought is not organized, trimmed, prettified; it flows, dips and glides; it *sinks,* and the prose that reflects honest thought must sink with it.

There are of course innumerable ways to prevent one's writing from rising to an unnatural, artificial level. Some of these can be mastered only after years of experience. But some are within the average reach of average us.

I.1. The Simple, Straightforward Mistake. Ever since that great American poet, or poet of American, T. S. Eliot, set the world afire with the grammatical error with which he begins his great poem, "The Waste Land" (Let us go then, you and me?),[1] the world has known that truly *big* writing and speaking must contain many *little* errors. Does one wish to avoid the charge of traditionalism and pedantry while attacking the modern linguists? Mr. —— —— solves the problem simply and clearly, with a direct prepositional onslaught:

> It is with the practice of writing that we must get ahead with anyhow, not with the lint-picking philosophical distinctions that the linguists are presenting us with . . .

Or, does one need to establish rapport with a convocation of average students and teachers? The President of the Board of Trustees of a university in Utah wins everyone with one stroke:

> My daughter has never been able to have children because of the 4-H factor.

Finally, you will be surprised at how much can be accomplished by simply slapping down whatever word first comes into your head, without bothering too much about its meaning. In writing about "masscult" and "midcult" in *Partisan Review,* for example, the author (Dwight Macdonald) ran a real danger of sounding condescending towards the masses and mids. But he saved himself by proving, at one stroke, that he is one of us:

> There were two Byrons, the public swashbuckler of *The Corsair* and *Childe Harold's Pilgrimage* and the private mocker of the same romantic attitudes, and this split between the two was to become congenital.

Exercise for I.1: Write a sentence containing three creative solecisms and at least two errors of fact. Be careful to make the whole thing seem inadvertent. Note how quickly the skills you are developing become congenital. . . .

Principle II: Repetition Is Economy

Assume that your readers cannot get a point if it is made only once. The Average Reader in the up-to-date world of today—a

---

1. Unfortunately there is no record of whether the Fisher King used good grammar or bad. But as somebody has said, a booboo should not mean but be.

global world if we ever lived in one—is in a hurry. If he misses the point, he doesn't want to have to worry his way back over the passage to figure it out. GIVE IT TO HIM AGAIN, and he'll thank you for it. Here are three versions of a notice before and after revision into true American:

Worst	*Medium*	*Best*
NO CLASSES WILL BE HELD SATURDAY, JULY 9, since both the written examinations for master's degrees and the graduate record examination are to be given then.	Due to the scheduling of the written examinations for the master's degrees and the administration of the graduate record examination on Saturday, July 9, it is found to be not practical to attempt to hold classes on Saturday, July 9, 1960.	"Due to the scheduling of the written examinations for the master's degrees and due to the administration of the graduate record examination on Saturday, July 9, 1960, it is found to be not practical to attempt to hold classes on Saturday, July 9, 1960. Because of this, all classes originally scheduled for Saturday, July 9, 1960, are cancelled." —Dean —— ——, School of Education, State University of —— ——.

Principle III: Always Make Your Reader Feel Good

There are many ways to make your reader feel good, but never forget that straightforward flattery is still as useful as it ever was. "You are already writing," a brochure from Antioch College, advertising their Writing and Publishing Seminar, tells me, and immediately I feel more productive than I've felt in months:

You are already writing, or trying very hard to do so, if you receive this notice [they absolutely refuse to *send* the notice to the slothful?]. You have sorted out your ideas [see BAREFACED LYING, Chapter VII below]. You have exposed yourself to skills and techniques. You have discovered that writing is a hard won art. You have decided in which categories you would like to publish.

Exercise for Principle No. 3: Write a brief reply to this brochure, flattering Antioch into giving you a scholarship to the Writing and Publishing Seminar.

Principle IV: All Men Are Brothers in Ignorance

No author was ever hurt by being ignorant of his subject matter. When in doubt, write on. Our British cousins are often better at this sort of thing than we; I have yet to meet an Englishman who felt that having nothing to say should lead a man to say nothing. Observe the skill of Mr. —— ——, surely an Englishman, as he finds himself—unexpectedly, one assumes —writing on the subject of "Bronzes and the Minor Arts: Jades, Lacquer, Enamels, etc.," for a volume called *Chinese Art: An Introductory Handbook.* "I think this picture is signed Wen Chia, whose sixteenth-century uncle, Wen Ch'en Ming, was so famous," Mr. —— tells us when the going gets rough. "To me it seems as good as a Cézanne, though nothing could be less like one." Having exhausted what he has to say about the painting, all of it carefully confined to what you or I or the next man might as easily have said, Mr. —— suddenly sees his path clearly. "But what is the use of looking at Chinese paintings unless you know something about European ones?" he goes on, without a blush. "Cézanne's water-colours are better than anything I have ever seen in Chinese art, except perhaps some paintings by Chu Ta reproduced in Japan." Noticing, perhaps, that this contradicts flatly what he has just said about Wen Chia's painting being as good as Cézanne's, he hurtles ahead:

Moreover, the Chinese are as keen on Cézanne as we are when we see good specimens. Professor Liu Hai-su, formerly Director of the Ecole des Beaux-Arts of Shanghai, was a good judge of such matters; he was himself a good painter in all styles, and wrote a book which was to appear in English. So has Mr. Chiang Yee. It is possible for such men to have some idea about whether Chinese pictures are good or bad, or by this or that artist.

I hope I have given the impression in these notes that, unlike many other writers on Chinese painting, I cannot even read Chinese; my opinions are usually quite valueless unless I have fortified myself by reference to someone else. My feelings about Chinese pictures, however, and my enjoyment of them, I hope gradually to refine. 'The heart I can use; the head I can borrow.'

Now I think that any careful student comes out of such a passage feeling that he too could be an art critic, and not only that but a critic of Chinese bronzes and other minor arts.

Exercise for Principle 4: Write a paragraph comparing the Nō plays of Japan with pre-Aeschylean tragedy. Study Helps: Mr. Gilbert Murry and men of his stamp can, or could, tell one play from another pretty well.

Summary and Controlling Idea

The Democratic Writer will not impose unnatural coherence or clarity on his materials. His overall purpose will be to show that he is at least as safe as he is sound. In the words of the Marquis Publications blurb for *Who's Who* [note the difficulties in being genuinely democratic when advertising what for many is the Final Rung on the Ladder]:

> The duty of Marquis Editors is an entirely impersonal one. It is to select, impartially and to the best of their abilities, those they consider fall under carefully established standards—tested during more than half a century—for reflecting comparative subjectivity to reference interest on meritorious scores. Once so selected, the maintenance in print of an accurate, down-to-date, life record—to serve the indisputably important purposes just cited—must of *both* fairness and equity, depend principally on your responsitivity.

Conclusory Exercise: Contrast, using maximum responsitivity, the role of fairness and of equity in deciding who's who.

CHAPTER II
GOOD AMERICAN IS EXTREMELY DYNAMIC

Before beginning Chapter Two, we should begin by giving the summary and controlling idea of Chapter One. The hard-hitting point of Chapter One was that *good American is democratic American.* It is often a good idea to use a title that, like this one, gives a clue to your general idea.

The Summary and Controlling Idea of Chapter Two is different. It can best be summarized as *good American is extremely dynamic.*

Now, then, in terms of some rather fundamentals.[2] First, how can writing be Democratic and still be Dynamic? This problem has been dealt with dynamically by P. T. Barnum, Dale Carnegie, Hollywood, and Madison Avenue for years. The results are what we know, an imaginative mingling of productive trends that has done our industrial and social structure proud. . . . The following few general principles should help the dynamism spread upward fast.

> *Principle II.1: Dynamic American Is Self-Confident*
> *American*

Note how the following applicant for a teaching job inspires confidence in the mind of the chairman receiving his letter:

> As I have said above, I am ill-prepared to teach 18th Century English Literature or American Literature, but uniquely suited to teach such a course as World Literature, if you offer such a course.

This is crude but forceful. It has a certain primitive dynamic quality like drawings in old caves and is not to be scorned. For a more sophisticated, professional example of II.1, however, we must turn to *The New Yorker*, which until recently was among the least illuminated of our cultural centers in the art of dynamic democratic. From this it is clear that *The New Yorker* not only caught up but is now ahead of the field:

> *The New Yorker* is a humor magazine with an underlying seriousness, a serious magazine imbued with the comic spirit. In its articles, its fiction, its cartoons, its satirical writing, and its reviews, it reports and comments on contemporary life in a responsible, humane manner, and with a light touch.
> *The New Yorker* is edited in New York and from a New York point of view. The editors look around them *in* New York and look out upon the world *from* New York. . . . The editors have many clear-cut objectives. . . . With its large reportorial staff, both here and abroad—trained in *The New Yorker's* ways of thoroughness, responsibility, good writing and objectivity—the magazine presents (to the extent that any magazine can) a true picture of the contemporary world.[3]

2. The idiom is taken from an address by a full professor of education. Verbatim.

3. From a 14-page circular advertising *The New Yorker*. It was nice to find, accompanying the booklet, a letter I never finished reading: "Dear Reader: The enclosed booklet was prepared to introduce *The New Yorker* to those who do not know it well. It supplies . . ."

Exercise for II.1: Write a dynamic description of your own writing prowess, throwing in an occasional qualification ("I understand the world to the extent that any man can," etc.) for democratic flavor.

> *Principle II.2: Dynamic American Uses Concrete Details and Avoids Abstractions*

II.2A Concrete Details. We can do no better here than borrow from another little handbook, a handbook which, for reasons that will perhaps be obvious, is now undoubtedly being superseded by our own, but one which nevertheless has its points. And I quote.

Before	*After*
A little woman came out of the house and slowly made her way down the hill to the water's edge.	An old woman with a face like a crumpled leaf crept out of the gray, weather-worn house that frowned down on the sea from beneath two ragged pines. She was dressed in black, and she carried a small pillow, a book, a red plaid blanket, and a black cotton umbrella under one arm. Leaning heavily on a silver-headed cane while she picked her quavering way along the slippery, grass-grown path that squirmed over the bluff and down to the sea, she looked like a fairy-tale cricket, a lame one.

Now if the editors of *The Macmillan Handbook* can achieve effects like this without even seeming to try, surely *you* can do as well. That revised passage *lives*. It makes you *see* that little old crumpled woman staggering under her load and listing to the left under the weight of that pillow, book, blanket and umbrella.

Exercise for II.2A: Re-write the following vague generalities, to achieve dynamism through concreteness: "All men are mortal." "Do unto others as you would have them do unto you." "Power corrupts; absolute power corrupts absolutely." (Hint: "All men and women, from great square-shouldered football players to little old women with faces like crumpled leaves, are subject to the ravages of fate, chance, kings and desperate men.")

II.2B: Showing Is Better than Telling. Again we must quote another little handbook, *A Guide to Fiction-Writing,* by Mr. —— ——:

Now consider this bit of writing: "I heard many years ago that Grandpa Russell had married again and had another son, John. The family moved to the fen country, where these events I am about to tell you actually occurred."

Now that form of telling is obviously not *dramatic* telling.

Now notice this: "The great car took the hairpin bend on two wheels, and the fugitive cast an agonized glance down the winding mountain road. Far below him, but drawing ever closer, was the pillar of yellow dust that was the avenger."

Now that *is* dramatic telling. The story *is* telling itself, please note.

Fortunately Mr. ——'s principle is by now universally accepted; entire schools of creative writing have been founded and built upon it. But it might surprise the beginning student to know that writers occasionally still violate it. There is, in fact, an army of critics lying in wait to pounce upon the violators, and pounce they do. Listen to Joseph Cowley's complaint in his review of Paul Horgan's *A Distant Trumpet:*

Everything is softened, watered down—brutality, fighting, love, sorrow, the commonness of the soldiers. Even the adultery of Kitty Mainwaring, one of the officers' wives, first with Matthew and then with Corporal Rainey, is not given us as direct experience.

Well, perhaps Mr. Cowley is asking for too much. But still one can find examples of what Horgan might have achieved if he'd tried:

Seeing me standing there, momentarily paralyzed, the man straightened to his full height and catapulted himself upon me, forcing me back across the room to my bed [query: would this not be improved by calling the bed "my fourposter with the scarlet valence and the mauve lace pillows?"]. Into my mind came the certainty that this was an insane rapist. I would be murdered. I remember thinking, "When they find me I hope they will realize that I fought as hard and long as I could."

We *do* realize it, we really do; we cannot help but feel that this writer (Anon., in the April, 1960, *Ladies' Home Journal*, "A Shocking Story") has come very close indeed to giving us her very own rape, as direct experience. The art of narration by showing can hardly be carried further than this. But the effort to do so is still the most worthwhile any young writer can undertake. If all students would take this principle seriously, I'm sure that we could "decimate one-third"[4] of the bad books being written today.

II.2C: In Choosing Concrete Details, Be Evocative; Be Metaphorical; Be Poetic

1. "I am no Masters fan, but it is impossible not to admire the dexterity with which he keeps his balls in the air; the interests are at once archaeological, historical, mystical, sexual, sporting and psychological." (Norman Shrapnel, reviewing John Masters' *The Venus of Konpara*).

2. "But contraception did not seriously affect the birthrate until, in the seventies, it returned from America, to which it had been carried by the younger Owen. Malthus had raised a spectre which could be neither ignored nor laid." (G. M. Young, *Victorian England*).

3. "She became impersonal and forgot her husband, only using him as a lay figure to give point to her tale." (Sherwood Anderson).

CHAPTER III
THE DEMOCRATIC GRACES

Again we are involved in paradox: the outstanding writer of American is he who stands out least, and who manages to do so by taking the most pains to stand, as it were, *in*. Just to the extent that he repudiates traditional and aristocratic rhetorical figures—I might mention zeugma, I might mention litotes—will he embrace *appropriate* figures like hyperbole, oxymoron, and anacoluthon. Furthermore, to the extent that he, by such devices, succeeds in standing out least, to that extent precisely

4. I borrow this idiom from *The New Republic* of May 16, 1960.

will he make the task easier for his teachers, teachers like the one quoted below (at One of the Better Universities in Cambridge, Mass.):

> We shall be having to face large numbers of these students in the office and having to discuss their cases individually. Quite naturally, most of them will feel that they are exceptional; and we shall have the unwelcome task of having to convince them—individually—that they are not.

My point in quoting this remark should be clear, and it is this: if we teachers of rhetoric succeed in *really* persuading our students of the virtues, nay the necessities, of Democratic, then no teacher will find students in front of him who would be caught dead *feeling* "exceptional," though they will be permitted (paradoxically, again!) to *talk* about themselves as if they were.

Principle III.1: Hornblowing Is Creative (Narcissism Should Be Hyperbolic)

We have already shown how important it is, when boasting, to commit the Big Boast. But it is not enough simply to exaggerate. Experiments have shown that unless your claims are so extreme that the *careful* reader will see that you're lying, the *ordinary* reader, who is, after all, your audience, will not think that you're making any sort of claim for your product—ultimately yourself—at all.

Once again here we academics might well turn to our more realistic brethren in the advertising mediums for a pointer or two. When, for example, the Family Classics TV series introduced the revolutionary concept of devoting two hours straight-hand running to a single great literary work, did they make the mistake of claiming that David Susskind hoped in this way to reduce a bit the mutilation that most TV arrangements commit? They did not. By taking two hours for each show, they said, Susskind was going to be able to give us such literary works as *Vanity Fair* and *Les Miserables* in "unabridged, unedited" form, and "in a manner in which we are confident the author would have approved."

Similarly, when the *Encyclopaedia Britannica,* which spends

more each year on advertising than it would cost them to re-
write themselves completely, wishes to tout some filmed lessons
on Shakespeare, do they think it enough to say that the lessons
might help some people to enjoy Shakespeare who might not
otherwise? Not they!

> The fourth filmed lesson acts as a crescendo employing Maynard
> Mack's unique ability to weave together the twisted skeins of Shake-
> speare's intricate play pattern into a clear and understandable picture
> of Hamlet as a young man facing some of the problems of growing
> up. . . . Now the student can place himself in the position of Hamlet
> . . . ready to accept the whole of our human situation, with all its
> tragic limitations.

These would be impressive results, in anybody's Encyclopaedia.
But of course neither Mack nor the Britannica really expects us
to believe that Mack has at last achieved the tragic effect that
was botched by poor, tangled-up Shakespeare. The whole point
is that they *knew* we wouldn't think they believed in their product if they didn't lie about it a bit!

> *Principle III.2: Good American Is Usage (Incorrect
> Is Correct)*

What beginning writers tend to forget, often even after they
have ceased to be, technically, beginning writers, is that since
there is, after all, no criteria except usage, the good writer will
make his writing sound like usage sounds; he will *handle his
usage equally as well as the next egalitarian.* (One cannot do
better in this regard, perhaps not even as well, than to follow
the guidance provided by the new edition of *Webster's New Unabridged Dictionary*, which is full of usage. As Mr. Philip B.
Gove, Editor in Chief, has said,

> An essential requirement for determining best usage is that it be ac-
> tual genuine usage of such frequency as to be indisputably prevailing.

(Though in editing the new edition Mr. Gove has overlooked
some of the richest examples of usage that are actually genuine
in my own milieus, he's done about all anybody could expect
in a first try.)

The silly objection that is sometimes made to this—namely

that to let usage establish usage is circular—is silly. How else
can men speak except as they speak, how write except as they
write? No way. So that makes our task an highly easy one, however badly it may make the pedants feel.

Let us now look at some usage. The first group are quotations
from letters of application and recommendation written by
professors and administrators within the last year; they are, in
short, contemporary academic usage type quotations:

1. Mr. —— is always ready to help the student develop a strong
interest in worldly affairs.
2. I can say with equivocation that this faculty member . . .
3. I presume it is to early . . . but I do want to summit this young
man's name . . . for future consideration.
4. As to my personal dissipation habits, I feel that my many years
of athletic training have been the influential basis for my nearly complete abstainance from smoking and drinking alcoholic beverages. I
do from time to time smoke a pipe or indulge in a drink once in a
while. I have always felt that I must set an example if I am to expect
my athletes to do the same.
5. Mr. —— has not, I sometimes feel, gone through the transgres-
sion from adolescence to maturity.
6. Every faculty member is, I suppose, fallable.

Exercise: Write three sentences of usage.

As we come to the end, now, of Part I of *The Art of Sinking
in Prose*, I am thoroughgoingly aware that many of my readers
cannot have fully and dynamically mastered the principles upon
which our work should be foundationed. As one of my own better students recently so well put it, "Confusion, I feel, is still
amiss." We shall move along in Part II to a new part, dealing
with the larger units of the writing learner's problems.

.   .   .   .

CHAPTER XXXVIII
CONCLUSION

It is approaching a time when I must tell my numerable readers
that the *Art of Sinking* has just about reached the stage of abort.
But one must recognize that all good things come to an end,
finalwise. To firm this up a bit, let me just sketch out for the
reader's consideration a few of the pointers that seem to me,
off the top of my cuff, to suggest what possibilities for further

study ought to be. Here is a rigorously selected set, chosen, as
my children say these days, from the set of all chapters that I
might have fruitioned if given a micro-modicum of encouragement.

> *One: The Reforming of American (General Cul-
> ture Division)*

What I would have done here is plug in a few new parameters,
or, more accurately, view the whole of American culture under a
different model. I am aware, of course, of the truth recently
enunciated by a Washington bureaucrat: we should all pursue
only those projects which are probabilistic of achievement. But
I ceased to be dubious after I had read the essay: "Prospectus:
Toward High Information-Level Culture," by Aaron Katz.
There I learned about the information gap which we all labor
under: "Man is not merely an organism, but he is an organism
programmed by nature to fill this information gap and thereby
achieve maximum adaptation for his species." Mr. Katz explains
that "Art can be considered as the accumulation of information
concerning the 'aesthetic' dimensions of human experience,"
and that "the vast literature of phenomenology and existential-
ism demonstrates how the vicarious daily life feelings—as well
as their long-term expressions—can be analyzed." Carrying on
his analysis of man as "information processor," Mr. Katz finally
gets around to defining the science that could save us (you):
"Social science, properly understood, is actually the study of
man performing maximally in the direction of fulfilling his
species' goal of maximizing information. In other words, social
science is the study of man performing in high information-
level culture."

The value of Mr. Katz's approach can be seen when we look
for, and discover, how effectively he deals with subjects that
used to give us great difficulty. Take religion: "When we ask
'What is the meaning of existence?' the answer is, in part, 'which
existence?' i.e., 'existence at which information level?' This
breaks up and disperses the excess quantum of wonder which
is generated in the mind of one who abandons low information-
level cultures."

Another thing we've been doing that is wrong is reifying the good. "In high information-level culture, 'the good' need no longer be reified, because we now possess knowledge of just what 'the good' is: it is the maximization of information (and behavior consonant with that goal)."

I was tempted to quote a large quantum of Mr. Katz's essay, but I was pretty sure that your information-level culture (*hypocrite-lecteur!*) would not prove up to it. Minimizing the length quoted, I thought I might maximize your efficiency as an information processing reader. What still worries me is whether any of us writing or reading *The Art of Sinking* are in fact prototype members of scientific culture. "The answer [to just about everything] is simply to identify the normal individual with the prototype member of scientific culture. He is that individual who is rational, in the sense that he is cognizant of all the mental levels which are influencing his behavior, who is moral because his culture is moral, and who is emotionally healthy in Freud's sense because such health is the cultural norm."

> *Two*: *The Reviving of Every Previous Subdepartment of this Department*

I thought I could develop the readers' capacity for creative metaphor by reporting on one of our deans who, within twenty-four hours, told us (1) that "speaking of our hospitals, there's some slack in our beds, but this is mainly in Lying-In," (2) that "In obstetrics we have been losing our shirts," and (3) that "as a young man he had been totally immersed in marine biology." I would then have gone on with Paul Samuelson's Inverted Iceberg: "To look at the [doctoral] thesis is to miss the point: it is only the submerged peak of an exposed iceberg." (From "Economic Thought and the New Industrialism," *Paths to the American Present*, ed. A. M. Schlesinger, Jr.).

This made me think I might do a bit of Programmed Instruction in Metaphoric Transforms to help out the many readers who have written saying that they need help.

Examples:

Do not throw out the baby with the disposable diapers.

Do not expose the bottom two-thirds of the iceberg until you have explored the submerged peak.

Three

I thought I might do a chapter consisting of great statements in history, as they should be commented on by up-to-date teachers of the new English of today. For example:

Cogito ergo sum	Be concrete
Veni vidi vici	Expand
Four score and seven years ago	Wordy
Power corrupts. Absolute power corrupts absolutely.	Evidence for this?
Was this the face that launch'd a thousand ships, And burnt the topless towers of Ilium?	Avoid rhetorical questions
Tomorrow and tomorrow and tomorrow	Redundant

As I draw to the close, I cannot resist commenting on the potential significance of my contributions. Anyone who has followed me throughout will discern three periods, early, middle, and late. I do not, of course, lay claim to any more than having opened the vein of American. The lifeblood of this book has been all of the writers, wherever they may be, who have been willing to dictate-and-not-read; who have been able to resist proof-reading and revising; who have believed, as we all *must* believe, that first thoughts are best; who have lived by the conviction that if God had wanted our sentences to be well turned, he'd have turned them Himself; who have learned that any language a machine can write a man can write as well. It would be foolish for me to thank each and every contributor individually, but I cannot resist in conclusion expressing my conviction that during the six years of my little adventure we have experienced, as a nation living in the modern world of tomorrow, more than ever before, less revising and more honest free flow. If the little I have done to contribute to this trend has, in fact, had anything to do in furthering what we all know to be the kind of thing that ought to be supported.

EINSTEIN, ELEVATORS,
THE FOURTH DIMENSION,
AND THE DÖPPLER EFFECT:
A HUMANITIES PROFESSOR
WHO KEEPS UP ON THINGS
LECTURES ON RECENT
DEVELOPMENTS IN SPACE

We now approach a new unit in General Humanities, a unit which I am happy to report has been inserted as a result of popular demand. Too many people who read the headlines about the challenge of Sputnik lack the historic and scientific knowledge that underlies these momentous, these massive, developments. Let me tell you, once and for all, that space with its many problems was not invented on the morning that Sputnik I blasted off. (If at any time during this lecture you fail to understand my use of technical terms, please feel free to interrupt.) Far from it. At least as early as 1904, an unprepossessing little man with a wild shock of silvery hair had laid out the general lines of twentieth-century developments in this large area. That man was Albert Einstein, the father of the fourth dimension. The fourth dimension, I need hardly tell you, is what most of the *successful* launchings have been aiming for, though we should not allow our patriotism to blind us to the fact that in general the Russians have been more successful in reaching it than we.

Reprinted with permission from *The Carleton Miscellany,* winter 1960. © by Carleton College.

We may as well admit from the beginning that you won't get anywhere with the fourth dimension unless you understand elevators. Elevators are absolutely basic. I will try to explain why. Most of us, when we get into an elevator, think that it is the elevator that moves and we who have the sinking feeling in our stomachs. Actually, according to Einstein, as interpreted by Barnett, this is not so: the *elevator doesn't move*—unless you *think* it does. And even then, the sinking feeling in your stomach is illusory; all you have to do is move into the fourth dimension (T) and you won't even notice it. For example, turn out the light in the elevator. That light, before you turned it out, was traveling at the rate *c*. *Now*, of course, it is traveling at the rate *o*, which might at first confuse you. But this is all cleared up if you look at the equation

$$E=mc^2$$

in which E stands for elevator, m stands for the motion of the elevator (sometimes called *mass*, when the reference is to the second law of thermodynamics), and c^2 stands for the velocity of twice as much light as there was in the elevator *before* you turned out the light. This is a *constant*—for no discernible reason labeled k—and it is, fortunately, not relative to anything (in scientific terminology—for those of you who are interested in that sort of thing—it is "invariant under the Lorentz-transformation.")

Now suppose the elevator stops suddenly—still with the light off. Pay close attention here; a moment's carelessness and you are lost. With the light off—but first we must be sure whether the elevator is going up or down, and whether it is accelerating at a uniform velocity or just traveling along at a comfortable speed. If it's just traveling along, the tricky thing is that you'll float, just absolutely float in the air, groping for that light switch. If it's accelerating at a uniform velocity—upwards, of course—you'll think you're simply standing on the ground, being pulled downward by gravity (g; we don't have an equation for g yet, but we may get to one). As long as you have that light off, you'll never know *what* has happened, which is why the windowless elevator is so useful for experiments in relativity.

Now *general* relativity is the principle that if you're in the elevator, with the light off, the light traveling at a negative rate (that is, *-c*), you'll never know whether the elevator or the building is moving. But this is getting ahead of my story. The fact is that there is still a raging controversy among physicists over whether it is more important to understand elevators or trains. Some say one, some say another. It's hard for an outsider to see what all the fuss is about, really, because it looks to me as if a train is just an elevator traveling horizontally. But this must be due to the ignorance of a layman, because the elevator people always insist on having no windows, and the train people always insist on having windows to see the lightning through. I feel a little embarrassed about this part, because I know you're going to be upset by it. But let me remind you here, in the consoling words of Dr. Harold Lyons, inventor of the atomic clock, that we should not "try to understand this just by thinking about it." At any rate, if you just imagine two trains going so fast that if you are traveling on one of them and look at the other, it just looks like a blur, then imagine that they are going a little faster, so that you don't even see the blur, *then* you know what special —or rather, *general*—relativity is. This is the experiment that was proved at Greenwich Village in 1942, when it was first recognized that the sun has a curved corona magnetically attracted away from it by the moon during an eclipse. It is interesting to note that this is still disputed by some, which produces some uncertainty—known as the Heisenberg principle.

You musn't think, however, that everything is uncertain, just because some physicists are uncertain on principle. Everything is relative, but it's not necessarily uncertain. Take for example mass and energy. If you had read as many paperback accounts of mass and energy as I have, you'd soon see that mass and energy are absolutely basic. Some physicists, it is true, think that mass undulates and energy comes in corpuscles; that is, I believe, Barnett's interpretation of Einstein. But others think that energy undulates—that is, *waves*—and mass comes in corpuscles. This additional uncertainty is complicated somewhat by the fact that strictly speaking mass does not exist, as is shown by the equation I have put on the board:

$$Gx = \frac{B^2 l^4 v}{C^2} \int (Dy^{12} + Dz^{12})dS = \frac{Blv}{C^2} \int (Dy^{12} + Dz^{12})dS'.$$

What this *does* make clear is that the corpuscular theory—not to be confused with the monumental work of William Harvey, if you will excuse my little joke—says that electrons are about the size of corpuscles. The undulatory theory says that they are bigger. The same holds for light, since light is, of course, made up of electrons—quite small ones.

The thing is that relative to light's motion, which is quite rapid, everything else is rather stodgy. So all those people who, in the past, thought that the planets pulled each other about—"action at a distance"—are quite discredited. We must not forget, however, the warning of Conant of Harvard (among others): being discredited is not the same as being wrong. Take, for example, the Ptolemaic theory. This theory, translated into modern terms, would say, in effect, that if you're riding in an elevator, or for that matter a train, and someone steps on your toe, it's really you who put your toe under his foot. That is, whether one says that the elevator moves up the building, or the building slides out from under the elevator, it's all the same thing. Copernicus said, of course, that the *elevator really moved,* and he almost lost his head for it. Then for years people said that *Copernicus* was right and *Ptolemy* wrong (that's spelled with a P: PTOL; we may as well get at least *that* much straight). But *now* we know that Ptolemy wasn't exactly *wrong,* he was only inconvenient. It is indeed cumbersome to lead one's life as if the building slid down the elevator, especially once one gets the picture of the whole universe having to slide along with it, which is what *special* relativity advocates. (I might just refer you here to Ilse Rosenthal-Schneider.)

This of course leads us to quantum physics, which must not be thought for a minute to have superseded relativity. As I understand it, what the quantum people are after is Einstein's scalp—that is, in more scientific terminology, Einstein, with his broad, humanistic background, has been too much concerned with *qual*ities, and the positivistic quantum physicists want a return to *quan*tities, or quant*a*. I think it is also safe to say that the quantum physicists, particularly Max Planck, think that inertia is more inert than Einstein does.

I see that my time is almost up, and here I am just getting around to cosmic rays, atomic clocks, and the problem of whether or not elevator operators age as fast as the rest of us. In so far as I understand him, Dr. Lyons thinks that they age more slowly, especially on the trip up. If we can conquer outer space, as seems likely now that Lunik III is doing what it's doing, then we can send somebody out into space for a few years, knowing that when he comes back it will be too late: we'll all be on ahead of him in Time—*T*—dwelling in the fourth, or perhaps even the fifth, dimension. This raises some interesting questions, I realize, such as "What good will this do any of us, including the space explorer?" But I must confine myself to questions that can be answered somewhat more easily. We have time only to make explicit what you might in any case infer from the above: there are two kinds of cosmic rays, microcosmic and macrocosmic. Since almost everyone now admits that genes and chromosomes are nothing but microcosms, and since we can infer from modern physics that the universe is nothing but a macrocosm, it is clear that we are on the verge of one great unified science, the general, or unified, field theory. The problem of who will be the first to formulate this theory can hardly be considered by the layman as of fundamental importance. What *is* important is the obvious trend away from elevators and trains to colors. The best current theory seems to be that the microcosmic rays, which are of course somewhat smaller, are moving toward the center of the universe and are thus blue; sometimes these are called blue giants because, of course, as they get closer and closer they look bigger and bigger. On the other hand the red giants, or macrocosmic rays, are moving *away* from the center, at fantastic speeds. They are red because of the Döppler effect, or rather because there is *no* Döppler effect when we deal with light. As a matter of fact, nearly everyone now concedes that not just the earth, with its Sputniks, Explorers, and Luniks, but the whole universe is exploding out into the fourth dimension, a phenomenon which bids fair to make our past knowledge based on elevators and trains useless. All this presupposes, of course, that space is *not* curved negatively. If it *is,* then unless I completely fail to understand the whole problem, the inside-out, inverted, elevator, or "elevator-bubble," will come into its own. I personally hope that this will not prove to be necessary, for the sake of everyone concerned.

LADY CHATTERLEY'S LOVER
AND THE TACHISTOSCOPE

(Reading Time: One-half minute to two hours, depending on who you are.)

The Army has announced a new program in the improvement of reading speeds. Some graduates of the program are reported as reading at the incredible rate of 6000 words a minute. . . . (News Item.)

I. Excerpt from Start Now with Start,
by Dr. H. S. Haistye:

I sincerely pitied Mr. E. B. White when he confessed recently, with no apparent shame, that he is a slow reader. Since I am a very fast reader myself, the pity didn't strike me until three seconds of reading time later, when I was reading something else, but when it struck, it struck hard. I think I read White's statement in *The New Yorker,* sometime during the last six months, about two-thirds of the way down the far right-hand column. With the photographic memory I have developed in learning to read so fast, I can *see* White's statement exactly where it fell on the page. It might have been in *The Atlantic,*

Reprinted with permission from *The Carleton Miscellany,* spring 1960. © by Carleton College.

it might have been in almost any two-columned magazine. But I can *see* it, almost word for word. And what he said was that he reads few books because he reads books word by word.

Now whether Mr. White would admit it or not, that brief assertion, seemingly so candid, seemingly so disinterested, was really a deliberate slap at the modern reading techniques that have made me what I am today—the very techniques that can revolutionize *your* life. It may even have been a slap at the tachistoscope itself [Gr. *tachistos* superl. of *tachys* swift + -scope], but I don't want to make a charge like that without more evidence. What *is* clear is that White, of all people, has allowed himself to fall into that most illusory of all comforts: "I may read slowly, but look at my comprehension!"

Slow readers have to have *some* comfort, of course. I remember, to my shame, that in the days before my work on the Special Tachistoscopic Army Reading Training (START), I too felt sort of desperate when I heard about this or that prodigy who could read one thousand, or even two thousand words a minute. I *believed* in such people, I'll say that for myself, but that was the very trouble. If the best I could do was five hundred words a minute—and long hours of timing had convinced me that this was my best—how could I hold my own, to say nothing of getting ahead, in a world threatened by two-thousand-word men?

The answer is, of course, that I couldn't. Nobody can. And the answer to *that* is START. Though I'm only a 2000 word-per-minute man even now, I have seen friends of mine read 6000 words a minute, after completing the START course. Scoffers may claim that they *must* miss *something* in their reading, but our special Reader's Digest Comprehension Tests have shown that speedy readers get all the facts there are to get, and sometimes more. One of our students recently read at the unbelievable clip of 6333 words per minute; he was reading an account of the history, function, and table of organization of START itself, and when finished (reading time: 3/4 second) he scored 100% on the examination—not, I assure you, an easy one.

The question is whether we want progress or whether we don't want progress. E. B. White, apparently, is willing to remain at what one can only call the Hieroglyphic Stage in his reading. All right, let him. But if we are to meet the challenge of today, we're not going to do it reading at 500 words a minute.

Now the book that follows (Mean START Reading Time, SRT, 30 minutes; *Possible* START Reading Time, 10 minutes; *Your* Reading Time, chances are, two to three hours!) is designed to . . . .

II. EXCERPT FROM THE BULLETIN OF THE SLOWERS (SOCIETY FOR THE LOWERING OF WASTEFUL AND ENERVATING READING SPEEDS), VOL. I, NO. 1

Minutes of the Organizational Meeting, November 1, 1959

1. Professor Rhomson moved that the following section of Professor Petersloe's Laboratory Journal be incorporated into our new bulletin. The motion was seconded and approved. Although Professor Petersloe is—or perhaps I should say *was*—too modest to include personal praise in his journal, it should be recorded that he was the outstanding graduate of START, having attained just one month ago the incredible clip of 6033 words per minute, reading an account of the history, function, and table of organization of our enemy, START.

Journal of Arthur Petersloe, concerning the Effects of Start upon Full-reading-response (FRR)

Sept. 1

Established, with help of Rhomson, that to chuckle requires from $\frac{1}{2}$ to 15 seconds. Median, 2 seconds. Mean, $1\frac{1}{2}$ seconds. Ruled out, of course, all hypergelastics [*hyper* + *gelastikos* inclined to laugh (reading time, including time to look it up, 45 seconds)], in whom all chuckles turn to full laughs—another problem entirely—and those humorless persons who did not laugh at our materials.

Sept. 3

Spent day calculating. Assume chuckler reacts at mean, $1\frac{1}{2}$ seconds. How many words would a START reader read in $1\frac{1}{2}$ seconds, assuming *mean claimed-speed* (MCS) of 2000 words

per minute? Result, carefully checked for arithmetic by Rhomson: 49 words.
Sept. 4

Spent day reading, looking for 49-word sentences. Found
none. (Incidental effect: disastrous drop in reading speed.)
Query: Why does no one ever write a 49-word sentence, or
even a 49-word group of sentences? Seven times seven? Settled
for passages running from 45 to 50 words, always making sure, of
course, that they had several chuckles in them.
Sept. 5

Experimented on colleagues and students with following
passage from *Northanger Abbey:*

> No one who had ever seen Catherine Morland in her infancy
> would have supposed her born to be an heroine. . . . Her father was
> a clergyman, without being neglected or poor, and a very respectable
> man, though his name was Richard, and he had never been handsome.

Forty-six words, four, perhaps five, chuckles. Reading time
(SRT scale), for non-chucklers, $1\frac{1}{2}$ seconds; for chucklers
(CRT), $12\frac{1}{2}$ seconds to one minute, depending on how much
re-reading is required to bring the number of chuckles up to
five.

Spent evening looking into Austen literature to see if anyone had commented on slowing effect of her style. Found one
long, spirited complaint, by a Mr. E. N. Hayes; *Emma* a much
overrated book, in his view, because it slowed his reading speed
so much that it took him eighteen hours to finish the book.
Must see if this criterion has been used in judging other authors.
Interesting criterion.
Sept. 6

Rhomson and I established Tear-Duct Reaction Period
(DRP; Rhomson wittily dubbed this *Drip;* it is a great pleasure
to work with Rhomson). At first we tried melodrama, but got
no tears. Settled for torture. Median DRP, 5 seconds; mean,
$5\frac{1}{2}$ seconds, with some subjects requiring as much as 15 seconds
before the first tear started.
Sept. 7

The Sabbath. Spent day reading. Troubled to note that my

SRT still going up, while my DRP remains constant. Now reading at a flat 6035 words per minute.

Sept. 8

Experimented with Desdemona's willow-song scene: 753 words; expected SRT, 22 sec.; my SRT, $7\frac{1}{2}$. Theoretical DRP, counting 22 startings of tears, major and minor, 120 seconds, or two minutes, which, added to $1\frac{1}{2}$ minutes Ordinary Reading Time (ORT) makes $3\frac{1}{2}$ minutes at a minimum. I am told that on the stage the scene requires 7–10 minutes; don't know what to make of this.

Noticed curious disparity between theory and practice. My own SRT is now just under 6300 words, and after reading the whole of *Othello* in 3 minutes, 13 seconds, without a single tear, I turned for relaxation to *Scientific American,* only to find myself weeping copiously in the midst of a report on mating dances of migratory birds. Feel that am on verge of important new discovery. If SRT and DRP times diverge markedly, and if affective and glandular reactions, are inevitable, however belated, and however inappropriate the context of whatever one happens to be reading, then surely—but caution, caution! . . .

Sept. 13

Have spent week reading and thinking. Stumbled upon Stanley Kauffmann's review of *Lady Chatterley's Lover,* in *The New Republic.* "The erotic passages," he says, "are most certainly intended to evoke erotic responses. . . . If Lawrence doesn't make you feel in your very glands what it meant to Connie and Mellors to find at last a satisfactory sexual partner, then he has failed as an artist" (SRT, slightly less than 1/10 second). Rhomson and I spent Thursday reading in the Anatomy Library; no mention anywhere of the *very glands.*

Query: How to establish Very Gland Reaction Time (VGRT; Rhomson has already dubbed it Vagrant) without locating the Very Glands first? Rhomson suggested that I read *Lady Chatterley's Lover* and find out.

Sept. 14

The Sabbath. Read *LCL,* at constantly increasing speed. Total SRT: $3\frac{1}{2}$ minutes, at rate of 6731 words per minute. No noticeable reaction, anywhere. Am now turning, for relaxation, to the new issue of *Scientific American,* having noticed an article entitled Mating Practices of the Descendants of Margaret Mead's Mundugamor. Will report results later. . . .

III. A Note from the Editor of "Slowers"

Professor Petersloe has, I am sorry to report, disappeared from our campus, disappeared without a trace. Without a trace, that is, except his laboratory reports. I'm personally not trying very hard to find him; his work remains with us, and I have a feeling that even if he is alive, nothing he will ever do can equal what he has done. Prof. Rhomson is more convinced than I am that his taking with him two of our most promising secretaries indicates that he has plans for important research. I am sure that we in the Society for the Lowering of Wasteful and Enervating Reading Speeds can best honor him by combatting the forces that got him.

IV. A Hitherto Repressed Fragment from the Journal of Arthur Petersloe

Sept. 15

Rhomson and I both sheepish. How to account for our misreading of Kauffmann's obvious intent? Two hypotheses: we read it too slow, we read it too fast. Neither makes sense. But our chagrin more than compensated by sense of discovery—what Rhomson insists on calling *my* discovery. Discovery is, perhaps, too grandiose a term for it as yet, but the possibilities for further research do seem endless. Am pleased that Rhomson should suggest re-dubbing VGRT as PRT, after myself. But I must try to be more systematic.

What happened to me in reading *Scientific American* yesterday has led to a shift in my research program. Instead of trying to fight START, which will undoubtedly win anyway (look what they have done to *me*), why not exploit the possibilities stemming from the inevitable gap between SRT and chuckle, tear, and gland time, especially the latter (PRT)? The accidental correlation of *Chatterley* with the Mundugamor, with its astonishing effects, suggests the possibility of deliberately correlating, or *programming,* one's reading experiences, so that the inevitably lagging affective responses can be made cumulative. Just as one might read *Oedipus, Lear,* and *Death of a Salesman,* say, in sequence, with the tears earned by Sophocles watering, as it were, the pages of Miller, so one might begin with *Lysistrata* and go on—but wait. Why not correlate reading and *action?* One might . . . .

THE FIRST
FULL PROFESSOR
OF IRONOLOGY
IN THE WORLD

Unlike many revolutionaries in the history of thought, I am determined to claim no more than is my just due. Ironology did not spring full-blown from the head of Zeus, and it is now very difficult indeed to determine *where* the first faint glimmerings appeared. I shall have more to say of other claimants later, but for now the important point for us all to keep in mind is that it was not until 1948 (I remember the day and the hour) that I saw what had been wrong with all previous studies of irony, even my own.[1]

The day was December 11, 1948; the hour was 11:00 A.M.—a time of day when I am, modestly be it said, at my best. I was reading Edmund Wilson's commentary on his own earlier agreement with Edna Kenton's claim that it is the *governess,* not the *children,* whom we see trafficking with evil in *The Turn of the Screw.* In "Henry James to the Ruminant Reader"

1. As I am always telling my staff, irony is irony, old-fashioned study of irony is old-fashioned study of irony, and ironology is ironology. But more of this later.

(1924)—how many ruminants were to chew upon her suggestion she could hardly have guessed!—Miss Kenton had written: "So she [the governess] made the shades of her recurring fevers dummy figures for the delirious terrifying of others, pathetically trying to harmonize her own disharmonies by creating discords outside herself." Wilson had then written (1934): "The governess who is made to tell the story is a neurotic case of sex repression, and . . . the ghosts are not real ghosts but hallucinations of the governess."

In reading Wilson's 1948 footnote I was at first horrified to see signs of a recantation of his 1934 argument. He begins by admitting, somewhat grudgingly, that several scholars had used those fourteen years to poke some gaping holes in the Kenton-Wilson thesis. He confesses that he had "forced a point in trying to explain away the passage in which the housekeeper identifies, from the governess' description, the male apparition with Peter Quint." What is more, he admits that James's statements in his notebooks are hard to reconcile with Wilson's earlier allegations about the sex life of the governess. When I read this, my heart sank, as well it might. Much of my own work in the interim had been based on the unquestioned assumption that Wilson's Freudian reading had been sound. If the governess should prove, after all, to be a reliable witness to the children's fate, where was I to turn? I had not long to worry, however; within two paragraphs my new life was opened to me. "The doubts that some readers feel as to the soundness of the governess' story are, I believe, the reflection of James's doubts, *communicated unconsciously by himself.* . . . One is led to conclude that, in *The Turn of the Screw,* not merely is the governess self-deceived, but that *James is self-deceived about her.*"[2]

It may be difficult for many of my readers to understand the sense of exhilaration with which I read and reread that passage. The basic principles that it embodies have become so much a part of our heritage that younger readers may have difficulty in reconstructing how we pioneers felt at a time when we had not yet seen our path through the wilderness ahead. Even now I find that some of my sincere disciples are distinctly hazy about

2. That Wilson has since repudiated his repudiation [1959] is, I think, irrelevant to our purposes here.

their methodology; indeed, one of the purposes of this essay is to lay down, once and for all, the methodological distinctions that I first saw clearly on December 11, 1948. We have nothing to lose, and everything to gain, by rooting out from our midst those who would, by simple old-fashioned explications of straightforward irony, climb onto our bandwagon by imitating, in 1960, the sort of thing I was doing in the thirties![3] But back to Wilson.

What I saw on that December morning was that there are not one, not two, but *three* levels of dealing with irony. About the first, perhaps enough has been said, since the less said the better. Each of the other two has its proper set of principles, and the practice of either entitles a man, in my view, to membership in the newly formed IIII (my own role in organizing the Independent International Ironologists Incorporated is not important here). For convenience, we can use Wilson as our guide.

Level II (Wilson and Buthnot, 1934):

> *Principle 1:* No ironies are worth writing about unless they have gone unnoticed by all or most previous readers.
>
> *Corollary 1:* The most artistic ironists are those who deceive the greatest number of readers.

Now this level, old-fashioned as it may seem, still offers a good deal to the ironologist. From the simple motive of seeing in a work what no one else has ever seen have sprung (we may modestly claim) more books and articles than from any other single source. And from the corollary have sprung more reversals of traditional weightings than any other school of criticism can boast. I mention here only the Buthnot Index of Deceptivity (BID), which I developed in 1936 and which has been used by everyone of any importance since. Though I need hardly explain to the readers of *Ironology* the basis of the original index, I should point out that a new edition is now at the press, with an entirely new factor added to the original simple percentage count of readers deceived (RD). In the new test I have added a phi-factor, giving special weighting for the *quality* of deception (for example, a bright reader [BR] counts twice as

3. At the risk of seeming to repeat myself, may I point out once more that ironology is ironology?

much as a dull reader [DR]; a reader who has read 1000 ironic works [ER for experienced reader] counts twice as much as one who has read only 500 ironic works; and a reader who has read my own monumental guide to ironology counts twice as much as any other, in the unlikely case that he is bagged by the ironist). But I must hurry on.

Level III (Wilson and Buthnot, 1948)

> *Principle 2:* The most important ironies are those the author himself never suspected.

> *Corollary 2:* The most artistic ironists are those who deceive themselves.

If there is anyone who yet doubts the *seminal* power of our discovery, he cannot have studied much of the criticism published by myself and members of my department. From the many articles and books that might well have been dedicated to me, but for my policy of self-effacement, I shall cite here only the first book in the history of the world consisting entirely of criticism about *one short story: A Casebook on Henry James's "The Turn of the Screw,"* edited by Gerald Willen. (The suggestion by one of my colleagues that *Willen* is an ironic mask for *Wilson* is, I think, far-fetched) . The very existence of this book, made up as it is of *all the possible guesses* about the governess's character, should convince any doubter that our school of criticism and ours alone dominates the contemporary scene. Of the many passages in this book that exemplify the all-important *Principle 2,* I cite only a brief portion of the editor's own imaginative Introduction—just to show what can be done once a critic manages to free himself from the inhibiting traditional standards of relevant proof:

> Whatever one may think of Edmund Wilson's reading of *The Turn of the Screw,* the Freudian interpretation has triggered a great deal of discussion. . . . Is it possible, then, that Douglas is Miles? That the governess, in love with Miles (Douglas) , and unable to act in the situation, herself wrote a *story,* a fiction? And, finally, that Douglas as a child, as well as a young man down from Trinity, was in love with the governess? These implications may be inferred from the story, although Douglas's precise relationship to the governess is not closely defined. But even if there is an understated connection between Douglas and the governess, the interpretations developed by various critics are not necessarily invalidated. For the essential fact remains that the

story told by the governess needs to be read at varying levels. This is all the more true if we say that her story is, in effect, a fiction.

On the other hand, ruling out the possibility of an ulterior motive (involving Douglas) on the part of the governess, we may still maintain that her manuscript is not a true story at all, that it is a work of fiction she had already committed to paper before relating orally to Douglas. Or she may have made it up as she went along and then written it down. Whatever *The Turn of the Screw* is, however, a "true story" or a fiction, it still retains all its challenges.

I think it will be clear that Willen has here made explicit two more corollaries that have underlain all of our best work:

> *Corollary 3:* The more "varying levels" a story presents, the more challenges to the ironologist, and the more challenges the better the story.
>
> *Corollary 4:* The more hypotheses thrown up by the dredging critic, the better the critic, especially if these hypotheses can be seen to have come entirely from the critic's imagination, with no help from the author.

There was a time, I would be the first to admit, when some of my staff still tended to limit themselves to hypotheses that bore some relationship to specific statements in the work. Worse yet, I even hired a young instructor once who, without advance warning, published an interpretation based on paying attention to the *sequence* of words and events in the story, as if it mattered to an ironologist whether an interpreted detail came earlier or later in a story. But it can be seen that to work in that way was to rely slavishly on the author's assistance—tantamount to saying that he had some idea what he was doing! In firing that young man, I issued a little memo which has become a kind of classic among us, modestly be it said. I quote here only the most pertinent paragraph from a section which one of my colleagues ironically dubbed "The Ironologist's Catechism":

In short, then, to discover whether we have done what *can* be done with any particular text, we must always ask ourselves, before releasing our critical work for publication, the following questions—questions that were, one must painfully confess, largely ignored by young Straightley: Do I offer at least two hypotheses that have never occurred to anyone else? If not, try again. Are my hypotheses clearly guesses springing from my own fecund brain rather than dull reconstructions of possibilities from the text itself? If not, try again. Do my guesses

treat the text as a bumbling half-try by the writer, at best a starting
point for my own inventive powers? If not, try again. Will my inventions outrage all readers who have studied the original closely? If not,
try again. Have I treated *all* villains and villainesses as heroes and
heroines, and all heroes and heroines as villains and villainesses? If
not, try, try again.

Before turning to a final brief statement about the future
plans for the department, I must note two niggling matters that
have come to my attention. First, it is *not* true that I stole the
notion of *outrage* from Leslie Fiedler. I have in my files proof
that I was the first critic ever to state publicly the notion that a
critic should set out to offend all other critics. Secondly, I have
been accused by certain British critics of bias because of my
refusal to hire G. Wilson Knight. One correspondent has written: "Where could you find a fuller exemplification of your
catechism than Knight's reversal of Claudius and Hamlet?"
Well, I will admit that Knight's mastery of the Villain-Hero
Reversal Tactic is unquestionable. But anyone who studies his
statement carefully will find many obvious ways in which it
falls short of full ironology. "It is," he tells us, "a nihilistic birth
in the consciousness of Hamlet that spreads its deadly venom
around. That Hamlet is originally blameless, that the King is
originally guilty, may well be granted. But, if we refuse to be
diverted from a clear vision by questions of praise and blame,
responsibility and causality, and watch only the actions and
reactions of the persons as they appear, we shall observe a
striking reversal of the usual commentary." This, I must confess looks like ironology almost at its best. The striking reversal
(Principle 1) is good, though it would be better if it were clearly
a reversal of which Shakespeare himself was said to be unconscious. As it is, however, we have a fine bit of originality—a
stroke that is sure to prove a fructifying one—in Knight's request that we suspend our temptations to "praise and blame," in
order to come to a disinterested "admiration" for Claudius,
who "is distinguished by creative and wise action, a sense of
purpose, benevolence, a faith in himself and those around him,
by love of his Queen."

There is an extremely subtle distinction here between "praise
and blame," which we are to avoid, and our sense of approba-

tion for Claudius and disapprobation for the "cynical" Hamlet who is "a poison in the midst of the healthy hustle of the court." I will even concede that Knight has brought to a fine point a corollary we have not yet enunciated.[4]

And yet, and yet—why must Knight give the whole thing away by failing to make clear whether Shakespeare consciously intended Claudius to be hero and Hamlet villain? Needless to say, my mind is not closed on the question; I can still conceive of Knight as a full-fledged member of the department. But he has some way yet to go. There is too much, in his whole essay, of concession to his reader's desire for an air of providing evidence, too much of the conciliatory and too little of the outrageous.

But enough of such matters. I must draw to a close. There is no point in detailing the exhilarating history of how I wrested the department from the old irony crowd—though I do take some pride in the rigor with which I got rid of every last man who had ever published on *recognized* ironists like Lucian, Juvenal, Erasmus, Swift, or Butler. But I must just add a note about the future. It would not be fair to my colleagues for me to reveal the scope of their works-in-progress. But I *can* give some idea of the possibilities open to us by copying the table of contents of *my* new book, *The Secret Eiron: A Dialectic of Distant Personae,* to be published by Paradox Press this fall.

1. The Unreliable Narrator in *Paradise Lost*
2. Squire *All*worthy?
3. Dilsey, or Who Castrated Benjy?
4. Alyosha, the Androgynous Saint
5. No Crime, No Punishment?
6. Pap as Jim: The Father Surrogate in Blackface
7. Ishmael, the Secret Owner of the Pequod
8. "A" for A . . . . . . ? New Light on Hawthorne
9. Regan Vindicated: Responsibility and Piety in *Lear*
10. The Gothic Integrity of Becky Sharpe
11. The Hidden Satanism of *Four Quartets*
12. Jesus Christ and Judas Iscariat: The Duplicity of Sanctity

---

4. *Corollary 5:* In ironology, there is *always* a subtle difference between *a critical technique when used by your adversary and that same technique when used by the ironologist. In the last analysis, it is the difference between good criticism and bad.*

With the last two chapters, it will be clear that I am moving into a new dimension in criticism. I need not try to hide the fact that I have been asking myself for a long time: "Why confine ironology to imaginative literature?" I find no good answer to this question. On the contrary, if fruitful results can serve as a criterion in such matters, I find every reason for suspecting that until recently everyone *in all areas has taken everyone and everything* too straight. Few seem to have suspected the new reading delights that can come when one has at last seen that Adam Smith, say, *meant something else entirely*. Following this lead, my *next* book has chapters on the vices of Socrates ("The Hemlock Ploy"), Aristotle ("The Inner metaphysic: *Five Causes*"), Copernicus ("Geocentrism Disguised"), and a dozen others, leading up to "The Aesthetic Absolutism Implicit in Einstein's Ontology." The value of my approach cannot be given adequate statement in short compass, but it is at least suggested by the fact that we have so far found *not one single statement* in the entire history of western thought that did not turn out to be more interesting if turned upside down.

It is perhaps premature of me to suggest what our next step should be, but I cannot resist pointing out a very real sense in which God is proving to be the great ironologist. I hinted in my opening paragraph that I see ironology as the discipline of disciplines. While I am not yet prepared to go so far as to suggest that I have been explicitly chosen to see the Irony of Ironies, and to reveal in doing so the Supreme Ironologist, it may come to that in the end.

Meanwhile, with converts coming our way in droves, with more students than the department can handle, with a higher percentage of published books and articles per man than any other department, *in any subject,* in this or any other country, and with a consequent $5,000 raise for every one of us next year, I feel that my most seminal years are yet ahead. Unless, of course, the dean was being ironic in that last letter. Could it be possible—?

RAFFERTY ON RAFFERTY
A REVIEW OF
MAX RAFFERTY ON EDUCATION

This is one of the most effective satires ever written. The anonymous author—I would give anything to know who he is—has invented, in the guise of an essay collection, a wildly comic portrait of a hero who carries upon his frail shoulders the burden of every absurd educational pose known to man. The author (I shall from this point on call him X) has created in "Max Rafferty" a character sure to endure in our pantheon, a self-betraying narrator as egotistical as Sir Willoughby Patterne, as prosaic and utilitarian as Gradgrind, as authoritarian as Squeers, as fond of his own voice as Micawber.

"I tell you that . . . I tell you further that . . . And I say finally that. . . ." "I say 'Yes.' . . . For Pete's sake, let's encourage them. . . . So get with it. . . ." "Who insists on indoctrinating . . . teachers with the dogmas of John Dewey? I'll tell you who: the teachers colleges." What other satirist has so effectively echoed the voice from a Disneyland mountain top? The prophet harangues, snorts, chuckles, always through a hand megaphone, always in a slangy style derived about equally from Rudolph

Reprinted from *English Journal*, March, 1969, pp. 450–52, with permission of the National Council of Teachers of English.

Flesch and Little Orphan Annie: "Yes, siree. There we Cal-
ifornians stood with egg all over our faces." "Horsefeathers."

The voice is the voice of an ignorant man who would seem
learned. "Few modern writers, for example, can hold a scatological candle to Dan Chaucer at his filthiest. . . ." What a
scatological candle might be I shudder to think, and what old
Geoffrey Defoe would make of all this first-naming and nick-
naming only X could tell (the goddess Minerva becomes, for
example, Old Min!). Perhaps in consequence it is often the
voice of a conversational bully. Rafferty's enemies are never
simply mistaken; they are "fatheaded," and they utter "blatant
nonsense" and "fiddle-faddle" and "bunk," not the simple
errors that some men's enemies might utter. Mental institutions are the "funny farm" or the "booby hatch," and they lie
in wait, throughout the book, for anyone crazy enough to disagree with good old commonsensical, hard-headed Rafferty.
And they are not the only institutions that loom behind the
narrator's brutalized style. In "A Good Word for Capital Punishment" the style becomes the man; without quite arguing
openly for lynch-justice, Rafferty puts in his good word for a
large increase in capital punishment, or, as he puts it, "lowering
the boom," "promptly and vigorously," "permanently." "Instead of doing away with the gas chamber, I think we ought to
enlarge it." X may have overdone this chapter a bit; no one in
real life could be quite so awful, and the result is that the book
ceases, for a time, to be comic. (One cannot help wondering
whether X had some subtle reason for placing a chapter on
this subject in a book about education?)

But in general the satire is delightful, and it is extended to
matters that go far beyond stylistic eccentricities. X gives his
hero almost every major intellectual flaw.

1. *Confused Values.* Rafferty claims to be defending educational quality, but he reveals only the haziest notions of what
quality might be. And when he does become specific, he is
scary, as when he identifies quality with size: "I am not—alas—
a professor, although I have served a stint of graduate lecturing
in one of our *largest* universities. . . . I have been associating
rather intimately with the cap-and-gown set for more than 30

years. I serve on the governing board of the *biggest* state college system in the land and as a regent on the nation's *mightiest* university." (My italics.)

2. *Feeble logic.* Not since *Alice in Wonderland* have we had a book with so many delicious bits of topsy-turvydom. Censorship is a good thing, for example, when practiced by "educators," because "every schoolman practices censorship almost every day of his professional life" when he chooses what books to teach his students. Rafferty's proof for *this* is that his dictionary defines a censor as "anyone who exercises supervision over manners and morals." "If this doesn't describe one of the key roles of any teacher, I'll eat my mortarboard." Therefore censorship is no problem, right?

3. *Sloppy definition of terms.* We see in the last quotation how beautifully X has exploited Rafferty's naive faith in dictionary definitions. He can settle every question by choosing one or another definition from "my dictionary." Is "present-day literature" really literature? No, because "my dictionary defines . . ." X has deliberately deprived him of any awareness of how dictionaries work, of what questions they can settle and what questions they cannot.

4. *Inconsistency.* A lesser satirist might have bungled here. But X strikes just the right balance between too much inconsistency, which would have made his character unconvincing, and too little, which would have made him a serious proponent of a position worthy of attention. Does his hero on one page object to certain measures because they violate individual liberty? Well, let him then praise the "Golden State" for adopting and distributing its own textbooks and forcing "every public school pupil . . . to use them, with no ifs, ands or buts." Does he praise "simplification" in one chapter? Then let him, in the next chapter, make fun of other men's simplifications.

5. *Indifference to evidence.* X has on the whole kept Rafferty from offering any kind of evidence for his claims. The generalizations pour out fast and free, untrammelled by facts. But when on occasion evidence *is* offered, the effect is hilarious. Have some librarians argued that books cannot lead children to crime? Well, we can disprove that one. Look at Bluebeard, led

IRONIES AND THE NEW SCIENCE OF IRONOLOGY

to murder by books on black magic! Look at Hitler and the effect on him of *reading his own book, Mein Kampf!* Look at the Marquis de Sade and at the young murderer in England who *said* that Sade influenced him. Next question?

Etc.

Perhaps X's subtlest touches can be seen in the way in which he has handled those few perfectly reasonable opinions that he allows Rafferty to express. Just as we are beginning to think that all of his opinions are going to be whimsical (like calling Walt Disney "the greatest educator of this century") or obvious (like "Kids are education's main reason for existence") or inflammatory-disguised-as-tautological (like "A Teaching Credential is not a License to Corrupt"), suddenly he throws in a Sound Opinion or two. But it is here that X's skill is most evident, because in almost every commitment of a Reasonable View, the reasons are either left out or contradicted. Rafferty says, for example, that he favors the reading of children's classics rather than the Dick and Jane books, but he reveals himself as quite untouched by any reading of books, adult or juvenile. He says that he is in favor of voting for education bonds, but the effect of his book, if one took it in his own terms, would be to make one organize an attack on every school in sight. He says that he is in favor of eliminating courses in student grooming and telephone conversation skills, and that he wants to teach organized, disciplined, systematic subject matter, but the few hints he gives of the latter sound worse than the horrors his archenemy, John Dewey, was rightly trying to combat decades ago. There is, indeed, one moment when X almost loses control of his satire—when he allows Rafferty to begin a serious discussion of the question of what he means by "Education in Depth." He then devotes two whole pages to the "five purposes of education": "to pursue the truth; to hand down the cultural heritage; to teach organized . . . subject matter; to help the individual realize his own potential; and to ensure the survival of our country." Since these two pages come smack in the middle of the book, I feared for a moment that X would spoil his satire by allowing Rafferty to spend some of the remaining 160 pages showing us what these praiseworthy goals mean and how they might be attained. What a relief, then, to turn the page and find the subject changed to an impassioned claim that Will Rogers must have been lying when he said he'd never met a man he didn't like!

The supreme skill of this book, then, lies in its irony: the protagonist of "Education in Depth" never leaves the surface, the proponent of systematic intellectual discipline is unsystematic, anti-intellectual, and totally undisciplined. If X can only be located, he deserves the National Book Award.

LAST DAYS

Be thou faithful unto death.
        —Revelations

Eriger en lois ses impressions personelles, c'est le grand effort d'un homme s'il est sincere.
        —Remy de Gourmont

. . . a man who chose not to despair.
        —Helen Gardner on T. S. Eliot

LAST DAYS

It is said that there are more than two thousand separate "Christian" sects in South Africa alone, each founded by its very own prophet with his special revelation of truth. America can match that one easily, even if one keeps the "Christian" qualification. And if one expands the notion of religious sect to include any group with a leader chosen by divinity to reveal the last word, the count must go into the tens of thousands.

In contrast, the predominant rhetoric among intellectuals, at least until quite recently, has been either irreligious or ecumenical: let us drop our silly and indefensible ideological differences and build an international liberal world or international socialism or a single, genuinely catholic church. Exclusivist and often fanatical religious and political sects have gone on multiplying at a great rate—possibly even an increasing rate in the past two decades. And recently—if I may hazard one more grotesquely unsupported generalization—intellectuals have stopped anticipating an "end of ideology" and have begun to predict a new age of ideological warfare. Every man can choose his own sign of the times, but for me the new age became real the first time a student "cut me dead," passing me on the sidewalk on campus, because I had said something in public disagreeing with his views. Or another one: yesterday I received word, here in London, that Stanford University will no longer play varsity games with Brigham Young University because of the Mormon church's policy of not granting the priesthood to Negroes. A time of religious wars is again upon us!

My own spiritual path through the decades of official liberal toleration leading to this new age of intolerance has been as unoriginal as could be: from complete faith in the unique truth of one quite remarkably intolerant church (one that happens itself to have spawned more than fifty separate and mutually hostile sects), through a period of what I called atheism, when most or all beliefs seemed equally irrational, on to various re-discoveries of truths I thought I had outgrown. I spare you the details of this commonplace journey, except for one that throws an ironic light on the three sermons that follow.

Picture to yourself a twenty-year-old Mormon missionary, brought up with the habit of "bearing his testimony to the truthfulness of the Gospel," struggling in 1943 to come to terms with what seems to be the prevailing view of all the intelligent non-Mormons he knows: that there *is* no gospel and that to bear public testimony to any sort of religious affirmation is square. Trying to find some way, as he puts it, to avoid throwing out the baby (spiritual truth) with the bathwater (Mormon dogma) , he reads, for example, a series in the *Partisan Review,* called "The New Failure of Nerve." John Dewey and Sidney Hook and others accuse T. S. Eliot and Aldous Huxley and a variety of other muddle-headed folk of a cowardly betrayal of progressive (though perhaps unpleasant) truths which every honest and brave man must accept. Seldom can anyone have been more confused than that young man, trying to find some new direction for his life and being told again and again by those who appeared to be the best "thinkers" of his age that every time he touched a traditional religious category he was betraying the intellect.

It is somewhat more fashionable now to make open confessions of faith and commitment. Our trouble, as I tried to show in part I, is that our affirmations seem more and more brutally divorced from anything that could be called a mental effort.

The result is a new kind of failure, a failure of intellectual nerve in a sense different from what was meant by that hard-headed crowd writing in *Partisan Review*: a general and bland doubt that anything need or can be said for my beliefs except that I believe them. *Sincerely*. And if my sincerity is not clear to you yet, I can prove it to you by laying my body on the line. But please don't slow down the movement (left, right, or center) by trying to discuss my reasons; I have seen too many cases of intellectuals who have used their minds to undercut all conviction and render all committed action silly.

It seems likely that most men, including those who think of themselves as intellectuals, cannot for long avoid choosing affirmation of some kind—even a mindless affirmation—rather than live with an emptiness revealed by the denying intellect. Men will choose sides and fight in the name of debased gods rather than live with no god at all. "If you will not give me a good cause that will stand up to the light of reason, I will invent my own miracle, mystery, and authority. But I *will* have a cause."

I read in this morning's *Times* (December 3, 1969) of a so-called hippie cult, led by a man who calls himself "Jesus," "God," and "Satan," that has allegedly been committing a kind of ritual murder in California. "Members of the band—a mystical, hate-oriented tribe of twentieth-century nomads . . . killed their victims, police believe, both to 'punish' them for their affluent life style and to 'liberate' them from it. . . . All [the suspects] . . . consider themselves his 'slaves,' willing to do his bidding without question. . . . The cult considered itself above the law and divinely guided. . . ."

Are we shocked? I hope so. Are we surprised? We should not be. We have taught these young people that the universe is value-free, that values are invented by man, and therefore that each man is free to invent his own. As Ivan Karamazov says, predicting these groups, once there is no law everything is lawful. We have gone on to feed them a diet of fiction and movies and TV preaching both the "meaninglessness of life" and the excitement of violence. We have set them a splendid example, Vietnam, of a nation that considers itself to be above all traditional laws. How can we then be surprised if they run amok. Nor should it surprise us that they find it necessary to support their crimes with a religious rationale—though of the feeblest kind. We can in fact expect more and more of these desperate gropings for a divine cause: "If I am the slave of Jesus-God-Satan, at least I am *somebody*." (I would not be surprised to learn that the account of the group has been greatly exaggerated; my argument does not depend on the detailed validity of the example.)

Surrounded, or so it sometimes seems to me, by bands of such mad cultists on the one hand and by apathetic unbelievers on the other, I have no embarrassment, then, in continuing a life-long habit of "bearing my testimony" to what I think of as a rational faith. Since for me God lives—in a sense that I am happy to explain at the drop of a hat—the only thing that has recently died is the rhetoric of theologians. What I thus naturally struggle for is a way to translate the tired old words into a language that can be heard both by men who think that it is intellectually disreputable to listen, and by men who have hastily embraced this or that makeshift faith.

I cannot claim that even now I completely escape moments of despair. But whenever I am sufficiently undistracted to *put my mind to it*, I find no doubt whatever that the search for harmonies of mind and heart is itself in harmony with the nature of things. There are many older ways of putting this faith, perhaps the most common being: God lives. *Our* most widespread belief seems to be that God is dead, but that his replacement will be shipped in sometime around the year 2000.

Futurism was invented by western society, I gather, as it tried to find a replacement for the Christian payoff, salvation. Communism and capitalism have generally recommended themselves by offering alternative payoffs, both promising happiness to untold millions in the future. It is interesting that even our critiques of the received forms of futurism are generally futurist: the New Left, like the old, the new conservatism, like the old, tests everything as a contribution to future fulfilment. Thus the Lord God Eternal, the same now and always, simply does not exist for most of us, even those who claim to believe in God: God himself has been horizontalized, laid out flat on the chains of time; even if he's still alive for some, it is as Lord of the great payoff at the end of the line.

I watch my fine freshman class grappling with Descartes' argument that the God whose existence the great doubter has just proved (by ontological argument, be it noted) creates the world (and hence *them*) in every moment in exactly the same sense that he can be said to have created the world "in the beginning." Most of them simply cannot get it, just as they cannot discern anything more than playful fancy in Plato's metaphysics. They can palpitate to the Descartes who decides to pursue his honest doubts without compromise; they admire independent minds that choose to go it alone. And they admire the Socrates who talks like a member of the New Left. But when Descartes moves to his proofs, and when Plato tries to give his religious reasons for repudiating the bourgeois Athenians, they get off the boat. They know that science has disproved—whatever is not scientific. In short, they come to college already indoctrinated with a vulgar version of a positivist science that probably no longer exists among genuine scientists. And they know that nothing *exists* but the simple causal chain of events from past to future. They have been taught to pay homage only to that Future; they have read our new theologians who speculate about the year 2000 with the same fervor that the scholastics put into the question of whether the good is dependent on God's will. Those who resist the futurist dogmas that come at them from all sides turn helplessly to an unredeemed present and try to find beliefs that can feel genuine *now* regardless of what is to come. But so long as they find inconceivable a Supreme Being who is unchanging first cause, prime mover, and law giver, operating "vertically," everywhere, now, and always, they will be as lost in the present as they would be if still hoping for a future redemption.

With God safely interred, in other words, our rhetoric about how to live is thrown into chaos: the difference between sermons becomes only a difference of skill, never a difference of truth. Appalled by what this would mean if pursued seriously, I go on preaching in various ways that for our new beginnings we must turn always to the Logos, that curious word with the capital *L*.

I know that my assertions will to many seem as "unproved" as the dogmas of the new cults seem to me, especially in passages like my little effort at a theodicy that somehow slipped into "The Golden Rule"; even to me this passage is shorter on hard reasoning and longer on bare assertion than is comfortable. I like to think that with more time than was offered on these three lovely ceremonial mornings I could have filled in some of the more obvious gaps; some of them are at least plugged *at* in other talks. But I cannot pretend, even now, to a developed, fully invulnerable correlation between my "Platonic" faith in the reality of eternal and incorporeal qualities or values and my insistence on a hard-headed "Aristotelian" battle against the evils that are done in the name of similar "abstractions" believed in by other men. In one branch of Platonic theory, a branch I cannot follow, particulars become unimportant—even if they are particular persons. And in my own version, the particulars of a man's life and death and of his joys and sufferings are less important than whether or not he has, at any moment, in joy *and* in suffering, entered into reality by achieving some sort of genuine human fulfilment. Followed out to the hilt, this position I suppose leads to precisely the sort of dialectical juggling with abstract ideas and violation of particular lives and works that I try to combat in "How to Use Aristotle." Such unresolved (possible) contradictions are troublesome to a man who has made fun of those who glory in paradox and who fail to pursue their self-contradictions rigorously. About all I can say in defense of my own self-contradictions is that I am still trying to work them through.

Meanwhile I end with no sense of a coherent metaphysic to buttress my plea for a rational persuasion; I can offer only a series of pleas for various loosely related truths that I claim to "know." They may not be fully "demonstrated," but I hope that they are more plausible and less destructive than the more popular alternatives that are offered, with considerably less evidence and with no concern for consistency, by those who believe that Meaning is either dead or is only to be found in this or that new mystery cult.

THE GOLDEN RULE REVISITED
A SERMON TO
ONE HUNDRED AND TWENTY-TWO
SINFUL SENIORS
BEING GRADUATED INTO
A SINFUL SOCIETY

I

One mark of an educated man is I suppose the ability to decide which of the clichés his society pours into him still have nutritive value. Some of them are poison; some are pablum, suitable only for infants; and some on examination turn out to contain more vitamins and proteins than he had expected. Among the latter I would place the host of phrases that cluster around the golden rule: "man's inhumanity to man," "the inhuman use of human beings," "spiritual cannibalism"—and on the affirmative side, "love your enemies," "you are your brother's keeper," "men must be treated as ends, not means," "the innate dignity of every man." This morning in thousands of college chapels around the world speakers are no doubt telling their listeners to love their seatmates as much as they love themselves. The endless repetition of such truisms ought to make us at least initially suspicious, especially in a world where men daily destroy each other, both physically and spiritually—and usually in the name of virtue. By choosing the right pious phrase, a

Baccalaureate address, Earlham College, 1960.

man can make almost any kind of bestiality seem virtuous, like the comfortable stage-coach traveller in *Joseph Andrews* who refuses to lend his cloak to the naked and freezing Joseph on the grounds that charity should begin at home.

One of the major justifications for true education, education that really takes, is that it makes such self-deception difficult. An educated man, as we all know to our sorrow, may do evil, but if he's truly educated he won't be able to disguise evil by making himself believe that it is good. One thing that your four years in college should have taught you is that most bad things travel under good names, or as it used to be put, the devil himself can quote scripture for his purposes. If this is true, if it is really one function of education to uncover our hypocrisies and to force us to distinguish between things that are only called good and things which really are good, then perhaps it is appropriate for us this morning, at the culminating religious service in a four-year educational program, to look behind our claims to believe that men should be treated as persons and not used as things. At the very least we may come to see our failures somewhat more clearly.

We should love our neighbors *as ourselves,* we say, and more than a fourth of all Americans, according to one survey, believe that they succeed in loving their *enemies* as themselves. What a blesséd land—one man in every four is a saint! But even if we assume a good deal of hypocrisy in our loving pretensions, they are *there*, and at least we should consider fairly closely what would be required of a man if he took them seriously. If we mean anything by them, we must mean that we set the same value on our neighbor, or in the extreme case, our enemy, as we do on ourselves. We obviously can't mean that we love our enemy as we love our latest steady-date, doting on his every move and longing to be in his presence every minute. We must mean that our neighbor—the man or woman sitting next to us here and now—*is worth as much as we are.*

Now how much am I worth to myself? The very question is almost meaningless: there is no scale of calculation, no measuring table that could ever translate my interest in my own well-being, regardless of how I define it, into figures, into hard cash.

If someone were to offer me all the wealth in the world in exchange for committing suicide, or in exchange for surrendering all my chances for happiness or well-being, the offer would seem ludicrous. It is not just that I'm worth *more* than that to myself. It's that my feeling about my value goes right off the chart; it simply cannot be put in measurable terms. Regardless of how low an opinion I may have of myself, my essential nature is not to me measured in any quantitative scale. I cannot be evaluated, in my own eyes, at less than infinity.

Now the dictum that we should love our neighbors as ourselves must mean that we should recognize the equal validity of other men's infinite self-value. As you sit here today, you have some sense of how much *you* are worth; most of us would "give anything," as we put it, for—and then we each fill in our own brand of salvation, however secular that salvation might be. But how many of us would give as much for the well-being of the stranger or near stranger, or even the intimate friend, sitting next to us this morning? Instead, we cut them down to a size which can be measured against other values, and we thus learn to deal with them as we deal with things: as useful or troublesome for our own purposes.[1]

There are many trite ways of describing this process of cutting down to a manageable, *usable* size. We can say that we violate their *divinity*, or that we deny their essential *dignity as human beings*, or that we deny their *humanity*. I should like to explore briefly two other ways of describing the same thing: we treat people as things whenever we reduce their worth to numbers, to quantities; and we treat people as things whenever we use them for our own ends regardless of their own well-being.

1. As I do a final editing of this speech, on December 2, 1969, I have just come from a reading of the London *Times*, with its many accounts of the My Lai massacre. The bland good humor of the sermon seems grotesquely inadequate to the realities of "Pinkville," and I find myself wondering whether any of my auditors have been graduated to their very own atrocity since that beautiful morning at Earlham. But of course at the time it was given the sermon was equally inadequate to the realities of Belsen or Hiroshima or the Moscow purges or the Thirty Years' War. The evil feels closer to me, now, and the tone thus becomes different when I speak (below) to the graduates of 1969. But the essential problem still seems to me unchanged.

These two terminologies cannot really be separated for long. To *measure* human beings, as the social scientists do, is often a first step to *using* them, and to use them we must always in one way or another reduce them to calculable size. But we can keep them distinct for awhile by beginning with a brief look at how we all quantify our neighbors and thus implicitly deny that they *are* worth as much as we, in our own infinite and genuinely precious dignity.

Think for a moment of what we are doing today. We are awarding approximately the same degree to 122 of you students, because you have been with us for four years and have managed to accumulate at least 120 hours of credit, as we say, meaning that you have sat in on about forty courses and received an average grade of C or better. But can we grade quality? We say that a student is a good student. Fine. We are judging a quality. But the registrar's office requires a grade, so we translate "good" into A or B and the A or B goes into the record. Then at graduation time the A is translated into a 3 and the B into a 2, and on down the line, and the student then has, as we put it, a grade point average of 2.649. Now the student is no longer a good student, he is a 2.649 student. We must now calculate honors and honorable mention. The cutting point between an honors student and one who only deserves honorable mention is 2.65. Oh, dear. This student has only 2.649, 1/1000th of a point below what it ought to be. Sorry, only honorable mention. (The seniors do not need to be told that this is an actual case from this year's class.)

Now any teacher who is honest will tell you that he cannot grade students with any high degree of accuracy at the A, B, and C distinctions. Even the mathematicians, as a Haverford experiment has shown, cannot translate their measurement of a student's mathematical ability into quantitative terms with any greater accuracy than about one full grade. In English and history and philosophy the judgments are even less reliable. Yet we insist on translating them into precise mathematical terms. Sometimes these numbers are measures of charity, too, as some of you know to your relief. The teacher weighs so-much charity against so-much knowledge (or ignorance), finds charity triumphant, and the student passes. Or truth triumphs, and the student fails. Whichever way he decides, he must reduce a complex human being to a simple and brutal mathematical symbol.

We may feel like condemning Earlham and other colleges for depending on this ridiculous kind of measurement, but before we do we should be very clear about how ineradicable the need to *quantify* our fellows seems to be. The God of the Old Testament, to name one weak mortal among many possible examples, constantly distinguishes the worth of different persons, and he seems to condone such judgments in men themselves. Abel is worth more to him than Cain, Noah more than the innumerable wicked souls who died in the flood. Was each of those who died of *infinite* worth? Jehovah certainly does not say so. When the Lord bargains with Abraham over the fate of Sodom, we seem to get a calculating comparison among men of differing worth. At first the Lord is determined, you'll remember, to destroy the whole city, good and bad. But Abraham plays upon his sense of justice: "Far be it from thee to do such a thing, to slay the righteous with the wicked, so that the righteous fare as the wicked! Far be that from thee! Shall not the Judge of all the earth do right?" God accepts Abraham's calculation that fifty good men are enough to balance his wrath against the many wicked men in Sodom. Then Abraham cautiously and shrewdly brings God down to forty-five, then forty, thirty, twenty, and finally ten. If there are ten good men, that is enough, God finally says, to save the city: "For the sake of ten, I will not destroy it." Now I have always wondered why Abraham stopped at ten. Why not five? Why not *one?* How much is the *goodness of one good man* worth, if it takes ten times that much to outweigh on the eternal scales several hundreds or thousands of wicked men? One-tenth of infinity? But you can't divide or multiply infinities. Yet we have said earlier that each man is of immeasurable, incalculable, infinite value.

I ran across an almost horrifying example of the same kind of calculation in a recent book called *How to Read a Novel.* The author has been troubled by a claim made by Albert Camus, in that wonderful little novel, *The Fall,* that Christ must have felt guilty about Herod's slaughter of the innocents.

After all, if it hadn't been for Christ's mission, the poor children wouldn't have been slaughtered; their killing argues, implicitly, that Christ and God were unable to avoid *using* human beings in the pursuit of their own ends. In the following passage, the author tries to exonerate Christ from Camus' charge:

A little research into the "vital statistics" of the times might have dispelled this curious delusion. In ancient times the number of Herod's victims was supposed to be great. . . . But modern hagiographers, beginning with Bishop Butler, point out that Bethlehem was a small place and, even when its environs were included, could not have produced more than twenty-five babies under two years of age, at the very most. Some authorities place the number as low as half a dozen.

A guilt complex as enormous as that which M. Camus' hero ascribes to the Savior of the World would seem to call for the slaughter of considerably more innocents than history gives us reason to believe in.

This absurd argument, assigning a little bit of guilt for one murder, a little bit more for two, and so on, may seem to you extreme. But we all perform similar calculations all the time. An obvious instance is that of the Justice Department's current effort to calculate how much compensation people should have whose lives are disturbed or destroyed by jet testing. How much is a child's terror, or a year of sleepless nights, worth? Calculate, go ahead and calculate. We all do it every day.

If we shift to the second way of talking about and defending such violations, the accommodation of means to ends, our daily guilt becomes more clear. Most of us will refuse to sell other men for cash, but when we are forced to weigh men against men, we land in difficulty. It is popular to condemn means-and-ends thinking—whenever we catch somebody else using it. The Communists are frequently and properly attacked for openly preaching that what is immoral by bourgeois standards is justified in working for the triumph of Communism. But one need not go to Russia to find the same line of argument: "After all, what is the misery of a few people now when weighed in the balance against the immense happiness of millions of men in the future?"

We simply do not see the issue so clearly when our own lives and our own future is at stake. I recently read a defense of our atomic bomb testing that was very interesting from this point of view. The writer admitted that several thousand people in the world were probably condemned to an early and horrible death every time another bomb is tested. But, he said, these deaths will be spread over the whole population of the earth, and when the potential danger for any one person is spread over three billions of people, it turns out to be "statistically insignificant." All of the fallout to date would not shorten the *average* lifespan even so much as one day. Surely a small price to pay for security.

Splendid. But small for whom? For those who die of leukemia? Is death *average,* is pain from cancer *average?* If each man is of infinite worth, is not one sacrifice-death infinitely tragic and infinitely vicious? What are we to say to the murderer who tells us that the effects of his murder, when distributed over the population as a whole, are statistically insignificant? The average lifespan is affected much less by a murder than by a bomb test.

Or take another form of daily sacrifice: We know, every time we get behind the wheel of a car, that there is a chance of our killing either ourselves or someone else, not a high chance but a lot higher than in the bomb example. One in every 8000 Americans is killed each year by a car. Is each one of them of immeasurable value in the sight of the Lord? Surely we don't mean that. If we did, how could we ever balance against their deaths the trivial advantages brought to us by the automobile. Two weeks ago a girl I know of got word one evening that her fiancé had been killed on his way to visit her. How much in the comfort and efficiency of our normal mobile lives is that girl's grief worth? You refuse to calculate? Well, we all calculate, willy nilly, every time we drive a car.

II

Now if what I have been saying is true, it means that we are all in something of a box. Certainly as speaker today I have myself thoroughly boxed in. I am saying that there are two absolute demands in human life, and that these absolute demands are in irreconcilable conflict. We all feel some kind of demand to treat our fellows in terms of absolute qualities; we grant them, in theory, an absolute, infinite worth; we all feel in ourselves what it means to be of immeasurable value, what it means to be an end rather than a means to someone else's purpose, and we cannot escape the conclusion that whatever worth we accord ourselves must be accorded to other men. Yet we all recognize the absolute impossibility of acting *without* judging our fellows and calculating their relative worths, and to some extent *using* them and weighing them on impersonal scales.

If I were driving a car down the road and the sudden choice arose between running over Albert Schweitzer or Adolf Hitler, there is no doubt in my mind which I would choose. If a maniac were about to kill my child, and it was my child's life or the maniac's, there is no doubt what I would do. Or let's come back close to home. Every year Earlham suspends a certain number of students. Of those suspended, whether for academic failure or misconduct, there are a few who would be better off, probably, if they could stay at Earlham. Not many, but some. How do we justify expelling them? It's for the good of Earlham, we say. Earlham cannot tolerate such behavior, because it would—well, what would it do? It would affect the quality of the lives of the remaining 800 students. This we say and this we believe. (It is true that sometimes we say that it is for the student's own good, but this is seldom clearly so.) And what are we saying when we cast these sinners from our presence?

We are saying that the lives of the remaining students and faculty are more important to us, more valuable, worth more, than the single life of the student who is kicked out. We may deplore this until doomsday, but the fact is that Earlham could not exist without making decisions of this kind every day of the week—and most of the compromises consist of weighing the good of some people against the good of some other people; the people in favor of whom we decide in any particular case we call "Earlham"—to salve our consciences. I must be clear: if I were in charge I would not be able to avoid such decisions; I could not preserve the Earlham I value without making them. In short, I am trapped in a situation which requires me, for inescapable reasons, to do things of which I do not approve, and to inflict suffering unjustly.

The difficulty we find ourselves in rests, then, or so it seems to me, at the very heart of our world; it goes deeper than most of us will ever see, and it would be a serious mistake for us to pretend to have resolved it simply by exalting, as one recent writer does, the "noble art of compromise." But there is some comfort in the fact that it is an age-old difficulty.

Each generation discovers for itself that in one sense the world seems to be made for man and that in another sense it seems to violate everything he cares for. Things on this earth have always been troublesome for anyone who tries to *think* about them: the latest crop of existentialists discoursing on absurdity are no more anguished as they face our problem than was Job. But if it is comforting to realize that men in the past have been in our box, it is also sobering to realize that we cannot, in this problem, expect the future to be brighter. Progress in science can remove some areas where this problem is troublesome: we might, for example, develop accident-proof automobiles. But the material progress we make seems to turn up more opportunities for the inhuman use of human beings, and more temptations in the form of global strategy based on grand ends which dictate cruel means.[2] Think of how not long ago we treated those Bikini Islanders. Indeed, I believe that there is reason to expect our problem to get worse rather than better: in short, to me the future looks black, if we think of what it will bring in the way of temptations to harm men for the good of other men or—what is worse—for this or that abstract cause.

But it is important again to remember that the future has always looked black, or almost always. Indeed, until a hundred or so years ago most men thought of things as deteriorating rapidly toward the end of the world, and most religions have been born in an effort to deal with the undeniable fact that our tangible world dies; we die and the world will most certainly die. As the ancient philosophers said, the world is radically contingent.

Yet what is this world that is dying and will die, and *where* is the future that is black? It is precisely in the world of time and

2. I did not know, or need to know, that the Vietnam war was just around the corner.

space, in the world of measurement and calculation, in the world of means-and-ends reasoning; it is there and there only that decay and corruption occur. The future is black and has always been black, but only for things, not for qualities. A century from now your bodies and mine will all be gone to dust—and perhaps radioactive dust at that. But the quality of this moment—good or bad—will remain what it always has been.

The world that is begotten, born, and dies, to quote Yeats, is the world in which men can be treated as things, because they *are* things in that world. Time itself treats them with bland calculation, sacrificing them to its ends as casually as it sacrifices the sparrow or the sparrow-hawk. But time, too, must have a stop; its realm is totally limited by our ability to enter another world, to experience each other as persons and to experience the quality of the world surrounding us. If I have been alive as a full human being in this moment, I have been living in a world that will never change. It will always have been true that this moment *is* what it *is*. Because whatever is really genuine about this moment was not invented by us this morning and will not be destroyed when we die. If there is love at work here this morning, you and I did not invent it. It had its existence in a world which repudiates absolutely the sovereignty of time, space and measurement.

We have heard some beautiful music this morning. Where does that music exist now, and how much is it worth? Is it the manuscript? Sold to the highest bidder. He takes it home, but strangely enough he has not bought the music. He can participate in it, but he cannot buy it. You and I own it as much as he, but we own it only in a very limited sense; if we were all wiped out, mowed down as we leave the building, the music would be unaffected. Even Bach owned it only provisionally. The Bach that lived in time died and ceased to own his music. But is Bach dead? I only wish I were as much alive at this moment as he is. He is very much alive, indeed, but *where* is he? The question is unanswerable, perhaps, except in negative terms. One thing we know clearly: he is not in the world in which calculations are made about grade-point averages.

This is all very well, you may say, but *we* exist only in these bodies; we are caught in that hierarchical world just the same. Try to get out of it, and see how many mystical visions you'll have *then*. True enough, in a way. For reasons which I can't pretend to understand, the timeless world is available to us only through the world of time. Though we are in one sense "trapped in a dying animal," we could never experience our moments of love and creation at all except at the cost of being born into the time-bound, destructive world.

Time present and time past
Are both perhaps present in time future,
And time future contained in time past . . .
               [But] Time past and time future
Allow but a little consciousness.
To be conscious is not to be in time
But only in time can the moment in the rose-garden,
The moment in the arbour where the rain beat
The moment in the draughty church at smoke-fall
Be remembered; involved with past and future.
Only through time time is conquered.

T. S. Eliot's beautiful poetry does not change the fact that once we enter the world of time, we are inevitably caught up in evil. Born as individuals with private egos, into a world that always seems to be cutting away at our edges, we seek to protect ourselves by extending our individual domain; we are naturally *egocentric,* as we say; originally sinful, as men used to say.

Why this should be so may be ultimately beyond answer, but I think it is instructive to try to think of any other way to make a world in which love and creativity are even possible. We *must* first be born as free individuals if we are to move beyond our individual limitations. If to experience love and creativity is good, if to *love* human beings rather than to *use* them is good, then individual consciousnesses, with all their attendant self-centeredness and evil, are necessary. You will notice that this is a form of the ends-means argument that I was earlier attacking: if we are to have such-and-such values, we must sacrifice such-and-such other values, and the price in this case is suffering and evil.

Whatever we discover of love and selflessness must spring, then, from this calculating world of original sin—that is, of unavoidable, natural, in-built selfishness. (I hope nonbelievers here see that I am talking to them as well.) It is always, and *absolutely*—I choose the word carefully—wrong to harm other men for our own ends. What may hurt another man may differ from society to society, but the commandment not to harm him does not vary. And yet we cannot live without to some degree harming our fellow men. Thus we live in a world we never made, full of problems some of which will no doubt never be solved. But most of us have experienced the wonderful inundation of joy and peace that comes on those rare occasions when we join a determination to love our fellows, rather than use them, with a determination to face ourselves squarely and honestly when we are unable to act in love.

I don't pretend to know what Paul had in mind when he said that the greatest of all human qualities was charity. But I like to think that it was a combination of love with honesty, that is, of unlimited respect for persons and unlimited respect for truth. We know that a true exercise of love and honesty will not solve all our problems. But we can be sure that the commandment we have is absolute: whether we look to the Bible, to the uncanonized prophets, to the prophets of religions other than our own, to the great philosophers and literary artists, or simply to our own experience, we are commanded to throw away the false scales and measuring tools of the world of time and enter into the eternal kingdom.

THE WORST THING
THAT CAN HAPPEN TO A MAN

About two weeks ago, a student came to me at my home and reported, in anguish, that because of the disappointing behavior of a much-admired adult, morality had lost its meaning for him. "When I came to Earlham," he said, "I was planning to become a missionary. Now I've lost my faith in God, and what's worse, I can't see that it makes any difference what anybody does. Everything seems meaningless." About a week before that, another student had said, "It seems to me that the most intelligent writers today all say that the universe is absurd. It obviously doesn't matter what *I* do, one way or another."

As all of us know, these students are not alone. A very large proportion of students today, like many of their elders, find moral choice difficult partly because it seems meaningless; they often feel that their sense of helplessness simply reflects the state of the "empty" universe, as portrayed by "the most intelligent writers." Now I am not so rash as to think that I can say what needs to be said to those of you who feel this sense of moral vacuum in your lives; if the answers were easy or clear,

Address delivered at senior recognition convocation, Earlham College, 1962.

we would not find ourselves in such anguishing controversy
about them. At one time in my life I did believe that the answers could be found simply by an appeal to God and revealed
religion; at a later time I thought they could be made by a
simple declaration of atheism and what I called "radical
humanism." In recent years things have not seemed so simple;
only this year I've found myself again revising my views as a
result of having been taught, by a small group of students meeting weekly at my home, that I don't know as much about the
issues as I thought I did. And now, after spending a long time
on this talk, I'm even more conscious than before of my own
inadequacies. The only excuse I can offer for tackling a problem that is bigger than I am is that these are, for many of us,
matters of life and death—sometimes even literally deciding
choices about suicide and murder. We all must answer, consciously or unconsciously, the question of whether values are
objective, and we should therefore try to answer it well rather
than thoughtlessly to repeat fashionable doctrines—what
philosophers used to refer to as "received ideas."

I

There are three different kinds of claim that are often disguised under the same heading when people say that moral
judgments are only relative or subjective. First is what might
be called radical relativism: all moral choices are strictly relative to the wishes and capacities of the individual: right you are
if you think you are.

Since the examples used to prove this position are often ludi-
crously weighted to make the point, let me do some weighting
in the other direction, by trying to dramatize with a few test
cases what we would have to accept if we really believed in
radical relativism. These examples are not offered as proof,
except in a very much curtailed sense of the word. We'll come to
something more closely resembling traditional modes of proof
in a few moments. Here are a few imaginary *Earlham Post* news
items, none of which report anything that could be judged
objectively bad *if* the relativist is correct:

Item: The administration of Earlham College revealed yesterday that Professor Wayne Booth has been, over the past three years, accepting bribes from his students. "I have found," he said when questioned about the morality of this practice, "that I can get as much as $100.00 for an A. I like money, and I feel that what a man likes is what is right for him. If other professors feel that grades should be assigned according to merit, that is their business."

Item: "It was revealed yesterday that President Landrum Bolling has been accepting an annual bribe of $25,000 from the NAM in exchange for a promise to recommend free enterprise whenever possible. When questioned, President Bolling said, "I need money for my family's education. I see nothing wrong in following my personal desires in this matter, especially since it's in a good cause. If other college presidents think they should lead their colleges for the good of the students and not for the welfare of the president's family, that is their privilege; such behavior is no doubt right *for them.*"

Final item: Professor Dan Levine revealed yesterday that he did not believe in his own progressive convocation speech but gave it in the pay of the Communist party. When questioned about the morality of this practice, Dr. Levine said, "It's just the way I was brought up. My parents took bribes, and all their friends took bribes, and therefore so do I."

If the thoroughgoing relativist is right, there is nothing unreasonable about the defenses in each of these cases, and there would have been no true moral superiority in the act of turning down the bribes. Though such examples do not prove that the relativist is wrong, I think they make his choice somewhat clearer than if we allowed him to talk about such matters as whether to steal a book from the bookstore, or such confusing matters as whether to have pre-marital intercourse. It's fairly easy in any case that seems to us borderline to confuse ourselves by pointing to statistics or Kinsey reports or an alleged lack of harmful consequences. But it's a little harder to dodge the real issues when we force ourselves to recognize that if *all* moral judgments are relative, we must declare meaningless the judgments *we* want to make as well as the judgments other men want to make against us.

Put in this extreme form, the relativist position may make us feel uncomfortable, but we still must ask whether it is possible to give proof that it is wrong. Can we prove that choices are not always subjective, that there can be objective validity to moral demands?

It depends a lot on what we mean by proof. Are we looking for proof that would convince a Hitler that he should not exterminate the Jews? If so, I'm afraid we're lost from the beginning. There can be no such proof, if we assume that Hitler has reached a point where he no longer, as we say, listens to reason. If there is such a thing as a wicked man—someone who *prefers* to harm other people or who has no inkling of what it means to consider the needs of others—there can quite obviously be no logical proof to him that he should be different. To what kind of evidence or first principles would we appeal? All proof must refer to some kind of first principle or assumption that is unproved, and all moral proof, since it tries to lead someone to a kind of action, must appeal to a first principle that includes within it a motive, an "I want"; nobody moves, presumably, without a motive. If any man really *wants* to harm others, then he can be perfectly logical (note that I do not say *reasonable*) in working out his harmful purposes. There is no logical proof that could dissuade him unless we could show that his behavior would bring his own destruction; but this would only be an argument for more caution, not for improving his intentions.

Sometimes people talk as if this were a scandalous limitation in moral discourse. Just think, we *can't prove logically* that a man should do what he knows is right. But ethics is no worse off in this respect than any other area of knowledge. If I ask the literary critic to give me logical proof that good literary works ought to be preferred over bad literary works, or the musician to prove that I should prefer beautiful music to radiator thumps, or the political scientist to prove that I should prefer good government to bad government, they may laugh at me, but they can't give me what I ask for. Some of us are surprised to learn that even the most positive of the sciences is stuck in the same trap. If I ask the physicist to prove logically that he ought to believe good evidence rather than bad, or that he ought to let the evidence decide whether he accepts a hypothesis, again he may laugh, but he can't give me what I want. If I really prefer to falsify my evidence in order to serve Communism or the cigarette company that has hired me to disprove the connection between cigarettes and lung cancer, if I really reject the basic scientific endeavor, the scientist cannot give me *logical proof* that I am wrong.

We cannot even *prove* that most certain of all propositions, the law of noncontradiction—the notion that two contradictory propositions cannot both be true at the same time, or that the same proposition cannot be both true and false at the same time, if all the terms remain defined in the same way. For all I can *prove*, in this sense of the word, Chris Clausen may be essentially a human being and essentially an electric light bulb at the same time; if he wants to be smart alecky and say, "Prove that I'm not," I can't think of any line of argument that will demonstrate the falsity of his position.

All I can do—but if I am right it should be enough—is show that the consequences of the opposing view are such that he cannot live with them. Even to get through the next hour he must assume the substantial continuity both of himself and of the persons and things around him; if he once tries to act on the assumption that he is both in this hall and out selling insurance or playing touch football at the same time, he's doomed to find his assumption contradicted at every step of the way. What's more, in our conversation he can only finally rest in silence, because if his denial of the "law" holds, then everything he says can be both true and false at the same time, and he thus cannot affirm or deny anything meaningfully. Again, his elected silence will be impossible to live with, because he knows, from a vast accumulation of experiences, that he has in fact something meaningful to say about many subjects; like every other human being who is not immobilized with some form of madness, he thus "knows" that the law of noncontradiction holds. He can thus honestly "bet his life" on the "unproved" law; it would be radically unreasonable to refuse to do so, because the principle always works, always is confirmed by my experience. Exceptions claimed by people who believe in such things as astral projection (I can be both here and on Venus at the same time) certainly bear the burden of proof, if proof is what we are looking for.

But when we turn to moral matters, things are not quite so easy. When we raise the question of whether our choices are simply expressions of subjective preference—and therefore always in one sense equally right and equally wrong—we again seek to know, not simply to guess. We must come to some sort of justified conviction, if we are to lead effective lives, that it is not simply sentimental, irrational twaddle when we urge each other to modify immediate impulses by considering other men's needs and desires. But the reasons here cannot be quite so decisive as they can be in dealing with the logical validity of logic itself.

Assuming, then, that we cannot hope to find final logical demonstration or scientific proof of the kind yielded by laboratory experiment, the question then becomes: what *good reasons* can we find?

My first reason consists of that dangerous and much discredited argument, the appeal to authority. It can never be very powerful in itself, but when as in this case it has been relied on extensively on the other side, one is surely justified at least in balancing authorities. When students are worried because "all the intelligent writers" talk of an absurd universe, they can properly ask themselves whether the claim is really so. And the authorities I would remind you of are the men, from ancient times to the present, who have thought hardest about our question. The appeal to authority is always weakest when authorities disagree, strongest when they are most in agreement. And what we find in the history of this problem is that not just a few old conservative diehards but almost everyone who has worked on the question for as much as a full day of hard thinking, has concluded that reasoning about our moral choices, and taking our conclusions into account when we choose, are worthwhile and defensible human activities: some actions are *in fact* better than others and therefore *ought* to be chosen. I find many students who will sometimes question this, or seem to, until one pushes them to give up beliefs they really cherish. I find a great many modern "middlemen" of ideas—journalists, popular literary critics, novelists, poets—who think they are reporting the most up-to-date philosophy when they defend relativism. But I find hardly anyone who has worked at the problem with any determination, hardly anyone, be it hedonist, emotivist, skeptic, pragmatist, existentialist, or whatever, who has concluded that thinking about choices is irrelevant since all choices are equivalent. Even those existentialists who think the universe is absurd argue passionately that we should study the question and make a meaningful choice of *their* kind.

It is of course possible, even so, that the philosophical tradition of respect for ethical reasoning is mistaken. But which, I ask you, which is more reasonable, more probable: that men who have been hailed by their contemporaries as the profoundest, most penetrating of their generations—something that has not happened, by the way, to you or me—should be all wrong, or that *I* should be wrong? Before I decide, I surely have some obligation to take a look at what they have to say for themselves.

My second reason—I think somewhat more forceful—comes from a close look at the logical consequences of denying the notion of oughtness or duty. If we take the question, "Ought I to do what is right?" there are two ways of answering it negatively. We might say, "No, I ought to do what is wrong." But this is logical nonsense, because what the word *right* means *is* that which I ought to do. If I want to talk nonsense, I may, but all discussion about everything must then come to a halt; the very demand for proof becomes meaningless. The second form of denial may look more reasonable: "No, the word *ought* and the word *right* are both meaningless. I have no duty to do the right, and I have no duty to do what is wrong. In fact, I have no duty at all." But this is to deny what is present in all of our minds, namely, a conflict between certain of our immediate inclinations and our sense that we ought to curtail them. We have a sense that we ought to follow some inclinations and deny others. It doesn't matter at this point which direction we feel we *ought* to go. Even the hedonist argues that we *ought* to pursue our pleasures, whether long or short-range; if we ask him, "Why ought we to pursue our pleasures?" he is in the same box we're in, and he must answer as we are answering—because it's right to do so, and to deny that you ought to do what is right to do is to end in logical nonsense. At least the burden of illogicality is more on the man who denies moral validity than on the one who affirms. If you deny that you ought to do right, you're in trouble as soon as I ask you whether you *ought* to so deny.

Perhaps this is enough about radical relativism, since anyone who still feels that he is a hardened skeptic can find fuller arguments than I have given in *any* major philosopher, ancient or modern. And even the minor ones are often helpful. I might suggest Stephen Toulmin's *The Use of Reason in Ethics* as one up-to-date and hardheaded defense of the meaningfulness of reasoned moral choice.

II

The most frequent answer to these and the many other arguments against radical relativism is to move to the second main form—cultural relativism. Though the actions I have described are wrong in our society, in other societies they might be right. Os Cresson told me that in Ceylon, or some such place, professors normally accept bribes to supplement their meagre income, and we all know about the use Eskimos are supposed to make of their wives when guests are entertained. The relativist position here becomes, "If it's good *in a particular society,* it's good, and if it's bad it's bad, and there's no objective standard." I'm afraid that this argument from cultural diversity seems much less striking to me than it once did. If you told me that at DePauw University all senior virgins with grade point averages above 2.65 were honored by being thrown into live volcanoes, I wouldn't be terribly surprised, and I *certainly* wouldn't think your facts any sort of argument about whether DePauw's or Earlham's method of honoring seniors was right. Cultural relativism is, in fact, on shakier ground than radical relativism; once the relativist has given up his radical ground of denying *all* oughtness, he's much easier game.

In the first place, he's almost certain to sneak the concept of duty into his argument; anthropologists often try to convince

us that we *ought* to act as if the concept of ought were culturally
determined, that we *ought* not to take it so seriously, or that
our society *ought* not to think our values superior. I want to
ask them whether, in their view, a society in which most men
had the attitude of cultural anthropologists would be superior
to one in which most men were racial bigots. If so, of course, I
have them where I want them!

Secondly, I find it hard to believe that the cultural relativist
means what he says. He asks me to believe, for example, though
he does not use this example, that a country that practices racial
discrimination is right, so long as it believes it is right, and that
there is therefore no arguable moral difference between the policy of the South African government and the policy of that old
southerner, Joe Elmore, who spends his summers in Texas
working for integration. Worst of all, he asks me to believe that
any effort to improve my own society is morally indifferent,
since whatever form of society I might improve *to* would be no
better, objectively, than the one I left behind. Yet none of the
cultural anthropologists I know has *acted* as if improvement
were undesirable or impossible. I am forced to conclude that
they do not really mean that all forms of society are equivalent
in value, but that what they are really saying is something like
this: "We wish you would be more tolerant and understanding
toward other forms of society; many of them are far better than
they look, and some may be better than ours." Now this is a
highly defensible moral plea in which I hope we can all happily
join them.

But there is a third difficulty in their position. Granted that
if I were an Eskimo, my marital practices would be different.
But the real question is not whether in one society I ought to
do this and in another that; the real question is whether, in each
society, I ought to respect what is thought to be right. Must I
take the community into account in my decisions? Every particular requirement relies on some general notion of duty to
others, and we can thus see that underlying all the diversity of
moral demands there is a question common to all societies: Will
you ignore the community and its highest code in the pursuit of

your own conflicting ends? Every community is based on the notion that you will not. (There's an excellent little essay by Solomon Asch which elaborates this point.)

III

I think that this is enough to establish that if there is any morality at all, it is transcultural in its basis, though it may express itself in different forms from culture to culture. But are there any specific transcultural values with more content than simply "You ought to respect the code"? To ask this question is really to ask whether there is such a thing as human nature that *ought* to be respected and fulfilled, regardless of whether a particular society's code calls for it or not. If one society believes that it is my duty to exterminate Jews or persecute Negroes, and another does not, is there any cross-cultural norm that can be appealed to? If not, we haven't really got very far.

It wouldn't do us any good at this point to take a survey of all cultures to find out whether there are any values that all of them would vote for. What we need, rather, is some notion of universal values that all cultures *ought* to vote for. It is the very existence of such values that the cultural relativist denies.

I think it very probable that we could work out a rather large list of specific values shared by most or all cultures—such things as moral and physical courage (though its forms would vary greatly), loyalty to the family or clan, the keeping of promises, and so on. If there are any cultures that do not in fact share these, we would feel justified in describing them as Erich Fromm describes ours: the Sick Society.

I'd like to conclude by seeing whether there is not a rational way of defending, as one transcultural value, perhaps the supreme one, the notions embodies in the golden rule. What proof have I that men and societies ought to regard men as ends in themselves, not to be used as expendable means, as mere things? Aside from our conventional maxims and the authority of Jesus and the prophets, why *ought* I to treat other men as I would like to be treated? Is the burden of proof on the man who denies the validity of the golden rule or the man who upholds it?

It would seem to me that reason is all on side of the golden rule, and I find only my irrational feelings on the side of deny-ing its validity. If I consult my feeling alone, unschooled by ex-perience and reason about experience—let's say my feelings as a very young child before I've learned about the needs of others —they tell me to regard in every situation only the question, What's in it for me? Even if I consult my own feelings at this moment, with forty-one years on my snow white head, I find an overwhelming conviction that I am the center of the universe, and that *my* welfare is more important than yours. And look at *you* out there, uneducated little monsters, knitting away, writ-ing letters, convinced of your own centrality, convinced that this speech is *my* problem, not yours—and here *I* am, with this tight little center of self-awareness and a conviction of *my* su-preme value. Irrational feeling tells us all quite clearly which of us is right. But if I start *thinking* about which of us is right, if I look at the astonishing similarities between your external ap-pearance and my own—two eyes, two ears, a prattling mouth, and so on—and especially if I talk with you and listen to you talk about your ego, I am forced to conclude that you feel as central as I do, and—horror of horrors—your pain and plea-sures are as important to you as mine to me. There may be saints among us who manage to *feel* this truth—and that would be what we mean by really loving our neighbors as ourselves— but for most of us the *feeling* persists that our happiness is worth more than other people's.

We have no rational grounds whatever in defense of this feel-ing. If you are fundamentally like me, as reason teaches me to believe, then I can have no rational grounds for giving you pain to serve my own ends. In fact, to put myself first is fundamen-tally irrational—the most basic irrationality perhaps of all. Now this is no surprising conclusion, even though it is often de-nied. Men have always tended to use terms like "irrational" to describe those of their fellows who ignore the rights of others completely. But think then of the strange position the man is in who would deny the rationality of duty. Only *he* would argue that his own emotional drives are supreme—against every evi-dence provided by his reason that other men are as central as he.

Now of course the relativist can still say, "But you've still not provided me with *proof* that I ought to take other people's equality into account." But I think I *have* shown that to earn the title of reasonableness, a different but very real sense of "proof," every man must choose to take his fellows into account. And if this is so, how can reasonableness lie on the other side? Where does the burden of rational proof lie? Must not the relativist find some rational, rather than merely personal, emotional, grounds for his position?

I see no way out of this trap I have set except to deny the validity of reason itself, in which case the relativist is reduced to denying all knowledge, or to insanity. Men and societies can go insane, men can refuse to discuss, men can become convinced that there is no meaning to the universe or to their own choices. They do it all the time. If a man really believes that it is irrational to take his fellows into account, we cannot, of course, convince him that he is wrong, not with direct argument; he has repudiated by his very stance precisely what would make reasoning possible. But we have surely shown that such men have no rational grounds for claiming that only they are being reasonable.

If all this is true, then it is also true that societies *ought* to take moral truth into account, whether they do or not. The society that denies it, by practicing slavery or racial discrimination or whatever, is objectively, morally wrong to do so, and we *know* that this is so because we know that if they will listen to reason, as the phrase goes, we can show them that they are violating what they know to be true. Note that we do not know it because we feel it; morality has now become something much more than "what feels good," as Hemingway once claimed it was.

You may want to say, at this point, that all we have come to is another form of relativism, humanistic relativism. The values we are arguing for are all relative to man's nature. They don't apply to dogs or angels, and therefore we've not found any absolutes. But remember that we did not set out to look for absolutes. We've been trying to find out whether moral choices are merely expressions of personal preference or whether there is an objective rational difference between good choices and bad choices, good reasons and poor reasons. It doesn't bother me if we've ended in another position that can be *called* relativism; it is, in fact, sometimes called objective relativism. The important thing is that we need not feel apologetic when we try to decide which values and which choices and which reasons are best.

I must add, however, that this humanistic relativism is not finally satisfying to me. I see no ultimately satisfying answer to the question of values short of deciding whether they are independent of human valuers. Are they in any sense eternal, independent of man's valuing? Or, to ask the question another way, are they invented by men or discovered by men? Will it matter, anywhere, after that final cataclysm has destroyed all men, whether I have sold A's to my students? I'm sure you'll be relieved to hear me say that I know better than to try, this late in the hour, to convince you that it does.

IV

Many of you have guessed, by now, what I think is the worst thing that can happen to a man. Plato had a fancy way of describing the fate that is indeed worse than death itself: The worst thing that can happen to a man, Socrates says, is to become a misologist, a hater of the logos, a hater of the word of truth, a man who has lost his faith in human reason. There are perhaps few men who have ever become complete misologists; but we are all threatened, in the twentieth century, with forms of misology that would lead us to become less than men. To order our sex lives, for example, on the same grounds as are used by the tomcat is to become a tomcat. To order our moral lives generally on the personal preferences of the moment, without a constant reference to the accumulated wisdom of ourselves and other men, is to resemble—even if our preferences are generally amiable—at best a nice little house puppy. The worst thing that can happen to a man is to cease to exist as a man. Socrates lives, as a man, here this morning, because he was willing to pursue the word wherever it led him. Many of us here, *looking* perhaps somewhat more alive, are, as men, much closer to the grave than he.

The worst thing that can happen to a nation, as a nation, is to give up the idea of a common nationality based on common respect, and resort to civil war. The worst thing that can happen to a world is to deny, by war, the possibility of a reasonable settlement of differences—the denial of common humanity. The worst thing that can happen to a man is to deny the possibility of controlling his impulses by taking human thought about them. When I settle my own disputes with myself by a simple war of the passions, letting the strongest win; when I settle my disputes with my personal acquaintances by a simple appeal to power or superior cleverness with words; when I settle my disputes with my fellow countrymen by force rather than persuasion; when I decide to settle disputes with other countries by destroying them so that the problem of difference is simply wiped out rather than thought through—when I do these things, I act against reason. I may, of course, use impressive logic in pursuing my unreasonable purposes, but I have forfeited my claim to rationality. And I no longer exist, really, as a man, even if I survive my animal battles.

We all must die sooner or later, and for most of us most of the time that seems like a pretty bad prospect. But that other form of death, loss of faith in reason and its grounds in human community, is a far worse fate—and it is a fate, incidentally, that seems in this century more of a threat to the "educated" than the "uneducated," since the latter are usually less tempted to defend their moral failures by saying that "it doesn't matter anyway." The man who makes faith in reason a part of himself will himself survive, in a very real sense, wherever reason itself survives. The man who repudiates the very possibility of sharing a meaningful code with his fellows dies before his time.

If you think I am wrong, friends, let us reason about it, together.

THE AUTHOR OF
THE SINGLE STANDARD

My text this morning is a modern parable, one that happens to be literal history:

There was once a professor at a university who happened to catch the president of that university in a lie. The lie was verily a small lie, told semipublicly unto a small group of potential donors, in the hope that they would think well of that impoverished university and give money unto it. The outraged professor said unto his friends that he was tempted to resign from the faculty, so corrupt had it revealed itself to be by that lie. "How can we honorably remain," he asked, "at an institution whose president does not recognize the difference between truth and falsehood?" Now it came to pass that when that professor had served his time, he was not rehired by that university because the professor's teaching had driven away all students within the sound of his voice. And the professor came unto his Graduate Dean and said unto him, "Friend, I have a favor that I would ask of you. I shall need letters of recommendation to other colleges, and I pray from my heart that you will write me a letter praising my teaching and not mentioning the fact that I am not being rehired by this university." And when that Graduate Dean raised his eyebrows, as to betoken that meeting the request would be to deceive the world

Convocation Sunday sermon, Rockefeller Chapel, the University of Chicago, May 1969.

for the professor's personal advantage, the professor said unto him, "I wouldn't ask this of you if it were not terribly important to me."

None of us can fail to recognize that professor's sin, because we are all guilty of it: it is the sin of the double standard, applying a less rigorous code to myself than to my friend, and a less rigorous code to my friend than to a stranger, and a less rigorous code to a stranger than to mine enemy. How different such a procedure is from that of Amos in our reading this morning. Amos, the rube from the sticks, comes roaring into the city and tells everybody that the Lord is going to be just as rough on them as on their worst enemies:

> Thus saith the Lord; For three transgressions of Damascus, and for four, I will not turn away the punishment thereof because they have threshed Gilead with threshing instruments of iron:
> But I will send a fire into the house of Hazael, which shall devour the palaces of Benhadad. . . .
> Thus saith the Lord; For three transgressions of Gaza, and for four, I will not turn away the punishment thereof; because they carried away captive the whole captivity, to deliver them up to Edom:
> But I will send a fire on the wall of Gaza, which shall devour the palaces thereof. . . .
> Thus saith the Lord; For three transgressions of Tyrus, and for four, I will not turn away the punishment thereof; because they delivered up the whole captivity to Edom, and remembered not the brotherly covenant. . . .
> Thus saith the Lord; For three transgressions of Edom, and for four, I will not turn away the punishment thereof; because he did pursue his brother with the sword, and did cast off all pity, and his anger did tear perpetually.

And so on, through the transgressions of the children of Ammon, and the transgressions of Moab, and the transgressions of Judah, each of them to be destroyed; and finally down to the doors of home:

> Thus saith the Lord; For three transgressions of Israel, and for four, I will not turn away the punishment thereof; because they sold the righteous for silver, and the poor for a pair of shoes.

Scholars say that Amos moves in here, geographically, from the furthest outreaches right down to the town square, a fine way of dramatizing that *nobody escapes*. Though their sins may differ, country by country, they have each violated a central standard, and each must die. Here at home, at the seeming center, here in Israel, the code is the same as it is everywhere else, because it all comes from the same true center—that single center which the Jews discovered and which is one of the many things that travel under the name God.

A Gallup poll last week announced that more Americans than ever before believe that religion is declining in this country. Seventy percent of all persons polled say that belief in religion is declining; for young adults the figure is eighty-five percent. Yet I am constantly told on this campus that there is a revival of religious interest, that more students and faculty are taking religion seriously than at any other time in the past fifty years.

These contrasting claims may result from a simple difference of definition; the pollsters report a drastic drop in churchgoing, and nobody at Chicago would claim that there is a great increase in *that*. Or it may be that students at Chicago are the vanguard of a new swing to a different kind of religion. But I suspect that both reports—the national report of decline and the local report of growth—are based on the most superficial signs imaginable, the one a decline in the number of people who believe in Santa Claus and the other an increase in the number of people who are having exciting spiritual experiences which they cannot explain. On the one hand God is dead; on the other my mystical experience, tailor-made to comfort my very own personality, lives.

I don't suppose it matters very much whether we decide that religion is declining or expanding, unless we are talking of something that in itself matters. And most of us would say that what is called religion usually does not matter very much. Religious choice is, we have learned to say, a "matter of opinion." We have been trained to reduce everything—the ten commandments, the golden rule, the law of survival, even $E = mc^2$—to "a matter of opinion," and then, having in this way asked "What is truth?" we can, like jesting Pilate, split without waiting for what we know would be an absurd answer.

Well, my absurdly conventional point is that it is *not* a matter of opinion, that the essence of religion—the passionate effort

to live in harmony with the author of the single standard—
matters more to mankind than any other single thing. William
Ernest Hocking, whom I daresay you've never heard of, once
defined religion as a passion for righteousness and for the spread
of righteousness, conceived as a cosmic demand. How absurd
can you get! Nobody today "pursues righteousness," or even
mentions it; righteousness is what narrow-minded dogmatists
display when they are trying to push their forms of behavior
onto us. But it shouldn't require much semantic sophistication,
for people who talk as easily of moral outrage and commitment
as we do these days, to juggle the definition a bit and see that it
says something with interesting consequences.

What Hocking meant, I think, is that religion is essentially a
faith in any value so long as that faith embraces, *as a command
from the cosmos* (or "from the nature of things"—choose
your own vocabulary) a passionate serving of that value in the
world. In this view, my religion, whatever its name, will be the
sum of commands issued to me or through me by the universe
itself, or as some would say it, Himself. Thus the man who feels
that there is something deeply and inexcusably wrong about
the Vietnam war and who feels called, as men used to say, to
try to change the world to fit his views, is expressing his religion,
whether he thinks of himself as an atheist or a believer: he has
a passion for righteousness, and for a spread of righteousness,
conceived as something spoken to him from the nature of things
as they are, the great *I Am*. He may be right or wrong in his
reading of the cosmic demand. To have a religious commitment
has never protected anyone from making mistakes, and as we
all know it can often lead to a compounding of mistakes; the
sense that one's commitment is not merely personal but comes
as a command often accompanies acts of fanatical cruelty—one
of the things that has given religion a bad name.

No doubt it has been a sense of horror about past fanaticisms
that has led many modern clergymen to define religion in more
agreeable, less threatening terms. The pious and puritanical
tradition of commands and restraints and conflicts drove men
from the church; the up-to-date thing is to invite them back by
writing letters to *Playboy* saying that the Playboy philosophy is

a great religious breakthrough, that sex is really religion after all, and that since God intended us all to be happy, we touch the divine whenever we touch a human pleasure.

It is indeed comfortable to learn from those charged to teach us that orgasm is a form of prayer, or that—as Gully Jimson says in *The Horse's Mouth*—laughter and prayer are "the same thing, brother," or that listening to Bach or the Beatles is an act of ultimate worship. But it is too late to go on kidding ourselves in this way, with what is really a simpleminded inversion of the old and equally silly notion that everything pleasant is *against* religion. If everything one wants to do is made into a religious act just by the wanting, then in effect religion no longer has any content.

We are all free, of course, to use words as we want to; if you don't like my definition because it raises unpleasant questions, there's not much I can do about it; I certainly cannot appeal to the supreme lexicographer whose Word is in question. Short of his aid, which even if delivered would no doubt be ambiguous, about all one can do is look at what the word has usually meant to other men. And there is no question but that originally— whatever may have happened to it in recent years—it contained inescapably the notion of cosmic rule or command or restraint. Though etymology can never settle the question of contemporary meaning, it is surely significant that *religion* is supposed to have come from *religio,* meaning taboo or restraint, akin to *religare,* to hold back, bind fast. Its primary meaning is thus its Biblical meaning. As Leviticus says," You shall afflict your souls by a perpetual religion" (Leviticus 16:31).

Afflict our souls? Perpetual? You've got to be kidding. Religion as a restraint or compulsion upon us from God, from the Supreme Being, from the Cosmos? Not on your life! We've just been through all that, for decades, for centuries. The modern age has been achieved precisely by struggling successfully against the evils of repression and the psychological and social miseries that such ideas produced when they were dominant. You are opening the floodgates—I can hear some of you saying—to the worst excesses of puritanism. We know that fanatical, mind-destroying dogmas and cruel crusades are always defended in the name of cosmic demands that are undebatable just because they are thought to be cosmic. "I must send you to the stake for the salvation of your soul." Modernity may have its evils, but at least it does not justify ungodly communal actions in the name of the Lord. The whole development from the Reformation—in the name of the independent Protestant conscience—to modern nihilisms and existentialisms and pragmatisms can be described, with oversimplification but with an essential rightness, as a reaction against the very notion that any man can speak for more than himself. No man can speak for the cosmos, and if this is true, then we may as well admit that there is no cosmos, for all practical purposes; cosmic demands are unknown. Speak for yourself, John, because when you try to speak for me, you soon begin forcing me to speak with *your* voice.

But while we are remembering these well-known excesses and dangers of religious conviction, it might be well to remind ourselves of the consequences, some of which we now live with, of life lived without arbitration by the author of the single standard. One of these, it seems to me, is the wild proliferation of pseudoreligions that are sucked into the vacuum created when God died. Men are in general unhappy about speaking for themselves alone. We all want the support of being right, or of being thought to be right, and if traditional religion will not provide me with a validating God, why then I'll just invent me a little God of my own: astrology, spiritualism, scientology, Eselen, astral projection, futurism in its many forms—not all of these idolatries are called religions by their inventors, but they thrive, I am convinced, only because our society has failed to provide less destructive and more defensible versions of a cosmic order.

To some extent we are all struggling with the need to invent gods to replace those that have died. If I have learned that there is no absolute objective status to the drive for a value like justice—since God is dead—and if at the same time I have a deep personal feeling that it is wrong to starve my neighbor in the ghetto in order to live in luxury in Hyde Park, I can either oppose the injustice as a mere personal preference (and a part of myself will feel outraged at the notion that it is merely a pref-

erence equivalent to another man's preference for *in*justice),
or I can invent some other suprapersonal value, like the forces
of history, or the building of the movement, to support my
claims. If there is no objective artistic standard—that is, no
God—to validate in any way my impressions that some works
of art are nobler achievements than some others, then I can
either shout my artistic wares from the housetop, hoping to
capture a vanguard whose approval will somehow validate what
I am doing, or I can retreat into cynical silence or equally cynical attacks on the phoniness of *all* art. And if there is no such
thing as a supreme standard of truth to validate in any way the
superior truth of some scholarly conclusions and the untruth of
others, then I must repudiate the scholarly endeavor, either by
withdrawing from the university entirely or by transmuting
the university into the service of my immediate feelings or convictions. In short, if goodness, beauty, and truth are not in any
way objective and real, in *some* sense independent of my efforts
to reach them, my whim becomes supreme; and if, as the intellectual world has been telling itself for decades, values are invented by man, not discovered, if there is no cosmic demand
upon me to embrace some views and to reject some other views,
then of course I can do with the university and with my life in
the university whatever happens to feel agreeable to me at the
moment. What is agreeable and what is right have become identical, and I may as well use any means that lie at hand, so long
as they are used in what *feels* like a good cause. Right you are if
you think you are.

The result is, of course, a world shattered into thousands, perhaps millions, of different standards. In place of the single
standard imposed upon the universe by the traditional God of
law, we invent a valueless universe giving equal lack of support
to all. Our double standards result because, as could have been
predicted, when everything is permitted, the permissions are
somehow granted more liberally to me and my kind than to my
enemies. If all moral and intellectual norms are merely personal
or social inventions, then of course I may make use of them for
my personal convenience; I may commit injustice in defense of
my side, and I may still be "justifiably" outraged when my

enemy commits injustices. I may lie for my cause, but lying is of course vicious when my enemy does it. I may harm anyone who opposes my cause, since the circle of rightness is drawn by my cause, and anyone inside that circle is judged by a different standard than should be applied to anyone outside the circle.

Thus illegal and disorderly actions are committed by the police in the name of law and order. Some students have committed acts of cruelty in the name of a loving community, willing to make this specific living person miserable in the name of an abstraction. A faculty member, believing without check certain rumors about a particular student's participation in the sit-in, tells him that he will no longer work with him on his Ph.D. program—applying, you see, standards of scholarship about those rumors which would outrage him if they were applied to himself. Last fall a black student phoned me to rebuke me for my "attack on Woodlawn" in my orientation speech, which she had not heard. Since I had not even mentioned Woodlawn, I was shocked that such a rumor was going about and that she had not bothered to check on its validity before allowing herself the luxury of anger with me. "Oh, but you're an administrator; you've got to expect these things." At which point I gave her an impromptu sermon and conceived the first idea for this sermon this morning: "Now look," I said in indignation, "we're all in this thing together. If I judged the behavior of black students on the basis of every rumor coming my way, you would rightly be outraged. But as a religious person you know that we're all judged here by the same standards—administrators, faculty, students; there's only one judge, and he's neither a white dean nor a black student."

To which she did not reply, then or later. But she *might* have replied with the two routine questions that men in all ages have put to those who have asserted the existence of a supreme judge: "How can you prove it?" and "Even if you think you can prove that the author of a single standard exists, how can any human being pretend to speak in his name? Since we live in a relativistic or pluralistic world in which every judgment anyone makes can be cancelled by the judgment of someone else, how can there be a single standard in actual daily fact—even if there were a supreme arbiter in theory?"

Obviously I cannot pretend to answer either of these questions adequately in my remaining time, but I cannot say strongly enough how important it seems to me that academic communities struggle for new forms of the questions and new ways of trying to answer them. Universities have struggled many times in the past to relate themselves to the cosmos. But perhaps never before has there been such a large number of intellectuals who thought that negative answers to the two questions were self-evidently the only answers: there can be no proof of the existence of a Supreme Objective Standard, and even if there could be, there can be no way of determining which men are closer to it than others.

But if anything should be clear by now it is this: a university simply cannot survive unless there is some kind of consensus within it on essential values. The consensus need not be an intellectualized one, and in fact it has usually not been; most societies, including academic societies, have had available to them strong traditions which made it seem self-evident that there *are* standards of thought and conduct. Only when all faith in traditions or traditional creeds has been lost are we forced to look for what might be called a rhetoric of communion, a way of convincing each other that we are after all children of the same father, or brothers under the skin, or scholars in a universe and university, not a pluriverse or pluriversity. We must either learn to think together about suprapersonal values or perish.

If this is so, it is a time when we should expect a revival of inquiry into the traditional proofs for the existence of God. A Sunday morning sermon is hardly the place for extensive discussion of these proofs. Like many other men these days, I am especially interested in the ontological proof, but I invite you to look into the others as well if you have serious interest in whether there are respectable intellectual grounds for living in pursuit of the Supreme Arbiter.

For now, I can only touch on the moral grounds of our intellectual woes. Our "community" here came breathlessly close to perishing this year—some would say that it did perish, as a community, never to be revived. It did so because it became fragmented into different moral universes, each applying its own double moral standard with an absolute sense of self-righteousness. All about us men were using means against their new enemies that they would have been outraged by if employed against themselves. Think only of what would have happened, if a group of administrators had sat in on the Student Government offices, refusing to leave until students met their demands about student behavior. Or of how certain arrogant and cruel faculty members would have reacted if students characteristically treated them with the same contempt they show to students. Regardless of where we stand on the events of this year, it is clear that we cannot survive increased fragmentation in our notions of what is permitted. But what will establish the limits? Is it really wrong to use one standard for my crowd and a different one for all the others, whoever they may be? Who says so? If my crowd are fighting for justice and the other crowd are obviously bastards, why not?

The chief support for such a position, as I have already said, seems to be a kind of prevailing climate of opinion that the universe is itself indifferent or cruel or absurd, and that therefore men have for support only the values they invent. Without attempting a systematic reply to such a position, I cannot resist giving you a piece of scripture I found in an old desk. It is a fragment of a dialogue between the universe and a questioner:

"You're mean and brutal and absurd," says the Sartrean student.
"Who says so?" asks the universe.
"I say so," shouts the existentialist.
"Is your judgment sound?" asks the universe.
"Of course," the absurdist replies.
"According to what standards of soundness?"
"Cruelty is cruelty and absurdity is absurdity," replies the rebel.
"You are of course right," says the universe, "but only because I give you the right to say so. If I did not concur with your judgment that the suffering of little children is a terrible thing, then your judgment against me would be mere personal feeling. But of course I do concur—and therefore I am on your side in your judgment about the cruelty which you find mixed up in my nature. If I did not support you at least in some sense, you wouldn't have a leg to stand on. But of course it was I who made you capable of discovering and formulating these judgments; you did not make yourself nor invent your marvelous moral sense."

Such a dialogue, even if pursued at length, would not answer that second and most pressing question we have raised several times already: Who is to judge? What right have *you* to say that you speak against *me* in the name of universal standards? Certainly the deepest wounds during our hurtful year came from the sense many of us in all camps had that others were presuming to have a direct pipeline to the truth, without taking our different notions into account. But who *is* to judge whether the students sitting-in were righter or wronger than the professors punishing them for it? Isn't it really just a matter of who wins? If there is a continued swing toward revolutionary tactics in this country, the leaders of the sit-in will finally be made into heroes of the people. But if the right wing wins out, the faculty will be seen (unless they have meantime battled the right wing) as the vanguard of those who fought the rebels.

But if I am saying anything this morning worth saying, we cannot rely on historical validation to tell us who was right or wrong. Even if we could say easily what *is* historical success or failure, the answer would not tell us whether the Author of the Single Standard found us justified or damned. If as I have said *God* is a convenient traditional term for the totality of cosmic demands upon us, we are judged neither by our own conscious judgments nor by how things turn out, but by whether we have indeed acted in accordance with the law. We think we discover God in many ways, and no doubt we sometimes do, through tradition, through reason, through mystical experiences, through daily loving encounters; we find him or fail to find him in history, but it is he who judges history, not we.

The painful result is that no one *knows* whether he or anyone else is qualified to judge. No one can ever impose any judgment on other men with confidence. But we are not left entirely without a clue—the clue provided by those standards which we believe can be justly applied to ourselves. "Judge not that ye be not judged, for with the same measure that ye mete withal it shall be measured to you again." No man can avoid judgment about the rights and wrongs of the world, and every man knows when someone else is using a double standard against himself. In fact I usually discover the ideal of the single standard as I experience what I take to be injustice; all of us, even the most hardened criminals, think that we are entitled to "fair treatment," and we all respond to injustice against ourselves with an absolute sense of speaking not just for ourselves but for something fundamental in the nature of things. "It's just not fair." "I don't deserve it." We somehow *know* that when we say such things we are not simply saying, "I don't *like* what's being done to me." We are saying that those who are treating us as worth less than themselves are wrong, *really* wrong.

The only *leap of faith,* then, is taken when this inescapable feeling is reversed—when I require myself to apply a common measure to other men in passing negative judgments on my own acts of injustice. Once the leap has been made, one has left the private, godless world of the isolated ego and entered a world of suprapersonal truth: Anselm and Augustine would say, if I understand them, that at that moment of self-transcendance, one has declared one's faith in God. But this leap is a leap of "faith" only in a very curious sense, because it is a leap that is required of us by every rational criterion one can think of. I have no rational grounds whatever for thinking myself to be a glorious and unique exception among men, fundamentally worth more than they are. They all resemble me in every *essential* respect, and it is only rational to suppose that their right to just treatment is worth exactly as much as my own, no more but no less. My feelings get in the way of this rational judgment, true enough; I *feel* supremely important. But unless I am willing to say that injustice against me does not matter, I cannot rationally conclude that there is no meaning to the notion of injustice. And if I admit that notion, I have embarked on a road that will lead me inevitably to recognize that Standards exist. Either it is right, really right, to say that some acts are unjust, or it is not. But to say that such a judgment is meaningless when it applies to myself is impossible for any man who is not playing games with words: I know that *I* really deserve justice. But if I *really* do, so do you.

The discovery of the Single Standard was one of the most astonishing achievements of man's history. All feeling was against it. Every accident of tribe and province and family was against it. Many arguments from superficial differences were against it—how can I possibly say that those creatures across the river, who don't even speak Hebrew, are creatures of the same Lord as I am? Yet the achievement was made.

As we all know, it does not stay made. Unlike many of man's astonishing works, this one leads a precarious existence among us. Individuals forget it; whole societies deny it. But it has a curious power to get itself reborn again and again. At every instant of its rebirth it is challenged—as always—by some of our deepest feelings: "Stand to one side, Number One is coming through!" And it is challenged by our daily experience of an inescapable plurality requiring a pluralism of human codes and methods. But the universe goes on quietly applying its reasonable standards on our ego-centered violations of the command to love our neighbors as ourselves and our ego-limited intellectual systems. There is a single standard here, whether we perceive it or not: Either we learn to treat other men with infinite respect, which is love—and which means, among other things, in accordance with the highest possible standards of truth—or we will ourselves suffer the tortuous twistings of soul that universally punish men who cannot love. And the community we build, with or without revolutions or counterrevolutions, will be a twisted corrupt hateful thing.

The Author of the Single Standard has decreed it, now decrees it, and will decree it always. Praise Him.